Flawed Texts and
Verbal Icons

Flawed Texts and Verbal Icons

Literary Authority in American Fiction

Hershel Parker

9618

Northwestern University Press

Published by Northwestern University Press
Evanston Illinois 60201

Cloth ISBN #0-8101-0666-3
Paper ISBN #0-8101-0667-1
Library of Congress Catalog Card #84-61439

Cover photo "RUBE" by Jon Naar, New York NY

Cover design by William Seabright, Glencoe IL

This book is dedicated to
my wife, Heddy-Ann Richter

CONTENTS

CONTENTS (continued)

Preface

This book grows out of prolonged, repeated attempts to reconcile evidence of writers' lives and histories of their compositional processes with the prevailing trends in editorial theory and practice, literary criticism, and literary theory— especially the persistent tendency to treat any literary text as a verbal icon, a unique, perfect, and essentially authorless entity. My arguments are easily stated, although it will take the book to elaborate them. All valid meaning is authorial meaning, but in standard literary texts authorial meaning may be mixed in with non-sense, skewed meanings, and wholly adventitious meanings which result from tampering with the text, by the author or someone else. Because the creative process is by nature determinate, revising authors very often betray or otherwise blur their original achievements in ways they seldom intend and seldom become aware of. The dominant editorial theory of the last three decades, W. W. Greg's "Rationale of Copy-Text," is invalid in most cases of belated revision because it is grounded on the assumption that every author retains full authority over anything he has written for as long as he lives. While textualists have scolded critics for blunders based upon misprints or other trivial errors, they have, under the aegis of Greg, created many new texts exemplifying what Bruce Harkness identified in the 1950s as the "novelistic fallacy," the habit of thinking that there are so many words in a novel that a few dozen (or a few thousand) can't matter much. Literary critics from the time of the New Critics have often systematically ruled out the possible relevance of biographical and textual evidence which I would call crucial to cogent literary theory as well as to responsible interpretation, and they have done so, often enough, while they were reading unreadable texts. From the 1960s through the mid-1980s literary theorists (whether building a foundation for structuralism, affective stylistics, subjectivist reading, an aesthetics of reception, or an aesthetics of feminist criticism) have recurrently sabotaged their arguments by accepting, in one form or another, the New Critical dictum that authorial intention is irrelevant to interpretation and is in any case irrecoverable. Even deconstructionists blithely set about their demolitions before they know what they are deconstructing, placing as much faith as any New Critic in the authority of the text they take in their hands to unauthorize.

To exemplify the general neglect of a textual-aesthetic approach to literature I choose the opening of Lawrence Lipking's essay on "Literary Criticism" in the MLA's new pamphlet, *Introduction to Scholarship in Modern Languages and Literatures* (1981), a replacement for the 1963 *Aims and Methods* pamphlet directed once again toward all the members of the MLA and their students. Lipking begins by quoting Northrop Frye from the 1963 "Literary Criticism" chapter:

> We have to avoid of course the blunder that is called the intentional fallacy in criticism. The question "What did the author mean by this?" is always illegitimate. First, we can never know; second, there is no reason to suppose that the author knew; third, the question confuses imaginative with discursive writing. The legitimate form of the question is: "What does the text say?"

Recapitulating the "development of literary criticism" in the last decades, Lipking points out that now certain critics would find in the study of the author's intentions "the surest single ground of interpretation." Citing E. D. Hirsch's argument in *Validity in Interpretation* (1967) that the author's intention at the moment of writing is the only possible standard of validity in interpretation, Lipking observes that "even critics who disagree" with Hirsch have shown "an increasing interest in the author's readings or misreadings of previous texts. A new revitalization of Freudian theory, in recent criticism, opposes the distinction between the author's psychology and the meaning of the text. Biographical speculation has returned as a permitted analytical tool." Conspicuously, in this untendentious survey, one plainly aiming at historical accuracy, Lipking does not think to mention the possible relevance of the most textual of textual evidence, evidence of composition and revision of that nebulous thing we call "the text itself," whatever that is.

As Lipking's significant omission indicates, I have not exaggerated the isolation of biographical-textual scholarship from literary criticism and theory. Identifying an academic infrastructure weakened by such institutionalized gaps, I busy myself in this book with repairing old bridges and building some new access roads between and among literary approaches —biographical-textual scholarship and criticism, editorial theory and critical theory, editorial theory and creativity theory, scholarship and critical theory. The book comprises an insider's history of recent American editorial and textual theory and practice; an outsider's critique of recent literary criticism and theory; some detailed demonstrations of the implications of biographical and textual evidence for interpretation of literary works and for general aesthetic theory; a personal account of the aesthetics and the politics of reconstructing a novel which had become a classic in a truncated text; and some conclusions about some of the most problematical concepts in modern literary theory.

This book could not have been written twenty years ago, or ten, or even five. I owe much to the 1930s generation of American scholars both directly, through association with Leon Howard and others, and indirectly, through prolonged if intermittent association with Harrison Hayford, one of the students of the Yale Americanist Stanley T. Williams, but a glance through the early issues of *American Literature* will reveal how very different the work reported in this book is from the few "genesis" studies which appeared there in the two or three decades after its founding in 1929. In any case,

World War II and the post-war triumph of a new literary methodology, the New Criticism, combined to divert the attention of the first generation of American scholars from sustained textual research. Scholars who turned afresh to textual investigation after the early 1960s could benefit, as not even the most dedicated scholars of the 1930s could do, from advances in technology (such as the miracle of cheap photocopying) and from massive, coordinated research funded by the federal government (mainly through the Center for Editions of American Authors) as well as greatly increased university support for research. By the late 1960s there finally existed in American biographical and textual scholarship enough data, in accessible form, for anyone to begin to think seriously about it and with it.

Insofar as this book deals with editorial theory, it could not have been written before the dominant theory, W. W. Greg's rationale of copy-text (first printed in the 1950-51 *Studies in Bibliography*) had been promulgated and applied on a grand scale in CEAA editions and then analyzed by editors and textual critics, most notably by G. Thomas Tanselle in the 1975 *Studies in Bibliography*. Insofar as this book draws on creativity theory, it would not likely have been written until the late 1960s, when enough editorial problems had been identified to compel a scholar-critic to seek out descriptions of the creative process by philosopher-aestheticians like John Dewey in *Art as Experience* (1934), as Brian Higgins and I did to clarify and justify our arguments about *Tender is the Night*. Insofar as this book reconciles editorial notions of authorial intention with the use of the term in other disciplines, it could not have been written until after G. Thomas Tanselle had written his comprehensive essay on "The Editorial Problem of Final Authorial Intention" for the 1976 *Studies in Bibliography*. Furthermore, this book would not have been written as it is if at USC in 1975 I had not had both a typescript of Tanselle's paper and a student who was struggling to reconcile the odd things he was learning from me with the odder things he was learning from Stanley Fish. I mean Steven Mailloux, who in 1976 began leading me and his fellow graduate students into greater familiarity with current literary theory, some of which was using the same vocabulary I was (I don't know how any editor or critic could avoid the test of "reader response" in judging the effect of textual alterations) and some of which challenged me to defend or alter my assumptions about textual authority.

While you will find in my footnotes more references to biographers, editorial theorists, textual critics, literary critics, and aestheticians than to clinical psychiatrists, cognitive psychologists, and philosophers working on mental states and the "mind-body" problem, I have repeatedly taken courage from relating my evidence to research and theoretical work in these last-named fields. I have frequently quoted the clinical psychiatrist Dr. Albert Rothenberg in these chapters, for his detailed analyses of the creative process in *The Emerging Goddess* (1979) have proved more specifically applicable than John Dewey's powerful general formulations. Two wide-ranging collections will suggest why I look to the Cornell school of cognitive psychologists for ultimate help in understanding how we read unreadable texts: *Perception: Essays in Honor of James J. Gibson* (1974) and *Perception and Its Development: A Tribute to Eleanor J. Gibson* (1979). Following the lead of Ralph Rader, I have relied on James J. Gibson's *The Senses Considered as Perceptual Systems* (1966). When I was speculating about human memory and belated literary revision, it was heartening to turn to the research reported by Ulric Neisser, another member of the Cornell group, in *Memory Observed* (1982). John R. Searle's *Intentionality* (1983) has likewise provided a philosophical theory on which I can rely. Rothenberg, the Gibsons, Neisser, and Searle have in common an empirical approach: Rothenberg, who works from a variety of controlled experiments, two decades ago was already studying the manuscript of Eugene O'Neill's *The Iceman Cometh*; James J. Gibson cheerfully calls himself a "naive realist"; Eleanor Gibson is concerned, likewise, with "what happens in real life"; Neisser and his associates are specifically concerned with memory in "natural" or "naturalistic" contexts; and Searle is concerned with intentionality in "real-life" situations. My literary approach is equally empirical. However much editorial theory you may find in this book, however often I become entangled with the problematic concepts of contemporary literary theory, I deal with theoretical issues only as they loom up amid the rubble of the author's false starts, discarded openings and endings, rejected passages, rough drafts, magazine printings, expurgations, and sober (as well as drunken) second thoughts. What I say from my empirical analyses of literary composition and revision (and from my equally empirical analyses of literary critics and theorists at work) often disputes the prevailing opinions in editorial and critical theory and casts doubt on the way literary criticism is practiced, but it is in harmony with the evidence observers and thinkers like Rothenberg, James J. Gibson, Eleanor J. Gibson, Neisser, and Searle provide about the workings of the human mind.

I am alive to the comedy some will see in the spectacle of a textualist tromping onto the rarefied terrain occupied by critics and theorists. High claims advanced for textual criticism, such as Fredson Bowers's pronouncement in the 1963 *Aims and Methods* pamphlet that "the discipline lies at the base of all intellectual endeavor in our cultural heritage," have always struck most critics as deliciously droll. Yet one of the secret jokes which sustain textual bibliographers and textual critics when their work is undervalued or ignored is the knowledge that the truism is really true, that literary criticism and theory really do depend upon textual knowledge. In the last decade, I have paid for giving away the joke with humbler variants of Bowers's claims—the price of a series of reprimands in *American Literary Scholarship* for saying that better scholarship might lead to better criticism, the price of an outraged headline reprinted around the country: "MAILER BATTLES ACADEMIC CHUTZPAH." Made thus aware of the threatening nature of some of my observations, such as my saying in all honest blandness that criticism on, say, the theme of slavery in *Pudd'nhead Wilson* has been an exercise in futility, I have taken pains to couch most of my claims mildly throughout this book, however sweeping some of the judgments will be. I intend to persuade you by kinds of evidence you have rarely had a chance to think about, evidence offered here in abundance and variety.

Abundant as my evidence is, I have restricted it to American fiction, the field I know best, and my choice of texts is determined by the range of issues they can illuminate, as well as the fact that I picked them up as I found them in my way, from teaching and from working on volumes sponsored by the CEAA. It may well be that students of other genres will qualify some of what I say: some may argue, for instance, that a lyric poet may find it easier to reassert control over an altered work or easier to create what we might agree was either a new version or a new work of art, discrete from an earlier poem it was revised from. Critics of some of the great modernist writers may reasonably scent unwariness in my frequent emphasis on the sequence of composition and my skepticism toward reordered texts. For them, the brief discussion of Faulkner novels in Chapter 2 may clarify the difference betwen inadvertent, uncontrolled disjuncture and juxtaposition and disjuncture and juxtaposition as a literary method. Although specialists in British literature of the last three centuries will readily point to textual situations comparable to those I deal with here, and although specialists in both British and American literature have recently produced very useful studies of the making of various literary works, I believe that with only a few exceptions the aesthetic implications of such textual situations and evidence have not been rigorously scrutinized. Certainly the general academic community, as represented by the annual MLA program, has of late manifested almost no interest in the creative process, which I called "The Outcast of the MLA" at the 1981 meeting, and which (aside from a few sessions on teaching composition to undergraduates and teaching creative writing) was represented at the 1983 MLA by only a few talks on a program which listed 693 sessions, with perhaps an average of three speakers in each.

The closest parallels to what I am doing in this book range between two extremes, one quite esoteric, the other journalistic. The Society for Textual Scholarship has begun promoting international, interdisciplinary conferences which deal with textual problems in many languages, ancient and modern, and with textual problems in such diverse areas as musicology, art history, legal history, theatre history, and cinema studies. It now prints some of the proceedings of its conferences in the annual *Text*. The even more esoteric *New York Literary Forum* (again international and interdisciplinary) devoted the 1981 annual to *Fragments: Incompletion & Discontinuity*. Without being programmatical, *Critical Inquiry* has opened its pages to a "pan-textualism" which at times (as in some art criticism) uses historical, biographical, and textual strategies much like those I employ in my "demonstration" chapters. I would like to think that in conventional literary scholarship what I am doing is comparable to Jane Millgate's "The Limits of Editing: The Problems of Scott's *The Siege of Malta*," *Bulletin of Research in the Humanities* 82 (Summer 1979): 190-212 and her "Text and Context: Dating the Events of *The Bride of Lammermoor*," *The Bibliotheck* 9 (1979): 200-13. In the academic study of popular culture, some recent film studies are especially close to my work. I point to Paul Seydor's chapter on *The Wild Bunch* in *Peckinpah: The Western Films* (1980) as an analysis of the aesthetic implications of textual evidence so much like my own work that I wish I had written it, for with a change in my subtitle it could have been run into this book. At the other extreme, some of the most thoughtful comments on problems of authenticity, authority, intentionality, restoration, and revision, especially in film and music, have been written by journalists such as Janet Maslin and Donal Henahan for the New York *Times*; and Herbert Mitgang, the cultural affairs editor for the *Times*, has taken special interest in some of the novels I discuss in this book. Conscious of the hazards of defining my study strictly, I console myself with the knowledge that the man or woman who is ambitious enough to undertake a comprehensive study of textual integrity and authority in literature and the other arts will build upon the arguments and demonstrations in this book, the first on the subject of textual authority in American fiction, the first directly to challenge the textual ideology explicit in W. K. Wimsatt, Jr.'s note on his title *The Verbal Icon* (1954).

Acknowledgments

This book began during a long talk with James B. Meriwether in 1967 on authorial second thoughts, and much of it will only confirm what he has known all along. Harrison Hayford stands behind the book in ways different than he thinks and more numerous than I admit. Brian Higgins has proved an unparalleled friend and collaborator. I am not reconciled to Leon Howard's not being alive to read this book, for he was preeminently the student of the geneses of American texts, and preeminently the mentor of younger scholars. Heddy-Ann Richter has earned the Dedication.

After Cleanth Brooks has so generously and thoughtfully read some of these chapters, and reminded me how firmly biographical scholars (few of the calibre of Stanley T. Williams) once controlled English departments, I would be remiss not to call attention to his long uneasiness at being labeled a New Critic and being associated with ideas he never held and practices he never condoned. I hereby exonerate him of any and all malpractices which in this book I attribute to the New Critics and their witting and unwitting followers. I am concerned with what those followers actually said about authors and novels, not with how carelessly they may have read Brooks and Robert Penn Warren, or W. K. Wimsatt and Monroe C. Beardsley, or René Wellek and Austin Warren, and not with

xvii

whether they read any of these people for themselves or were merely imitating other practitioners of the dominant literary approach.

Most of this book was written during my year as a Fellow of the Center for Advanced Study at the University of Delaware and during the subsequent semester when I was allowed to teach it all, week by week. For their extraordinary support I am grateful to the President of the University of Delaware, E. Arthur Trabant, Provost L. Leon Campbell, Dean Helen Gouldner, and Chairman Zack Bowen. It was good to work near my old friend and new colleague, J. A. Leo Lemay, and our neighbor Bern Oldsey.

I am still grateful to the John Simon Guggenheim Memorial Foundation and its President Gordon N. Ray for a Fellowship in 1974-75. To employ an aesthetic formulation which I challenge in my fourth chapter, this is the book I ought to have written then but did not know how to write. In that Guggenheim year I discovered, at least, what kind of work I wanted to do, and in the next years at the University of Southern California Chairman Max Schulz and Dean David H. Malone were unfailingly generous toward me and my graduate students.

I am also grateful to the editors of periodicals for printing portions of this book and for allowing me to reprint them here in much the same form: *Critical Inquiry* (part of Chapter 1); *College Literature* (Chapter 2); *Resources for American Literary Study* (Chapter 5); and *Bulletin of Research in the Humanities* (Chapter 7). A few other passages are also recycled from reviews and essays.

For thoughtful readings and for practical help with ending the book I am grateful to Gerald Graff, the Director of Northwestern University Press. The then-anonymous reader for the Press, Lawrence Buell, was so obviously right in everything else he said that I reordered a chapter at his suggestion. If no textual anomalies have resulted, it is only because scholars have to be more careful about polishing their manuscripts than novelists do—have at least to glance through a work in its new order. I thank Alma A. MacDougall for her help with house styling and for her meticulous reading of the page proofs. For encouragement and support I thank Warner Barnes, John Benedict, Henry Binder, Watson G. Branch, James T. Cox, Frederick Crews,

Acknowledgments

David V. Erdman, Franklin Everett, William Frawley, Robert H. Hirst, Jay Leyda, Robert Lucid, Murray MacQuarrie, Thomas L. McHaney, Steven Mailloux, Jane Millgate, Michael Millgate, James Nagel, Martha Parker, Quanah Parker, Noel Polk, Nellie Richter, Charles E. Robinson, Edward Rosenberry, Paul Seydor, James L. W. West III, and Charlene Afremow and Randy McNamara.

My heroic research assistant at the University of Delaware, Robin Gaither, scouted out a Wang Word Processor and put this book into it, and the imperturbable Ruth Leo taught her how. They made it seem like child's play, and after a while they kindly let me play too.

CHAPTER 1

Lost Authority and Cheap Thrills

This chapter is an introductory survey of some of the vicissitudes which can afflict the authority of the author over text and meaning and the follies even good critics can commit when they assume that a text is authoritative merely because the author authorized its publication. Two recent studies can focus my argument. The first is *Interpretation*, in which P. D. Juhl clarifies and improves upon some of the arguments of E. D. Hirsch, Jr.[1] The second is a controversial *Critical Inquiry* essay, "Against Theory," in which Steven Knapp and Walter Benn Michaels attempt to correct both Hirsch and Juhl on some points but follow them in referring to "the meaning of a text" without asking how the text reached the state in which they encounter it.[2] Defining the argument of *Validity in Interpretation* as "unabashedly and I think necessarily theoretical,"

1. P. D. Juhl, *Interpretation: An Essay in the Philosophy of Literary Criticism* (Princeton, N.J., 1980), pp. 66-89 (the title of Chapter IV is "The Appeal to the Text: What Are We Appealing to?"); see in Chapter VI the subsection "Are the Meanings of Textual Details Unintended?", pp. 129-32.

2. Steven Knapp and Walter Benn Michaels, "Against Theory," *Critical Inquiry* 8 (Summer 1982): 723-42; the quotations later in this paragraph are from pp. 725, 726-27, 730, n. 8; and 727. In introducing the section "Critical Response: For and Against Theory," *Critical Inquiry* 9 (June 1983): 725-800, the editors say

Hirsch had paid almost no attention to the possible implications of evidence about the history of a text except in some offhand speculations which strike me as more incisive and ultimately more fruitful than anything American textual theorists were then saying:[3]

> With a revised text, composed over a long period of time (*Faust,* for example), how are we to construe the unrevised portions? Should we assume that they still mean what they meant originally or that they took on a new meaning when the rest of the text was altered or expanded? . . .

It was without recourse to evidence of composition, revision, and transmission that Hirsch defined "textual meaning as the verbal intention of the author" and treated "a text" or "the text" as an immutable arrangement of words, if not of punctuation marks also.[4] In asking what we are appealing to when we appeal to the text, Juhl likewise did not allow for a challenge of "Which text?"—not even when he went so far as to insist that the meanings of minor textual details are intended by the author. Echoing Hirsch, Knapp and Michaels insist that "the meaning of a text is simply identical to the author's intended meaning" and that "all meaning is always the author's meaning." Echoing Juhl, they insist that "all local meanings are always intentional." For Knapp and Michaels there can be, in short, no "intentionless meanings."

As a textual scholar I applaud Knapp and Michaels for admitting the existence of the author and welcoming him back from the banishment first imposed by the New Critics then reimposed by subsequent critical juntas. But their arguments against theory do not, empirically speaking, get us much farther than the theories of Hirsch and Juhl, and for much the same reason—the failure to pay attention to what lessons can be learned from "particular texts."[5] One lesson is that authorial

---

that the number of responses received within one month was "surely a record of some sort." As one of the responses, part of this chapter was entitled "Lost Authority: Non-sense, Skewed Meanings, and Intentionless Meanings," pp. 767-74.

3. E. D. Hirsch, Jr., *Validity in Interpretation* (New Haven, Conn., 1967), p. x.
4. Hirsch, p. 224.
5. Knapp and Michaels, p. 723.

meaning is not something an author pours into an entire literary work at the moment he puts the last touch to it, as Michael Hancher seems to argue.[6] Still less can intentionality be conferred upon a literary work in the form that is published and at the moment of publication, as James Thorpe so magisterially contends.[7] Rather, as John Dewey says, meaning is built into the text at the moment each part is written. The "artist is controlled in the process of his work by his grasp of the connection between what he has already done and what he is to do next." He must "at each point retain and sum up what has gone before as a whole and with reference to a whole to come"; if this does not happen, there will be "no consistency and no security in his successive acts."[8] Writers fail repeatedly to achieve their previously intended meanings during the actual creative process, even though their control over the emerging work is then at its strongest. At best, as Murray Krieger argues, they turn these failures of original intention into opportunities for success in some unexpected direction, but flaws which result from shifting or imperfectly realized intentions commonly survive into the printed text in the form of "contrary details" which we override in our compulsion to make sense of what we read.[9] If writers fail to achieve their full intentions during composition,

6. Michael Hancher, "Three Kinds of Intention," *Modern Language Notes* 87 (December 1972): 827-51; see p. 831, n. 10 for Hancher's only mention of authorial intention during the process of composition. I review Hancher's categories in more detail in Chapter 2. In *Intentionality: An Essay in the Philosophy of Mind* (Cambridge: Cambridge University Press, 1983), John R. Searle's term which would seem to apply to an intention during the process of composition is "intention in action." In this book I deal with authorial intention as (in Searle's term) a "mental state" directed at particular "objects" (p. vii)—words, as they are written. This mental state "imposes" intention on words ("entities that are not intrinsically Intentional," p. 27), in the process of thinking of the words and (usually) putting them on paper, embodying meaning in the words as they are written into the existing verbal context.

7. James Thorpe, *Principles of Textual Criticism* (San Marino, Calif.: The Huntington Library, 1972), p. 38.

8. John Dewey, *Art as Experience* (New York: Minton, Balch, 1934), pp. 45 and 56. I give warning here that I will quote these words more than once in the course of this book. Seldom has anyone said anything better about the creative process.

9. See Murray Krieger, *Theory of Criticism* (Baltimore: Johns Hopkins University Press, 1976), p. 27 (on the unlooked-for opportunity) and p. 41 (on the reader's compulsion to make sense). Since Krieger is almost as essential to my arguments as Dewey, I will reuse some of these words also.

they are even more likely to damage parts of what they had achieved when they belatedly alter a text, whether at someone else's suggestion or at some whim of their own. In revising or allowing someone else to revise a literary work, especially after it has been thought of as complete, authors very often lose authority, with the result that familiar literary texts at some points have no meaning, only partially authorial meaning, or quite adventitious meaning unintended by the author or anyone else.

In the following paragraphs I sketch a few textual histories even though I later, at the risk of some redundancy, elaborate my comments on *Tender is the Night* and devote a chapter each to *Pudd'nhead Wilson*, *The Red Badge of Courage*, and *An American Dream*. My first point is that often a part of a text we all read (and write about) has no meaning at all. This is easiest to demonstrate at the level of syntax. The Appleton edition of *The Red Badge of Courage* (1895) has no possible referent for the plural "matters" in this sentence in the last chapter: "There were small shoutings in his brain about these matters"; in Chapter 7 of the Dial version of *An American Dream*, the hero, Stephen Richards Rojack, speaks out of "that calm" when there is no longer any previous mention of a calm in the scene.[10] It is easy enough to identify a range of meaninglessnesses in longer passages. In Chapter 16 of *Huckleberry Finn*, for instance, Huck and Jim are going downriver at night on the raft, having passed Cairo in the fog without knowing it. In one paragraph they plan to watch for a light so Huck can paddle ashore in the canoe and ask someone how far down the river Cairo is, and in the next paragraph Huck concludes that there "warn't nothing to do, now, but to look out sharp for the town, and not pass it without seeing it." This nonsense was created when Mark Twain agreed to drop, from between the two paragraphs, the raftsmen episode, which contained the reason for the decision not to ask anyone else but just to watch out for the town.[11] In *Pudd'nhead*

10. I first suggested reconstructing the manuscript version of *The Red Badge of Courage* in *Nineteenth-Century Fiction* 30 (March 1976): 558-62. See Chapter 6 for more on *The Red Badge of Courage* and Chapter 7 for more on *An American Dream*.

11. See Peter G. Beidler, "The Raft Episode in *Huckleberry Finn*," *Modern Fiction Studies* 14 (Spring 1968): 11-20.

Wilson, as we have long known, several passages refer to the Italian twins in ways that make sense only if they are conjoined, as they were (two heads, four arms, one trunk, two legs) when the original version was completed.[12] In Chapter 13 of the published novel occurs a meaningless passage not involving the twins. A delegation of Democrats calls upon Wilson, the village butt, a lawyer who has just tried—and lost—his first case during his more than two decades in Dawson's Landing, and offers to support him for mayor. These men look like fools afflicted with a political death wish, but Pudd'nhead's desirability as a candidate survives from the original version, where he had just been catapulted into popularity by successfully defending his first client and winning his first case, a defense of the twin Luigi against the charge of kicking Tom Driscoll. The verdict, of course, rested on the impossibility of proving which twin did the kicking. Chapter 17 of Stephen Crane's *Maggie* was rendered meaningless in the Appleton edition (1896) by the excision of the title character's climactic encounter with the huge fat man. In this strange text, as I explain below, Maggie no longer explicitly goes down to the dark river, with anyone else or alone, although the setting shifts to the river; and tall buildings magically seem to jump down to the river from their location which had earlier been identified as farther away, in a "final block" of buildings.[13]

Often enough revised texts will contain passages which make a minimal kind of sense but lack the specific meaning they were invented to convey, even when that meaning is literally their reason for being. In *Pudd'nhead* the twins are present at all only because when conjoined they had for months served

12. I made brief comments on *Pudd'nhead Wilson* in "The 'New Scholarship': Textual Evidence and Its Implications for Criticism, Literary Theory, and Aesthetics," *Studies in American Fiction* 9 (Autumn 1981): 181-97. See also Philip Cohen, "Aesthetic Anomalies in *Pudd'nhead Wilson*," *Studies in American Fiction* 10 (Spring 1982): 55-69. I am not always distinguishing between anomalies which were created by the addition of the Roxy-Tom plot as the manuscript was being completed in December 1892 and the anomalies which were first introduced in July 1893 when Mark Twain pulled out half of his typescript for publication as *Pudd'nhead Wilson*. A detailed account is in my Chapter 5.

13. See Hershel Parker and Brian Higgins, "Maggie's 'Last Night': Authorial Design and Editorial Patching," in my special Crane issue, *Studies in the Novel* 10 (Spring 1978): 64-75.

Mark Twain as a source for hilarious inventiveness, and taking them out of the final text would have required more work than he was willing to perform. Once the twins are (most of the time) separated, Luigi's kick becomes commonplace, and other passages are lifeless: Mark Twain would never have had the twins play duets on the piano if they had not had four hands to put on the keyboard and only one bottom to sit on. (The book illustration shows one twin sitting on the piano stool and one on a chair—no fun at all.)

Clues to specific authorial meanings are sometimes removed with enough of the context left for the reader to arrive at a vague sense of the authorial meaning, although not the precise meaning the author had intended, as in this sentence from *Sister Carrie*: "In her own apartments Carrie saw things which were lessons in the same school." Since the 1900 edition omits the page and two thirds which Dreiser wrote to precede this sentence, the reader has to undergo a process of imperfect self-correction which the author did not set up: he has to assume that "lessons" refers to the conclusion of the once-distant paragraph which now stands just in front of the sentence in question, specifically to the law that "If a man is to succeed with many women, he must be all in all to each."[14] Then as he

14. First a comment on a windfall of a textual anomaly. For whatever reason, the *Critical Inquiry* printing of the second sentence of this paragraph replaced "undergo a process of imperfect self-correction" with "try to do that"; the result is that, as printed, the subsequent reference to Stanley Fish stands foolishly uncontrolled by any prior reference; nobody, of course, commented on the incoherence.

See *Sister Carrie* in the Pennsylvania Edition, textual editor James L. W. West III, general editor Neda M. Westlake (Philadelphia: University of Pennsylvania Press, 1981), p. 102, and in the Norton Critical Edition, ed. Donald Pizer (New York: W. W. Norton, 1970), p. 77. The Pennsylvania Edition is based upon a fresh transcription of the manuscript, the Norton upon the much abridged first edition (1900).

The Pennsylvania edition has sold well in the Penguin paperback despite being repeatedly attacked, notably by Donald Pizer in a review in *American Literature* 53 (January 1982): 731-37; my review in *Resources for American Literary Study* 11 (Autumn 1981): 332-36 (actually published in October 1983) was cast as a rebuttal to Pizer's. After Robert H. Elias and others criticized the Pennsylvania edition at a session of the 1983 MLA convention in New York City, I was allowed to speak from the podium briefly to repeat the textual anomalies I mention here and to challenge the audience to look carefully at the unintended consequence of all the "block cuts." As I said at the session, attention has been too much focused on the effects of the different ending. Worrying about endings is often unprofitable because they are frequently more contingent than the rest of the novel and in any

proceeds he is forced to revise that conclusion and take "lessons" as referring rather vaguely to the longings awakened by the sight of prosperous people, but he could never arrive at the original lessons in the crucial difference between having money and being poor. Any resemblance to the process of reading as described by Stanley Fish is coincidental: this is a case of needless, unintended fumbling ignorantly imposed upon the reader by careless excision.

A text can lose some authorial meaning but retain enough to serve as a clue to the right meaning, although the effect of that meaning on the reader will not be precisely the one intended by the author: compare the meaning and effect of the "mental conflict" Carrie experiences in the restored original text in the Pennsylvania Edition (p. 91) with that she experiences in the Norton (p. 71), a reprint of the 1900 edition. In the Norton, the reader can scour the preceding page and then correctly deduce that the voice of conscience is in conflict with the voice of want, but Dreiser wrote "mental conflict" to refer to the dialogue between the voices in the immediately preceding twelve paragraphs, not a word of which is retained in the 1900 text which the Norton follows, a text which does not carry full and precise authorial intentionality.

Sometimes a passage in a text will embody two different and contradictory authorial intentions rather than one consistent authorial meaning. For the English edition of *White-Jacket* Melville added to Chapter 27 two new short paragraphs which piously modify the democratic protest worked into the chapter as originally written, where the question for discussion, twice posed, is "Are there incompetent officers in the American navy?" This is the second of the inserted paragraphs: "And the

---

case are connected to the rest of the text only at one side. The tougher test for textual superiority, I would say, is within the body of the book, where the 1900 omissions create many dozens of disjunctures as serious as the two I cite here. The fact that readers have always overlooked such anomalous passages merely means that we have to make some sense of what we read if we are to persist with a book. It does not mean that readers may not have been so bothered by such awkward spots, however subliminally, that they have put the book aside, concluding, consciously or not, that Dreiser could not write coherent sentences, paragraphs, and chapters, and could not create interesting, consistent, characterizations. Pace is not merely a matter of brevity versus length, for the pace of a coherent longer book may well be faster than that of an incoherent shorter book.

7

only purpose of this chapter is, to point out as the peculiar desert of individuals, that generalized reputation, which most men, perhaps, are apt to ascribe in the gross, to one and all the members of a popular military establishment."[15] Purpose not being a quality which can be infused through an unrevised passage by an act of retro-declaring or retro-wishing, no one assigned to define the purpose of the chapter as first written could possibly come up with anything resembling the one Melville added in what looks like a perfunctory retrenchment from political radicalism. In the Appleton *Red Badge*, little regard was displayed for what if anything was left as meaning after cuts had reduced the original, objectionable evidence of Henry Fleming's persistent self-absorption, vainglory, and self-delusion, but there was also a deliberate if perfunctory effort to impose a new meaning on the remnants of the original meaning through the addition of a tiny upbeat last paragraph: "Over the river a golden ray of sun came through the hosts of leaden rain clouds." Yet throughout the much-scissored final chapter and the earlier portions of the text as printed in 1895, clues to Henry Fleming's vanity and self-delusion survive despite the excision of the most blatant evidence. The result of the Appleton expurgation was a maimed text which reached classic status because of the power it still retained, but which, once the vogue of close reading set in during the 1940s, became the ground on which a generation of critics battled inconclusively, armed with contradictory indications in the text.

Sometimes passages embodying one authorial meaning are so placed as to read as if they embodied a different one. What we know as Chapter 11 of *Pudd'nhead* was written when Tom was merely a local white youth, a sneak-thief and a scamp. In the published book, "Tom" from the start is not Tom at all but a changeling, part black and a slave, and Chapters 9 and 10 deal with his learning the horrible truth and undergoing great, if temporary, anguish about the news. In writing what is now Chapter 10 Mark Twain took some pains to make it plausible that in later (and earlier written) scenes Tom would act much as usual, despite his brief mental turmoil, but he did not bother to

15. See my "Melville and the Concept of 'Author's Final Intentions,'" *Proof* 1 (1971): 165-66.

8

work Tom's new condition into the parts already written. When he put *Pudd'nhead* together, he hoped in a general way that Tom would seem black in the passages written when he was all white, but he did not make any attempts to *make* him black in those passages, not even erratic attempts such as he made to separate the twins in some of the passages where he retained them as characters. As it turned out, Mark Twain got an accidental bonus on the level of local meaning, for any reader of Chapter 11 will think that Tom snatches away his hand so the palm-reading Wilson will not find out that he is part black and a slave, not merely that Wilson will find out that he is a thief. Judging from the abundant evidence that Mark Twain did not read all through what he salvaged as *Pudd'nhead Wilson*, he probably did not ever specifically "intend" the new meaning of the gesture, even retroactively, although he would have been delighted to get something for nothing. And judging from the contemporary reception and from modern academic criticism, there was no need for the author to have invested any more labor on the salvage operation than he did, for no critic has complained about Tom's being distractingly white in some middle chapters of the book.

Adventitious meanings which accrue to scenes in altered texts are more often than not obtrusively out of keeping, despite the happy fate which befell Tom's gesture. An example occurs in *Pudd'nhead* near the beginning of Chapter 13, written when Tom was still white and the love-rival with the fairer of the conjoined twins, Angelo, for the affections of young Rowena, who is, of course, as white as Tom. Moping along a lane, Tom thinks of calling Rowena in order to have some "cheerful company," then realizes that "the detested Twins would be there." Seeing Tom's unhappiness, Wilson starts to ask if Rowena has rejected him, but Tom explains that the trouble is that he has been disinherited by Judge Driscoll, his real uncle when the passage was written. Mark Twain was not titillating himself and his readers with a violation of the taboo against allowing a black to harbor casual thoughts of a tonic flirtation with a white girl; rather, in slapping together a salable text he simply failed to notice that the early written passage had accrued unintended racial implications.

9

Inadvertent, intentionless meanings riddle the 1951 edition of *Tender is the Night*, the one which Malcolm Cowley reordered chronologically in accordance with an intention Fitzgerald had had sometime in his last years, well after the publication of the book in 1934.[16] This text is in fact a showcase of adventitious meanings which the author could not possibly have intended and could not have wanted if he had become aware of them. They range from large-scale inadvertencies (such as the ludicrousness of the long mystery about what happened in the bathroom at the Villa Diana, when the reader of the reordered text knows just what kind of mad scene Nicole had enacted there) to small-scale inadvertencies (such as the luridness which accrues to the screening of Rosemary's movie *Daddy's Girl* when the reader knows that Nicole, who is watching the movie, was driven insane by incest with her father). Dozens of local details lose precise authorial meaning and seem to gain adventitious, nonauthorial meanings, even though almost all the words of the original text are retained. Authorial functions for parallel scenes, for instance, are subtly altered when the scenes are spaced either further apart or closer together, and authorial functions are altered even more drastically when scenes, images, and words are reordered, so that the reader encounters what was meant as an echo before encountering the occurrence which the echo was designed to recall. More recently, in revising the *Esquire* version of *An American Dream* Mailer made some tiny excisions which alter the functions of the characters in unintended ways. The ex-prizefighter Romeo, for instance, inadvertently seems to rise in the hierarchy of characters because the evidence has been blurred that the contest Rojack has with him was meant as a kind of hysterical parody of the more significant contest that had just occurred between Rojack and Detective Roberts, a psychological equal of the hero in the serial but not explicitly so in the book.

As these examples suggest, non-meanings, partially authorial meanings, and inadvertent, intentionless meanings co-exist in standard literary texts with genuine authorial meanings. It happens all the time, and almost nobody minds. The alert critic

16. See Brian Higgins and Hershel Parker, "Sober Second Thoughts: Fitzgerald's 'Final Version' of *Tender is the Night*," *Proof* 4 (1975): 129-52.

who progresses through such a maimed text will experience not only genuine authorial rewards but also some perfectly real aesthetic frissons which, although coming from words the author wrote, are haphazard and spurious. These adventitious thrills, which are not the result of outlandish literary experiments such as shuffling pages but are the everyday inadvertent consequences of a writer's imperfectly altering a text, are more abundant than anyone has suggested, and are of a significance which shames that notorious example of a fatuous literary response to a textual error, the cheap thrill F. O. Matthiessen felt when he was brushed by a "soiled fish," a single-word compositor's error (for "coiled fish") in a modern reprint of a nineteenth-century novel. These thrills are cheap, of course, because they cost the author (or someone else) nothing at all (or very little) to create; and they also cost the critic very little trouble to arrive at since they come readily to view in "the text itself."[17]

Confident that their aesthetic goosebumps are authorially planned, critics are lured into seeing authority where the passage they are reading contains nonsense. An instance is the Appleton *Maggie*, which the author himself expurgated under the direct orders of the editor Ripley Hitchcock, who may well have committed some of the textual mayhem after Crane had done his own worst to his bedraggled text. Whoever removed the fat man from the ending of Chapter 17, Crane himself or Hitchcock, does not matter. What concerns me here is that the ending of that chapter not only did not make sense but was not really supposed to make sense. That is, Hitchcock was primarily concerned with making sure that no reader of the Appleton text would know that Maggie had ever encountered such a gross, lascivious, and terrifying man, particularly not in a situation which in the original version involved an assignation not in even a cheap hotel, but, for all the reader could tell, in the open air, in winter, in the darkness of the riverfront warehouse district. Hitchcock did not bother to make sure he or Crane had left

---

17. Matthiessen's blunder was first pointed out in John W. Nichol, "Melville's '"Soiled" Fish of the Sea,'" *American Literature* 21 (November 1949): 338-39. In Chapter 3 I show how the vogue of the term "soiled fish" in the 1960s reflects a general ignorance about genuinely complex textual problems.

the chapter coherent in a new way: enough that it was not coherent in the old way. In the event, the Appleton edition contains nonsense rather than any particular meaning. The buildings seem to leap from the beginning of the block to the river's edge, Maggie seems to be at the water although she is not shown going there, light is seen and sound is heard in one paragraph and light and sound fade in the next, but that fading is not defined as a result of movement from the streets toward the river. Yet governing a number of essays on *Maggie* is the assumption that the text is coherent, when properly explicated. William M. Gibson insists:[18]

> Crane's intention in changing his text at this point is further sub-
> stantiated by his cutting two bits of dialogue which immediately
> precede. . . . Thus in Crane's revised text Maggie no longer solicits
> the last two men she meets, and the "huge fat man" whom she
> might accept has wholly disappeared—she has, plainly, made up
> her mind to drown herself. The ambiguity is gone and the logic of
> Crane's chapter and his whole story is improved, or remains
> unimpaired.

Under a similar conviction that the 1896 text must perforce make sense Fredson Bowers advances one of the most compli-cated arguments in American literary history in demonstrating, apparently to no one else's complete satisfaction, that Maggie from the beginning of the chapter has had one purpose and one purpose only, to commit suicide. She has been soliciting the men she meets out of "simple reflex," Bowers assumes, so if a man had responded favorably to her blandishments she would perforce have apologized and explained that she was really on her way to drown herself and, mindless chit that she is, just forgot momentarily.[19] All of the critics who have labored over the question of what happens in Maggie's last night in the Appleton edition have clung fiercely to the conviction that the words in the expurgated text must make sense, whatever their

18. William M. Gibson, ed., *Stephen Crane: "The Red Badge of Courage" and Selected Prose and Poetry* (New York: Rinehart, 1956), pp. xvii-xviii.

19. Fredson Bowers, in his Textual Introduction to *Maggie* in *Bowery Tales* (Charlottesville: University Press of Virginia, 1969), p. lxxxiii.

differing ideas as to the nature of that sense. So clinging, they have experienced cheap thrills unplanned by the author or anyone else.

While Cranians were writing about their thrills from the unintelligible text of *Maggie*, other critics were reveling in cheap thrills derived from intentionless meanings in *Pudd'nhead Wilson*, responding to authorial words which had lost their original authorial meanings and had seemed (by altered placement and altered plot) to acquire new meanings. Taking unintended, adventitious meaning as authorial meaning, Mark D. Coburn winces at what he finds in *Pudd'nhead*:[20]

> Twain devotes most of chapter 6 to an account of Aunt Patsy's reception, where Dawson's Landing swarms to meet the handsome young noblemen it has acquired. Twain's unusually heavy irony belittles the celebrants, compelling the reader to find their desperate need for public approval both amusing and pitiful. The contrast between the surface gaiety of the scene and the underlying blackness of Twain's satiric vision makes the chapter almost painful to read.

Coburn's almost visceral discomfiture is a cheap thrill, as cheap as the more tamely intellectual thrill John Freimarck has in deciding that Luigi's kicking Tom is "a direct reversal of Tom's kick which lifts Chambers over the doorsill" (this although Luigi's kick was written before Chambers was invented and before Tom had any black blood). James B. Haines thrills cheaply at a complicated set of correspondences when he declares that "Luigi by kicking Tom—as one might kick a dog—, is literally launching him into an orbit of subsequent actions and reactions, all of which have as their animating and sustaining force, the thrust of Luigi's foot, the impelling power of blackness" (this despite the fact that the foot belonged both to Angelo and to Luigi when the passage was written, despite the

---

20. Mark D. Coburn, "'Training is everything': Communal Opinion and the Individual in *Pudd'nhead Wilson*," *Modern Language Quarterly* 31 (June 1970): 213. The following two quotations are from John Freimarck, "*Pudd'nhead Wilson*: A Tale of Blood and Brotherhood," *University Review* 34 (June 1968): 306; and James B. Haines, "Of Dogs and Men: A Symbolic Variation on the Twin Motif in *Pudd'nhead Wilson*," *Mark Twain Journal* 18 (Winter 1976-77): 17.

fact that Tom was not black when it was written, and despite the fact that many of Tom's subsequent actions and reactions date from the time he was all white). Critics are particularly apt to thrill to what they take as authorial preparation but what is in fact their own imposition of order onto the sequence of pages they confront. They pay tribute to the construction of *Pudd'nhead Wilson*, commenting upon what happens "as a novel develops," on what the author did "from start to finish," on a phrase that "echoes threateningly and ambiguously throughout the novel," on "the novel's chief concern, from the first to the last chapter," on an "inexorable process" in the book, on how the "opening chapter, with considerable adroitness and economy, prepares us for the major ironies of the narrative to follow," on the "long, carefully plotted preparation," and on the author's coming "to grips with the animating issue of slavery in a sustained effort which, challenging him more deeply as he wrote, called upon the deepest resources of his imagination."[21] Malcolm Bradbury, finding purposeful ambiguity in *Pudd'nhead Wilson*, scoffs at critics who have tried to pretend that the plot is simpler than it is or have blamed the author for "evading the significance of his 'slavery' theme," while in reality the "very variety of their interpretations suggests the ambiguous quality of the book," and therefore its high literary merit.[22] This ambiguous quality of the book, of course, is the result of the way it was composed and later salvaged for print.

In reading the Cowley edition of *Tender is the Night* Wayne C. Booth experiences a complex set of adventitious frissons as he praises authorial preparation:[23]

21. These quotations are all genuine but I identify the author of only the last in order to stress that even the best critics make the same assumptions routine critics do: James M. Cox, *Mark Twain: The Fate of Humor* (Princeton: Princeton University Press, 1966), p. 221.

22. Introduction to *Pudd'nhead Wilson* (New York: Penguin Books, 1969), p. 29.

23. Wayne C. Booth, *The Rhetoric of Fiction* (Chicago: University of Chicago Press, 1961), p. 195. In writing a version of this chapter for *Critical Inquiry* I deliberately chose examples from the celebration of the Cowley text of *Tender is the Night* by a co-editor of *Critical Inquiry* and from a text Walter Benn Michaels cited in "*Sister Carrie*'s Popular Economy," *Critical Inquiry* 7 (Winter 1980): 373-90.

Consider, for example, the scene in which Rosemary has learned that Nicole and Dick are to meet for love-making at four. If we read Rosemary's jealous reactions ("It was more difficult than she thought and her whole self protested as Nicole drove away") without ever having seen Dick's and Nicole's love in the early years, and without knowing anything of all the qualities besides sex that enter into that love, we can hardly avoid feeling all on the side of Rosemary: too bad about the poor man trapped by the mysterious and obviously dangerous Nicole. But in the revised version our sympathies are properly divided: we see the two women fighting over the drowning man, himself a victim of both, though each is in her own way sympathetic. A fairly trivial affair has been transformed, through proper preparation, into a significant step in a moral collapse that none of the principals sees as clearly as we do.

This analysis is notable for the argument that authorial preparation is found not in the text into which Fitzgerald worked his developing intentions page by page; instead, "preparation" is discovered and celebrated in the text which was reordered without being rethought and rewritten. It is as if hunks of a novel were of the same consistency throughout, like processed cheese food.

It seems that treating the author as an abstracted, olympian power frees critics to celebrate nonsensical texts and adventitious meaning in texts where the words, but not all the meanings, are the author's; and treating the text the author created as if it were merely hypothetical, a metaphysical concept, frees them to identify "the text itself" as the published text or the revised and republished text. Joseph Katz goes so far as to say that the manuscript version of *Red Badge* is "a work that was never meant to exist," as if it had not in fact existed.[24] Wayne C. Booth talks coolly about the "restoration of chronological order" in *Tender*, when the surviving drafts show that there never had been a chronological order to restore, only the flashback structure, according to which the whole novel was built.[25] So much for the actuality of authorial achievement. As I will

24. Joseph Katz, Editor's Note to *The Portable Stephen Crane* (New York: Viking Press, 1969), p. xxii.
25. *The Rhetoric of Fiction*, p. 192.

15

demonstrate in the following chapters, all authority in literature comes from the author, but that authority can be blurred or wholly lost and, paradoxically, it can persist even when the author thinks it has been removed. Ironically, when the New Critics turned away from accounts of the creative process they cut themselves off from the best possible evidence for validity in interpretation and for textual unity; and when reader-response critics ignored both textual evidence and the findings of cognitive psychologists they cut themselves off from some of the best possible evidence as to how readers respond to literary texts. Throughout this book I view the problems readers have with imperfect texts not primarily as aesthetic (or moral!) but cognitive. That is, I ask the question James J. Gibson asks: "what happens to perception when the information is inadequate?" And I reply with his words: "In general, the answer seems to be that the perceptual system *hunts*. It tries to find meaning, to make sense from what little information it can get." I am talking, in textual terms, about what Gibson describes as the consequences of inadequate information—"information that is conflicting, masked, equivocal, cut short, reduced, or even sometimes false."[26] In this book about uncompleted texts, patched together texts, maimed texts, and meaningless texts, I celebrate the author's drive toward formal unity, and I celebrate as well (or sometimes commiserate with) the reader's drive to make sense of what he or she is reading.

26. See *The Senses Considered as Perceptual Systems* (Boston: Houghton Mifflin, 1966), p. 303. While for my purposes the best accounts of making sense come from the Cornell cognitive psychologists, John Reichert in *Making Sense of Literature* (Chicago: University of Chicago Press, 1977) draws support from "the language philosophers and philosophical psychologists loosely associated with Oxford—J. L. Austin, Gilbert Ryle, and their progeny" (p. x). In many ways, my book may be seen as a companion to Reichert's, and I would have made use of his arguments at various points if he had ever broken through the conviction that all texts "are written to be read" (p. 59), that all critics start with "a literary text" (p. 77) as a given. For Reichert, "textual evidence" (p. 101), means only what it means to a New Critic; "the text is the data which the interpretation attempts to explain or make sense of" (p. 104).

CHAPTER 2

The Determinacy of the Creative Process and the Authority of the Author's Belated Textual Decisions

In the last four decades editors, editorial theorists, critics, and literary theorists have all shied away from the creative process as if it were too untidy if not too embarrassingly indelicate for mention in public. It is easy to see why editors have tended to concentrate on printed texts, since many of them were most familiar with literature of the Renaissance, from which texts usually survive only in printed form. Ronald B. McKerrow and W. W. Greg illustrate this tendency, and certain of Fredson Bowers's editorial decisions are best explicable in terms of the same tendency.[1] McKerrow's great contribution in the late 1930s, in his *Prolegomena for the Oxford Shakespeare,* was to destroy the rationale under which editors had exalted the last edition published in an author's lifetime as the most authoritative text of a literary work. McKerrow realized that the earliest surviving edition would normally contain more of the author's own words and own marks of punctuation than any later text, and that each subsequent resetting would almost inevitably

---

1. I refer to the general failure to think in terms of surviving manuscripts; see Ronald B. McKerrow, *Prolegomena for the Oxford Shakespeare* (Oxford: Oxford University Press, 1939); W. W. Greg's "The Rationale of Copy-Text," *Studies in Bibliography* 3 (1950-1951): 19-36; and more particularly Fredson Bowers's abandonment of manuscript as copy-text even when it exists, as in his edition of William James's *Pragmatism* (Cambridge: Harvard University Press, 1975).

contain additional printing-house corruptions, even though they might be accompanied by new authorial corrections and revisions. McKerrow went so far as to realize that if what one wanted was an eclectic text containing the author's final intentions, the way to get it was to emend authorial changes in any later editions into the early copy-text, but he rather helplessly concluded that *all* the words from the later "authoritative" edition had to be adopted along with the obviously authorial readings, unless they were typographical errors or other blatant printer's blunders. Greg's contribution at the beginning of the 1950s was a plausible rationale for adopting most (if not always quite all) of an author's revisions while rejecting routine printing-house alterations (along with, perhaps, a few authorial changes so trivial or apparently indifferent as to be indistinguishable from printer's or editor's alterations). In reacting against the ignorantly sentimental exaltation of the authority of "deathbed" editions, neither McKerrow nor Greg showed any concern for going backwards behind the first edition in their search for the most authoritative form of a text. Indeed, Greg so fixated on the problem of editing printed texts that he left to Bowers and others the task of extending his theory to its logical conclusion that a final manuscript should be preferred as copy-text over the first edition set from it.[2]

In the 1960s the newly trained editors of the Center for Editions of American Authors accepted Bowers's extension of Greg's rationale to surviving final manuscripts, but they did not

2. The great propounder of Greg is of course Fredson Bowers, whose voluminous discussions up to 1976 are listed in the checklist of his publications in his *Essays in Bibliography, Text, and Editing* (Charlottesville: University Press of Virginia, 1975); the collection includes some of the more important of these discussions, such as the first (prepublication) explication of Greg, "Current Theories of Copy-Text, with an Illustration from Dryden," reprinted from *Modern Philology* 48 (August 1950): 12-20. G. Thomas Tanselle's two fullest explications of Greg's rationale are "Greg's Theory of Copy-Text and the Editing of American Literature," *Studies in Bibliography* 28 (1975): 167-229, and "Recent Editorial Discussion and the Central Questions of Editing," *Studies in Bibliography* 34 (1981): 23-65. Jerome McGann in "Keats and the Historical Method in Literary Criticism," *Modern Language Notes* 94 (December 1979): 988-1032, takes an airy view of questions involving the creative process, which he relegates to a footnote (n. 14, p. 1029): "what are we to understand as the point of origin? Is it the work's date of composition? The date of publication? And what difference would it make?"

evince complete easiness with a manuscript as copy-text, particularly if it differed greatly from the first edition.[3] A good many
editors chose to call the manuscript copy-text but for convenience resorted to marking up a printed text for their own
printer's copy, a defensible practice (since making a reliable
typescript printer's copy from a manuscript has its own hazards)
but one invariably strewn with pitfalls. The editorial language
of the late 1960s, well after Bowers's extension of Greg to manuscripts, was peppered with such odd terms as "pre-copy-text
variants," a phrase which, as used by some editors, obscured the
status of forms of the text prior to whatever edition the editor
was determined to use as copy-text. In the 1970s and thereafter
the fascination of the first edition is clear in the tendency of
some editors to define the manuscript as copy-text but to talk of
"restoring" a word from the manuscript rather than "retaining"
it in preference to a corruption in the first edition. In the same
period members of the CEAA advisory committee saw a number
of editors denigrating a manuscript as a "rough draft" which
was too imperfect to serve as copy-text, even though on close
examination it was found that the manuscript had been the
setting copy for the first edition—messy, to be sure, but demonstrably the setting copy and therefore not technically a rough
draft. In a kind of reversion to editorial policy before McKerrow,
editors seeking support from the National Endowment for the
Humanities have offered sample tables clogged with routine
compositional variants in late reprints while omitting the
changes which counted most, such as the author's revisions
between the serial version and the first book version; in effect,
such editors were asserting their kinship with the old champions of "deathbed" editions. During this awkward phase when
people were learning new concepts and new terminology, and
applying them in actual editorial work even as they were still
trying to grasp them, no powerful, coherent voice was raised
against the basic arbitrariness of Greg's modest essay, his dogmatic prescription that the editor's duty was to incorporate any
subsequent authorial readings into the early copy-text. Nor was

3. I avoid documentation in this paragraph because some of my information
was gained confidentially during work on the CEAA Advisory Committee or NEH
panels.

any powerful voice raised to protest the central assumption of Greg's rationale, that an author retains, as long as he lives, complete authority over his text; yet this assumption, as I will demonstrate in this chapter, is incompatible with what is known about the creative process.

At the same time that editors, leery of manuscript evidence, looked forward, away from the final manuscript toward the first edition (or, more often, looked forward, away from the first edition toward any subsequent evidence as to author's *final* intention), literary critics concentrated on the final product also. They ignored the evidence as to how any work had reached the printed form which they held in their hands as the verbal icon awaiting their criticism, the evidence as to what the work meant, in part or in whole, at any of the early stages of its composition. The Depression-born New Criticism attained its enormous practical power in the post-war burgeoning of established English departments and the creation of new departments in new colleges and universities whose libraries could rarely hope (at least for some decades) to become major repositories of books and manuscript materials essential for many kinds of serious historical, biographical, and textual research. Under this new methodology, tailor-made for the transformed conditions of academic life, a few lessons from a textbook by Cleanth Brooks and Robert Penn Warren along with a Rinehart edition, available anywhere, gave many a new assistant professor not merely a starter-kit but the whole stock-in-trade for setting up in the practice of literary criticism. And the New Critical avoidance of "textual bibliography" in all its aspects, including study of compositional evidence, has prevailed during all later fashions in criticism. In the 1960s, for instance, Paul Brodtkorb, Jr.'s phenomenological reading of *Moby-Dick*, one of the most sensitive and wide-ranging "readings" of the book ever published, reached a new pinnacle of intrinsicness at which all of Melville's factual errors and all the copyist's and compositorial blunders would have to be defined as Ishmael's.[4]

---

4. Paul Brodtkorb, Jr., *Ishmael's White World* (New Haven: Yale University Press, 1965), p. 5: There is "no necessity to blame Melville for the book's inconsistencies, because most of them are storyteller's mistakes, and Ishmael is pervasively characterized as a storyteller."

In the 1970s and 1980s, even the deconstructionists in practice treated any text as a New Critical given, however thoroughly they would then proceed to deconstruct it.

Theorists of the New Criticism, of course, had ruled extrinsic evidence, including compositional evidence, out of order. The nearest W. K. Wimsatt, Jr., and Monroe C. Beardsley came to discussing such evidence was the abrupt pronouncement that authorial revisions of an earlier work were merely late attempts to do right what the author had wanted to do in the first place, when he was not good enough to do it.[5] But theorists opposed to the New Criticism have been equally scornful of evidence about the creative process. In the 1960s E. D. Hirsch, Jr., for instance, declared that the New Critics had "very justly" attacked "the post-romantic fascination with the habits, feelings, and experiences surrounding the act of composition."[6] One is left to guess at what post-romantic horrors Hirsch had in mind, earnestly sentimental accounts, perhaps, of melancholy poets brooding upon parapets as they gushed forth their lyrics. Whatever the nature of his embarrassment with accounts of literary genesis, whether hopelessly maudlin and commonplace accounts now quite forgotten, or substantial, if theoretically naive, accounts such as John Livingston Lowes's much-praised *The Road to Xanadu*, Hirsch no more than Wimsatt and Beardsley wanted to descend to anything so gauche as talking about the creative process.

In the mid-1960s James Thorpe neatly avoided the grossness of the creative process by refusing to acknowledge the presence of literary authority in any stage of a work prior to its publication, the act of publication being the force which infused authority into all the words in the published text; a few

---

5. The collaborative essay was first printed in *Sewanee Review* 54 (July-September 1946): 468-88, where this passage appears on p. 470: "If there is any sense in which an author, by revision, has better achieved his original intention, it is only the very abstract, tautological, sense that he intended to write a better work and now has done it." In the reprinting of the essay in Wimsatt's *The Verbal Icon* (Lexington: University of Kentucky Press, 1954), p. 5, and the photo-offset paperback (New York: The Noonday Press, 1958), the passage appears in this form: "There is a sense in which an author, by revision, may better achieve his original intention. But it is a very abstract sense. He intended to write a better work, or a better work of a certain kind, and now has done it."

6. *Validity in Interpretation* (New Haven: Yale University Press, 1967), p. 3.

years later, Michael Hancher published an analysis of three kinds of intention which soon attained outsized influence in textual circles through G. Thomas Tanselle's acceptance of its categories.[7] Hancher applied the term "programmatic intention" to "the author's intention to make something or other," a "more or less approximate and generic" intention such as to write a sonnet or an epic. This kind of intention apparently precedes the actual attempt to write the sonnet or epic or whatever. Hancher then applied "active intentions" to those which "characterize the actions that the author, at the time he finishes his text, understands himself to be performing in that text." His third category was "final intention," an "intention to *cause* an effect of one sort or another: it defines whatever the author wishes to accomplish *by means of* his completed work"— such as the author's intention to cause a reader to change his belief about something or to have the work make money for him. Except for an offhand comment in one footnote, Hancher never took any account of the intentions a writer may have during the act of composition, never considered that if authorial intention in a literary work is there at all it might be built in, piece by piece, during the process of composition, rather than being bestowed retroactively, like a blessing. Hancher can accommodate the period before the composition, the moment of completion, and the indefinite period afterwards; but *during* —the ongoing creative process itself—has no place in his theory. For all practical purposes he does not seem to believe there is any such thing as the creative process. By contrast, when I talk of an author's intention to write something (from a sentence to

7. James Thorpe, *Principles of Textual Criticism* (San Marino: Huntington Library, 1972), p. 38, a revision of his "The Aesthetics of Textual Criticism," *PMLA* 80 (December 1965): 465-82; Michael Hancher, "Three Kinds of Intention," *Modern Language Notes* 87 (December 1972): 827-51 (the quotations are from pp. 829, 830, and 834; see n. 10 on p. 831). Tanselle's acceptance of Hancher's categories is in his "The Editorial Problem of Final Authorial Intention," *Studies in Bibliography* 29 (1976): 167-211, an essay extraordinarily important as the first attempt to reconcile notions of intention held by editors, literary critics, aestheticians, philosophers, speech-act theorists, and others. (Tanselle's footnotes constitute a superb annotated guide to discussions of intention from the early 1940s through the mid-1970s.) For another discussion of Hancher and Tanselle, see Steven Mailloux's chapter on "Textual Scholarship and 'Author's Final Intention'" in his *Interpretive Conventions* (Ithaca: Cornell University Press, 1982).

an entire novel) I mean what John R. Searle calls "prior intentions" (whether they are long prior to or momentarily prior to the act of writing). The actual composing process as I talk about it is what Searle calls "intentions in action." Like Dewey and like Krieger, Searle emphasizes that in the case of complex actions (such as—to invent an example—writing a paragraph of "The Whiteness of the Whale") prior intentions are relatively indeterminate. It seems clear that literary theorists must now take up the challenge of applying Searle to the process by which authorial intentions are embodied in literary works.[8]

For now, the most compelling recent descriptions of the creative process in literature (aside from some descriptions by writers themselves) is in the writings of a few aestheticians (notably Murray Krieger), and in the writings of a few clinical psychologists and psychiatrists (notably Albert Rothenberg); as it happens, both Krieger and Rothenberg are indebted to the philosopher John Dewey's *Art as Experience*.[9] The evidence presented by these three (like Searle's evidence) suggests that authorial intentionality is built into the words of a literary work during the process of composition, not before and not afterwards. Dewey's account laid great stress on the artist's moment-to-moment control over the relationships between what he has already done, what he is about to do, what he actually is doing, and what he knows, at least vaguely, that he must do later on. If what the writer puts down at a given moment does not "retain and sum up what has gone before as a whole and with reference to a whole to come," Dewey said, there will be "no consistency and no security" in what the writer later puts down. While genuine art is coherent, it can never be fully plotted out in advance; all finer artists "learn by their work, as they proceed, to see and feel what had not been part of their original plan and purpose."

8. John R. Searle, *Intentionality: An Essay in the Philosophy of Mind* (Cambridge: Cambridge University Press, 1983). See Chapter 3, "Intention and Action," especially the discussion of the "relative indeterminacy of prior intentions" in n. 10, pp. 93-94.

9. Murray Krieger, *Theory of Criticism* (Baltimore: Johns Hopkins University Press, 1976); Albert Rothenberg, *The Emerging Goddess: The Creative Process in Art, Science, and Other Fields* (Chicago: University of Chicago Press, 1979); John Dewey, *Art as Experience* (New York: Minton, Balch, 1934), pp. 45, 56, 139.

Like Dewey, and drawing from the discussion in *Art as Experience* which I have also relied upon, Krieger postulates an intense, hazardous process of composition in which a developing work "seeks to maintain its own integrity," even against whatever initial intentions the writer may have had for it.[10] Like Dewey, Krieger sees an author's choices as being diminished as the work grows: "there may be an action initiated that sends forth lines of probability that he must fulfill, characters who must in some sense be consistent, feelings aroused that establish a controlling tone, perhaps metaphors that later words will have to carry forward." By the time the author is well into the work, the nature of such of its aspects as action, character, tone, and metaphors "has become so formed that each of them insists on its fulfillment and dictates what is needed to bring that fulfillment about." Krieger describes a "drive toward oneness" which is "felt by the form-making writer in the throes of his give-and-take struggle that gives him his awareness of the growing monster whose demands to satisfy its own needs he must respect, even at the expense of his own original intentions." More clearly than Dewey, perhaps because he is dealing specifically with the art of words, not art in general, Krieger stresses the possibilities of small, local failures throughout a literary work—failures that do not amount to fatal flaws in its coherence, failures that readers overlook, most often, either recognizing no anomaly or assuming that the work is better than it is, and that the fault is in "the inadequacies in our actual response."

Where Krieger couches much of his description from the perspective of the literary work, the "growing monster," rather than its creator, Albert Rothenberg focuses his account of the creative process sharply on the state of mind of the artist. What Rothenberg describes as a result of his clinical investigations jibes with what Krieger says and with our commonsense impressions as to the phases of composition:[11]

Beginning with undifferentiated knowledge and experience, the creator proceeds through differentiation and joining, expansion and constriction, stray pathways and returns, diffusions and

10. Krieger, pp. 25, 25-26, 26, 32, 41.
11. Rothenberg, pp. 370, 342, 353, 355, 354, 355, 375.

24

sharpenings, fantasy and reality, world visions and narrow technical concerns, cultural concerns and individual preoccupations, art styles and personal styles, arousal and ratiocination, abstraction and concretion, breaking and making. Always, as there are factors and processes tending toward diffusion and expansion, there are equally strong factors and processes directed toward differentiation and joining.

All during the creative process the writer struggles "actively and adaptively to achieve certain goals," engaging "in a task that makes him increasingly anxious as he pushes onward." Though the process "characteristically involves a progressive uncovering of unconscious material with attendant anxiety, the progression...is slow, gradual—an arousal boost—and highly controlled." (Rothenberg defines "arousal boost" as "pleasure derived directly from moderate increments of arousal.") All during the highly conscious and controlled process of composition, anxiety is followed by relief, with "delicate balances between discomfort and relief, attraction and aversion." One of the "hallmarks of the creative process" which "justifies the risks and anxieties involved" is "the struggle toward psychological freedom," a struggle which is basic "to the value and appeal of art" to the artist, freedom attained with the composing and finally the completing of the work.

Krieger the literary theorist and aesthetician and Rothenberg the clinical psychiatrist are united in their depiction of the creative process as a struggle—toward growth to full size of a monster with a will of its own in Krieger's formulation, toward psychological freedom in Rothenberg's. Struggles end, for Krieger, with the completion of a literary work which has formed itself in its growth toward "oneness," literary unity. For Rothenberg, struggles end with the completion of the work and the freedom (or compulsion) of the writer to turn to the creation of a new work, it being a law of creativity that a writer will usually take up "another creative task as soon as he has finished the last one."[12] In either formulation, the author's authority is built, perfectly or imperfectly, into the text during the act of composition, during the moment-by-moment struggle to build a new

12. Rothenberg, p. 353.

sentence or paragraph or chapter upon the previous ones, and to build them, at the moment of composition, in such a way as to permit and to control what is already more or less inchoately envisioned as yet to be written. That is, in a literary work words written subsequent to a given passage will be written as they are because of the control already built into previous lines and because of the control already projected toward still later passages, although these later passages will take their precise form only from the innumerable local decisions, such as those governing choice of words and choice of sentence structure, which are made as the projected intention is, when the time comes, embodied, so that each achieved intention becomes an accomplished fact influencing still subsequent passages. I will consider later the possibilities of a writer's altering intentionality once it is worked into a passage, but for my purpose here it is sufficient to conclude that the coherence of any great literary work is the product of a multitude of decisions made—and opportunities lost or seized—during each moment of the actual process of composition.

At any point during the process of composition the writer's control may be imperfectly asserted, despite all the talk of achieved perfection which writers as well as critics may indulge in, such as Ernest Hemingway's claim about *For Whom the Bell Tolls*: "You see every damned word and action in this book depends on every other word and action."[13] Every word and action should depend on every other word and action, indeed, and sometimes that interdependence is so complexly coherent as to overawe any churlish or merely skeptical inquiry, but empirical evidence supports Krieger's intuition that every choice of sentence structure and every choice of phrase is a fresh occasion for partial failure, as well as a fresh occasion for solid craftsmanship or even for triumphant surmounting of the difficulty of the moment. Writers can fail to achieve coherence between sentences, between paragraphs, between larger sections of a work. They can relinquish a thought when it is too complicated to follow out, just at the moment, through all its

13. *Ernest Hemingway: Selected Letters, 1917-1961*, ed. Carlos Baker (New York: Charles Scribner's Sons, 1981), p. 514, Hemingway to Maxwell Perkins, 26 August 1940.

sinuosities. They can be robbed of a train of thought whenever they admit Coleridge's man from Porlock, the restless specter who knocks at their door in a hundred disguises, every day that they write. Hemingway ruefully, almost desperately, described to a friend his struggle to keep up his work rhythm on *For Whom the Bell Tolls* at Key West in the spring of 1939:[14]

> This is how it is. I went to Cuba intending to write three stories. I wrote the first one and it was good. Then I started on the second one and before I knew it I had fifteen thousand words done and was going better than I have gone since Farewell To Arms and I knew it was a novel. I interrupted it to come back here to K.W. Galaghers were comeing over from France and Bumby was down from school and I've been seeing people every day and being away from the novel and feeling as though I were loseing it has me almost nuts. I'm going back tomorrow and get in it again and I feel like you do before battle. I'm spooked of the necessity to interrupt again sometime the middle of May. If I lost it, and I feel so damned close to loseing it now, I should really be shot because it is the most important thing I've ever done and it is the place in my career as a writer I have to write a real one.
>
> I hope you understand it Tommy. Any guy who says he will do a thing and then rats out is a shit. But it would be a sin against the bloody holy ghost if I buggered up this book and I've got to stick with it until I finish it. . . .
>
> I know you understand about it where most guys think you can jump in and out of your work.

For Hemingway, the rare "belle epoque," the mood in which body, soul, and circumstances conspired to produce great writing, was to be cherished as something very like a divine gift of grace.[15] His struggle with *For Whom the Bell Tolls* may have been triumphant, but often writers struggle, as valiantly as Hemingway, to retain the mood in which they are progressing steadily on a complicated work, only at last to be battered into losing control. In the following examples I want to work from the perspective of the author, not the critic or theorist, pointing out

14. *Selected Letters*, Hemingway to Thomas Shevlin, 4 April 1939, pp. 483-84.
15. *Selected Letters*, Hemingway to Arnold Gingrich, 16 November 1934, p. 410; to Maxwell Perkins, 9 April 1936, p. 443; and to Arnold Gingrich, 16 September 1936, p. 451.

that distractions may come on such a grand scale that the book will be the result of more than one creative process, one or more of which may never have been completed, or that a book will be the result of an incomplete creative process.

In *Pudd'nhead Wilson* Mark Twain did not ever work his initial Siamese twins plot to its conclusion.[16] Instead, before he had completed the first plot he conceived a drastic plot shift and simply wrote straight on through an ending (newly conceived in some details, though probably somewhat close to the ending he earlier had more or less thought out), then continued from the ending to a new beginning and at last linked up, clumsily enough, to the point at which he had shifted to the new plot. Never during the composition of this big manuscript which contained what we know as *Pudd'nhead Wilson* and what we know as *Those Extraordinary Twins* (as well as many passages not ultimately used in either of these books) did a single, coherent creative process culminate in the completion of anything like a unified work of art. Months after completing this long manuscript, as I will show in Chapter 5, Mark Twain salvaged roughly half of it as *Pudd'nhead Wilson*, a text riddled with incoherencies that critics have rarely noticed. And Mark Twain's work in salvaging this material did not spring from a renewal of the creative process, as the grossness of the surviving anomalies show, but from a hardheaded merchandiser's hasty scrutiny of unsold goods.

Melville's *Pierre* is also the result of two very different and imperfectly combined creative processes, the second one destructive of part of the achievement of the first.[17] The biographical evidence indicates that Melville actually completed

16. My comments derive from my work on the California Edition of *Pudd'nhead Wilson* (in progress). See my Chapter 5.

17. See my "Why *Pierre* Went Wrong," *Studies in the Novel* 8 (Spring 1976): 7-23, and "Contract: *Pierre*, by Herman Melville," *Proof* 5 (1977): 27-44. These two articles are combined, revised, and augmented by me and Brian Higgins as the Introduction to *Critical Essays on Herman Melville's "Pierre; or, The Ambiguities"* (Boston: G. K. Hall, 1983), pp. 1-27.

While most critics find unity at all costs even in books known to have a strange compositional history, now and again a critic of the post-New Criticism generation (like a good many first generation American Literature scholars such as Leon Howard) is content to place less stock in formal perfection. Richard Brodhead, in particular, has displayed a remarkable tolerance toward Melville's altering the

(or all but completed) *Pierre* in a short version during an almost uninterrupted period of six or eight weeks in November and December 1851, a remarkably short period, even in view of his creation of both *Redburn* and *White-Jacket* in a four-month period two years earlier. The book he completed, or almost completed, was ready for sale to Harper's by the first days of January 1852, as a work of some 360 printed pages, his shortest book since *Typee* and *Omoo*. In all likelihood Melville had worked *Pierre* out to its tragic conclusion, very possibly rushing his hero pell-mell to disaster in a matter of days after he reaches the city, in a parallel to the several days of the action in the country which occupies the early part of the novel. We must assume from the evidence that Melville had freed himself of the original impulse by embodying it in a finished or all but finished manuscript before negotiating a contract for it. It was apparently the negotiating of a contract that triggered his abrupt shift of mood, for the Harpers gave him a contract which meant that, barring a near-miracle, he would have to give up his literary career: 20¢ on the dollar after costs, where the old terms of 50¢ on the dollar had not been enough to sustain his family. Stung by the contract and its implications, and faced with scathing reviews of *Moby-Dick* in the January periodicals, more than one of which called him insane, Melville began pouring out his new preoccupation with the failure of his career into the manuscript which he had intended as a psychological novel about the fate awaiting a deludedly enthusiastic seeker of Truth. Within a matter of days he had expanded the manuscript far beyond its original estimate, compulsively wrecking whatever unity the

---

direction of *Pierre* half way through the book as we know it. Brodhead observes, as Leon Howard and many others had done, that the second half of *Pierre* has little to do with the first, then with mild benignity decides that "Melville was wise not to let a foolish consistency keep him from exploring the subjects and methods he does" in "Chronometricals and Horologicals," "Young America in Literature," and "The Church of the Apostles," even though "their inclusion has a curious effect on the book's narration." Brodhead knows the book is split in two. Rather than demanding a verbal icon, however, he makes the best of a bad situation, finding interest where he can—but at the cost of closing his eyes to the agony that lay behind Melville's decision to record his rage against his reviewers and his fears about the death of his career as a writer, even if doing so meant wrecking what might well have been the most tightly unified work he had yet written. See Chapter 8, "The Fate of Candor," in Brodhead's *Hawthorne, Melville, and the Novel* (Chicago: University of Chicago Press, 1976), pp. 163-93; the quotation is from p. 182.

original work possessed with a new plot centered on the suddenly announced (and surely belatedly thought-up) writing career, past and present, of his young hero. At the beginning of Book 17, "Young America in Literature," Melville's "I write precisely as I please" signals his disastrous surrender to his new obsessions.[18] In the long book finally published, products of the two different creative processes survive, the product of the earlier process making up, most likely, the first half of the book, and products of the second process making up much of the second half of the book, inextricably mixed with passages imperfectly salvaged from the earlier version. The second process must be called creative, although it occasioned the destruction of part of the original conclusion of the book and made it a maimed work which can be celebrated as a literary unity only by rigorous exercise of critical will.

In other instances only a single creative process can be identified, although the writing may have been prolonged over several years during which it may have undergone changes of direction before being abandoned for other projects or left unfinished—and inconsistent—at the author's death. More than once Melville thought he had completed *Billy Budd, Sailor*, but was drawn into further revisions each time, so that what he left at his death was a "semi-final draft," according to the editors Harrison Hayford and Merton M. Sealts, Jr.[19] Not quite complete, the manuscript contained anomalies arising from the fact that Melville's intentions had changed at various points during his years of labor on the story. One instance is especially relevant here, the fact that Chapter 29 was left in a

18. See Brian Higgins and Hershel Parker, "The Flawed Grandeur of Melville's *Pierre*," in *New Perspectives on Melville*, ed. Faith Pullin (Edinburgh: Edinburgh University Press, 1978), pp. 162-96; reprinted with minor revisions in pp. 240-66 of the G. K. Hall collection cited in the previous footnote.

19. *Billy Budd, Sailor*, eds. Harrison Hayford and Merton M. Sealts, Jr. (Chicago: University of Chicago Press, 1962), p. 1. See especially their account of the "Growth of the Manuscript," pp. 1-12 and their "Analyses of the Manuscript," pp. 223-69. The following summary of Hayford and Sealts's findings is condensed from a discussion I wrote for a special issue on narrative endings in Hershel Parker and Henry Binder, "Exigencies of Composition and Publication: *Billy Budd, Sailor* and *Pudd'nhead Wilson*," *Nineteenth-Century Fiction* 33 (June 1978): 131-43.

state that revisions and additions in preceding chapters had rendered nonsensical. As Hayford and Sealts point out, at an intermediate stage of his work Melville wrote the news account which is now Chapter 29 to follow the ballad (which was the first thing he wrote); in the news account everything is misconstrued, Claggart being mourned as an innocent patriot and Billy condemned for extreme depravity. At the close of the account Melville appended four lines summarizing the moral of the entire work as he then saw it: "Here ends a story not unwarranted by what sometimes happens in this [undeciphered word, perhaps "conventional"] world of ours, innocence and infamy, spiritual depravity and fair repute." But when Melville began preparing a fair copy of the story he was led into another set of revisions in which the narrative took on new philosophical and dramatic dimensions and grew to some three hundred fifty manuscript pages. In this final stage of the story's growth, Hayford and Sealts show, Melville developed the character of Captain Vere, the tormented imposer of Billy's sentence, a man with an exceptional nature commensurate with Billy's own, capable of embodying the agonizing conflicts between intuition and duty, justice and law. The earlier-written news account and the coda did not "close" in any sense Melville's later-written dramatic scenes between Vere and Billy or resolve the issues raised by the strangely diverse ways in which Billy and Claggart could both be guilty. Consequently, when Melville ended the story in this third stage, he arranged three "brief chapters" as "something in the way of sequel." Chapter 28 reports that the injured and drugged Vere had murmured the name of Billy Budd just before his own death. Then as Chapter 29 Melville placed the news account, without the coda, since its ring of finality made it unusable anywhere except at the very end of the story. The last chapter consisted then of two parts—first a somewhat rewritten version of the prose headnote about a sailor from Billy's own watch who wrote the poem "Billy in the Darbies," then the poem, slightly revised from the version which years before had been the first part of the whole work which Melville inscribed.

Although Melville revised the prose beginning of Chapter 30 to include an allusion to the recently written "history of the spar from which Billy was hanged," he did not similarly recast the news account, a fact which, as Hayford and Sealts show, created anomalies in the text:[20]

> The news account, since it was written...before Captain Vere's role was developed...makes no mention of his part in the affair of the "the tenth of the last month," or of the engagement with the French ship (which would have been very soon after), or of his mortal wound, or his death—although all of these would have had to be known to anyone in a position to originate the report from which the account stemmed. As a matter of fact, since everybody aboard, as the later development had it, knew at least the "outside" story of the case and sympathized with Billy, no imaginable informant could have given "in good faith" a report subject to such diametric distortion as that displayed in the news account. These matters that were developed later than the composition of the account make its last sentence, particularly, anachronistic: "Nothing amiss is now apprehended aboard...." That Melville was aware of something of the sort seems implied in his pencil notation at the head of the first leaf (Leaf 340), "Speak of the fight & death of Captain Vere". He never went on to so do by revising the account, but canceled the notation.

Thus the impulse which made Melville bring the prose head-note to the ballad in line with the events he had finally described in the story also emerged as he reflected, at least momentarily, on what would be needed to salvage Chapter 29 as the middle one of three concluding chapters rather than the final chapter; but he had not fully resolved the inconsistency before he died, if in fact he fully realized that he needed to resolve it. As Hayford and Sealts wryly conclude, "no critic" had noticed anything anomalous, much less anything impossible, about the news account.

Even when a writer completes a literary work according to a single pervading thought which had impelled it from the beginning, he may very seldom be able to give it a "final polishing" which reduces unwanted repetitions, irons out inconsistencies, reconciles anomalies, elaborates echoes and images, plants forward-looking hints and backward-looking cross references, and

20. *Billy Budd, Sailor*, p. 269

takes care of such mundane housekeeping business as making sure that a character who lacks a father in the early chapters does not inexplicably acquire one later on or seeing that each character has the same name all the way through. Some writers, Ernest Hemingway among them, have been able to put a draft of a novel aside then some weeks later go back and rewrite it, but the rushed pattern typified by Melville is probably more common. Just as few writers have the chance to compose in what Melville called the "silent grass-growing mood" in which everyone should compose, but are forced to rush onward toward completion, so do writers rarely have a reflective yet hyper-alert period for final polishing between composition and publication.[21] In practice, a final polishing of one section may be contemporaneous with the composition of other parts, and one part may receive its final polishing before another part is written, so that the writer never has the chance to see, for instance, a serial version as a whole until after the last episode is published, a time that may be too late for conscientious revisings with equal attention to early, middle, and late episodes. In the last bustle of preparing a manuscript for publication (even a manuscript that had been in progress for years) authors tend to take shortcuts despite their awareness that spots here and there need a little doctoring. In *Huckleberry Finn* the reader never knows when Jim washed off his sick Arab makeup because Mark Twain struck out the passage where the Duke cusses Jim for keeping his blue paint on, then made a note to "shove" the information "back yonder to where they escape lynching & regain raft," but never followed through. Other housecleaning notes from Mark Twain to himself also got ignored: "Go back & burn the skiff when they escape lynching" ("burn" was a second thought for "sink") and "Go back & put on old clothes after escape from lynching."[22]

Rarely occurring in pure form, the phenomenon of final polishing may shade into haphazard or systematic censoring or

21. *The Letters of Herman Melville*, eds. Merrell R. Davis and William H. Gilman (New Haven: Yale University Press, 1960), p. 128.

22. DeLancey Ferguson called attention to these notes in "Huck Finn, Aborning," *Colophon* n.s. 3 (Spring 1938): 171-80, as reprinted in the second edition of the Norton Critical Edition of *Huckleberry Finn*, eds. Sculley Bradley, Richmond Croom Beatty, E. Hudson Long, and Thomas Cooley (New York: W. W. Norton,

other kinds of retractions an author suddenly sees a need for, as when he notices that he has been revealing all along something he would prefer, on cautious second thought, not to have the public know. On a given page, final polishing of one sentence may occur close beside a bit of self-censorship or correction of fact or editorial suppression. Final polishing of a sentence may accompany an adaptation of the whole work for a new audience, or may accompany the expansion or reduction of certain parts of the text. In practice, as I have said, writers almost never give equally meticulous care to each chapter of any novel they think they are subjecting to its final polishing. Just as we need to remember that any new edition or any revised printing will rarely be purely the product of a single impulse (such as an editor's desire to expurgate, a writer's desire to improve the style, a writer's desire to restore something earlier deleted), so we need to remember that seldom does a writer have the time and patience to polish a book to his heart's content at a time when he is still in fullest control, still remembers why he wrote each part as he did, and can still see the broad consequences of any local revisions.

Such authorial impatience should not be surprising, for the creative process is, after all, a process which by definition begins, continues (as clinical observation records, with varying admixtures and sequences of excitement, arousal, boredom, anxiety, and determination), then ends—ends with stubborn finality. The process is inescapably physiological as well as psychological and intellectual; the arousal can even be manifested sexually, Rothenberg shows (in a passage which may set people to musing over the tendency of some writers—male or female—to prefer their sexual partners to be nonverbal and therefore less disruptive to the writer's thought processes).[23] Since the process involves so much extreme bodily and mental strain, the writer tends to react against that strain by putting the

---

1977), pp. 314-15. My transcriptions are from *Adventures of Huckleberry Finn (Tom Sawyer's Comrade): A Facsimile of the Manuscript* (Detroit: Gale Research Company, 1983), Vol. 2, pp. 351, 448, and 448-A.

23. Rothenberg, p. 372: "Sexual impulses aroused during the creative process might induce conflictual anxiety because they are forbidden or because they require discharge. Or the alert, moderately tense state connected to creating gives rise to feelings of attraction and the need for sexual discharge."

work out of body, out of mind, as soon as it is finished. Many writers, as Rothenberg says, in a passage already referred to, are driven by inner compulsion or external circumstances into an immediate repetition of the whole exalting and exhausting process, turning at once to the composition of a new work, sometimes beginning it even before the old process is quite over.[24] At other times a writer may permit himself a fallow period where only what Melville called "silly thoughts and wayward speculations" about future projects are allowed to engage him.[25] Perhaps the finality with which thought of a literary work is left behind is commensurate with the grandeur of the task and the intensity and duration of bodily, intellectual, and aesthetic involvement in it. In any case, all empirical evidence should tell us that Greg is wrong, that in any mature human being, writers included, a state of indefinitely sustained arousal toward one object is unnatural.

Every reader of this chapter could supply a number of accounts by writers of the way they feel when completing one creative process and beginning another, or when beginning to think about the need to begin another. Melville comes readily to hand for my illustration. Some nine weeks after he had taken care of the last pre-publication details on *Mardi*, he wrote to Evert A. Duyckinck:[26]

> I am glad you like that affair of mine. But it seems so long now since I wrote it, & my mood has so changed, that I dread to look into it, & have purposely abstained from so doing since I thanked God it was off my hands.—Would that a man could do something & then say—It is finished.—not that one thing only, but all others —that he has reached his uttermost, & can never exceed it. But live & push—tho' we put one leg forward ten miles—its no reason the other must lag behind—no, *that* must again distance the other —& so we go till we get the cramp & die.

Melville's attitude is the normal one—in the altered mood which followed his initial relief at being rid of the book, he has "purposely abstained" from looking into it and even now

24. Rothenberg, p. 353.
25. Melville to Sarah Morewood, 12? September 1851, *Letters*, p. 138.
26. Melville *Letters*, 5 April 1849, p. 83.

dreads to do so. Instead, while wishing that human accomplishment could carry finality with it, he is impelled to think of the next task. In the event, he did not then attempt an ambitious book in which he would outdistance *Mardi*: he played the responsible family man and in one summer wrote two long books designed as commercial successes, *Redburn* and *White-Jacket*, before he could reward himself with the prolonged composition of another book such as he wanted to write, *Moby-Dick*. After a year and a half of intermittently intense labor on that book, Melville sent the American sheets to England in September 1851 and left his desk for autumnal chores and wanderings in the Berkshires. He was getting in his winter firewood in early November when he received from Duyckinck a clipping about the sinking of the ship *Ann Alexander* by a whale in the Pacific. The English edition had already been published, although Melville had not yet seen a copy, and the American edition was a week from publication. What Melville said in response to the clipping expresses the completeness with which he had put the whaling book behind him:[27]

> Your letter. . .had a sort of stunning effect on me. For some days past being engaged in the woods with axe, wedge, & beetle, the Whale had almost completely slipped me for the time (& I was the merrier for it) when Crash! comes Moby Dick himself (as you justly say) & reminds me of what I have been about for part of the last year or two.

Similar formulations can be found in a great number of writers: they have finished and dismissed the book, or the book has finished with them and dismissed them.[28] Many writers put the laborious efforts of composition and the mingled self-criticism and self-congratulation of completion resolutely behind them.

---

27. Melville *Letters*, 7 November 1851, p. 139.
28. Typical is what Eudora Welty says in *Writers at Work: The "Paris Review" Interviews*, Fourth Series, ed. George Plimpton (New York: Penguin Books, 1977), p. 276: "I correct or change words [in galleys], but I can't rewrite a scene or make a major change because there's a sense then of someone looking over my shoulder. It's necessary, anyway, to trust that moment when you were sure at last you had done all you could, done your best for that time. When it's finally in print you're delivered —you don't ever have to look at it again. It's too late to worry about its failings. I'll have to apply any lessons this book has taught me toward writing the next one."

When a writer takes up a completed work again, he may no longer be in fullest control of it, may no longer remember why he wrote each part as he did, and may no longer see the broad consequences of any local revisions he may be lured into making. The English edition of *White-Jacket* provides good examples of the mixed nature of variants in revised editions, for circumstances gave Melville a chance to polish the American proof sheets as he had not been able to polish *Typee, Omoo, Mardi,* and *Redburn,* a chance he would take full advantage of only once more in his life, when he revised "Benito Cereno" for inclusion in *The Piazza Tales.* He took the sheets of the American edition of *White-Jacket* with him when he sailed to London in the fall of 1849; he was free to revise them on shipboard, presumably, and later in his lodgings in London he made note of his looking the sheets over.[29] He was free to revise because the book was to be reset in London, if he found a publisher, so any changes he made could be accommodated with no expenses for altering standing type or plates. Melville did, the variants show, take his opportunity to do a limited amount of stylistic revising and to correct some factual errors and misprints, and at some point he wrote a delightful additional passage on the cook, Old Coffee, for insertion at the end of Chapter 68, one of his characteristic omnium gatherum chapters where insertions or additions of discrete sections would not be apt to disturb any aspect of the structure of the chapter or the book as a whole.

Yet a couple of his small additions damaged the coherence of the text which was eventually printed in London, conspicuously in Chapter 90, where Melville had written this hortatory footnote on British impressment of American sailors during the Napoleonic Wars:

> These things should be known; for in case the British government again goes to war with its fleets, and should again resort to

29. For a general account see Willard Thorp's Historical Note in *White-Jacket* (Evanston and Chicago: Northwestern University Press and The Newberry Library, 1970), 404-08, and the Note on the Text, 444-58. I categorize these and other examples in "Melville and the Concept of Author's Final Intentions," *Proof* 1 (1971): 156-68.

indiscriminate impressment to man them, it is well that both Englishmen and Americans, that all the world be prepared to put down an iniquity outrageous and insulting to God and man.

For the English edition, Melville expanded the passage at both ends:

It is not intended to revive old feuds. In one sense, let by-gones be by-gones. But these things should be known; for in case the English government again goes to war with its fleets, and should again resort to indiscriminate impressment to man them, it is well that both Englishmen and Americans, that all the world be prepared to put down an iniquity outrageous and insulting to God and man. It is hardly to be anticipated, however, that in case of war the English government would again attempt to revive measures, which some of its own statesmen must have deplored from the beginning; and which as [i.e., at] the present day, must surely seem iniquitous to the great body of Englishmen. Indeed, it is perhaps to be doubted, whether Englishmen could again be brought to submit even to domestic impressment.

This milder version obviously derives from a different attitude than the earlier one in Melville's most fervent oratorical manner, what Horace Greeley had called (in reference to the stump-speaking of Melville's brother Gansevoort) the "gas and glory" style. Presumably the additions were motivated less by Melville's own spontaneous literary impulses than by his desires to adapt the book to a British publisher and a British audience. He may have made the changes either just before he sailed for England or on the ship, but he also, and more likely, may have made them during the frustrating weeks during which he "wearily hawked this book from Piccadilly to Whitechapel."[30] When he came to terms with Richard Bentley, Melville had every reason for wishing to mollify the British in any convenient way, so a few adaptations for the new audience became mixed in with his corrections of fact, improvements of style, clarifications, the page-long addition about Old Coffee, and with, of

30. *The Melville Log*, ed. Jay Leyda (New York: Gordian Press, 1969) I, 361-62.

course, the usual assortment of printer's alterations, deliberate or inadvertent, and perhaps some minor editorial tinkering as well.

Stephen Crane's forced labor on the Appleton *Maggie* produced comparably mixed results.[31] In no sense was his work on the text early in 1896 a final polishing of the book he had privately printed in 1893. On the contrary, he made his new alterations under strict orders from his editor to remove, from throughout the little book, what Crane referred to as "the words which hurt." Crane doggedly plugged away at the chore, finding it so uncongenial, apparently, that he drew it out far beyond the time it should have taken, yet what he did was, in all likelihood, considered inadequate, so that probably the editor made further cuts (such as the deletion of the fat man in Chapter 17) once he had brought his expurgated copy of the first edition to New York City. Certainly Crane was not, contrary to what Fredson Bowers argues,[32] working his final aesthetic improvements into a text he was expurgating page by page; however, when he came to page thirty-one something, perhaps the amount of white space at the bottom of the page or on the facing page, tempted him to add a sentence to his depiction of a preacher who composed his sermons of "yous"—that is, who constantly harangued his congregation about the punishments awaiting them: "Once a philosopher asked this man why he did not say 'we' instead of 'you.' The man replied, 'What?' " The addition can hardly be said to do much damage to the text which was systematically being rendered lifeless and at points meaningless by expurgation, but it was an extraneous cheap shot, somewhat distracting because it intruded an alien perspective onto a passage which had been restricted to Jimmie's view of human nature and the world. The minister is appallingly hypocritical, to be sure, but the original point had been that he and his listeners, who were there for soup, not for castigation, were at cross purposes. As finally published, the 1896 *Maggie* contained corrections of typos in the first edition, the trivial addition about

31. See Hershel Parker and Brian Higgins, "Maggie's 'Last Night': Authorial Design and Editorial Patching," *Studies in the Novel* 10 (Spring 1978): 64-75.
32. *Bowery Tales*, ed. Fredson Bowers (Charlottesville: University Press of Virginia, 1969), p. xcvii.

the preacher, a couple of other slight expansions, many alterations of the style (eliminating extreme locutions), many deletions or modifications of curse words and other impolite
language, a cut version of the ending of Chapter 17, along with
some new typos and, presumably, other printer's alterations.
Crane could be trusted to do the preliminary excising of words
which hurt, but most of the stylistic alterations were probably
editorial, it being unlikely, in the case of strained locutions if
not outright solecisms, that in 1896 Crane would regard with
distaste so much of what he had been happy to publish in 1893.
A lesson of *White-Jacket*, *Maggie*, and many other textual histories is that even though textual variants first appear together in a
certain edition, we should not assume that they were all made at
the same time by the same person under the same impulse.

There seems no reason to doubt the obvious assumption
that the farther a writer gets away from the time the creative
process on a book ended, the more difficult it is for him to
remember the function of individual parts and the ways those
parts worked together. No hard and fast limits can be drawn:
some writers have better memories than others, some re-read
their own works more often than others, some wait until one
novel is published and reviewed before subjecting themselves
to the physical and mental distraction of undertaking a new
novel, and a great deal always depends on how prolonged and
overwhelming the creative process had been and how thoroughly the author is compelled to put it behind him and go on
with a new work. Certainly as authors get farther away from the
creative process they tend to become more cavalier about the
work. Henry James, for instance, felt no compunction about
touching up *Daisy Miller*, his early "study" of a nice American
flirt, three decades after writing it.[33] As he revised, he defaced
the tale. Forgetting, apparently, the charm of a Hawthornesque
echo in his reference to Geneva as the "little metropolis" of
Calvinism, he made it the "little capital" instead. He gave Winterbourne a new and hostile judgment on Daisy's appearance:
"she was composed—he had seen that before too—of charming
little parts that didn't match and that made no *ensemble*," and

33. "Daisy Miller: A Study," was first published in the *Cornhill Magazine* in
1878 then revised for Volume 18 of the New York Edition (1909).

she had "no idea whatever of 'form.'" (Here Winterbourne's view is not dissociated from the author's.) James made Daisy slangier (she says that she likes "hanging round," she says "He don't," she uses "ain't" instead of "isn't"). He made her coarsely say that her mother could wear her shawl "if she didn't mind looking like a fright." He made Winterbourne too obviously calculating: instead of hesitating a moment he pretends to consider something; instead of making the proper inquiries about his aunt's health he makes "a show of the proper solicitude." James gave Winterbourne a middle name which altered the effect from formality to ludicrous or even villainous pomposity: "Frederick Forsyth Winterbourne." Pervasively, he vulgarized the simple charm of the original without casting it into a mode where the heavy-handedness was somehow appropriate. Using the termless legal authority of the author, he violated the story, from first to last. This from Henry James—who is widely seen as an exemplar of the brilliantly revising author.

The 1931 version of *Sanctuary* is a classic instance of an author's attempting to reassert control over a novel by achieving the maximal difference in impact through a minimal outlay of revising. ("Minimal" is relative. Faulkner devoted much more labor to this task than Fitzgerald did to reordering *Tender is the Night*, but with comparable results.) Faulkner's inhibiting factor was that the novel was in galleys, having been set by the publisher when he had given up hoping the book could ever be printed. Once he saw the galleys, he wanted to make what improvements he could. He took the galleys apart, as he told the readers of the 1932 Modern Library reprint, and then reordered, mainly, rather than rewrote, as he did *not* tell the readers of the Modern Library edition. He drastically simplified the narrative technique, eliminating what he may have come to see as self-indulgent teasing of the reader through willful withholding and bestowing of information about episodes revealed only a bit at a time. The original narrative technique, self-consciously modernist in its structural disjunctures and juxtapositions, charged with hints of action only partially told, with results of actions before depictions of actions, with retelling of events from different perspectives, may now have struck Faulkner as

41

inappropriate for the material, a mechanical reuse of the techniques which had served him so well in *The Sound and the Fury*, where the strain on the reader's alertness had always been justified by the rewards.

Yet the genuine gains in clarity came at the cost of sacrificing much of the impact passages had when the reader approached them as he would have done in the original version, with or without specific information at a given point.[34] In the original text, for instance, the first thing we learn about Popeye is that Goodwin expects him to come to Jefferson and shoot him through the window of the cell where he is being held, apparently accused of some murder. Later in the chapter Horace recalls "Popeye's black presence" out at "that ruined house twelve miles from town," then circles round in his thoughts till he comes back to "Popeye's presence in black and nameless threat." The ominousness is powerful partly because we have already met Goodwin locked up and waiting for Popeye to kill him and partly because the threat is indeed "nameless" still, since we do not know what crime Goodwin is accused of and what actions Popeye is capable of. In the version Faulkner published, the same words about "Popeye's black presence" and "Popeye's presence in black and nameless threat" seem more than a little ludicrous, now that the book opens with a scene which, whatever else it does, establishes Popeye's own fears (Horace has to reassure him when an owl swoops at them), and now that intervening chapters have given substance to the threat conveyed in Popeye's presence, a threat no longer "nameless," even though we do not yet know precisely how he had hurt Temple Drake in the crib. Passages not only lose their precise meaning in the 1931 order, they also seem to acquire spurious meanings. In the first chapter of the original version when Miss Jenny tells Horace, "You were out there where it happened yourself not long ago," she knows more than the reader knows: she knows why Goodwin has been

34. See *Sanctuary* (New York: Cape & Smith, 1931); *Sanctuary* (New York: Modern Library, 1932); and *Sanctuary: The Original Text*, ed. Noel Polk (New York: Random House, 1981). Professor Polk now agrees with me that one should be very cautious in talking about Faulkner's "rewriting" of *Sanctuary*, as distinguished from his reordering it.

arrested, and she has called him a murderer. Furthermore, Horace's still unnamed sister has referred to Goodwin's woman as a murderess. The reader knows no basis for either charge, and has no idea whether one victim or multiple victims are alluded to. In the 1931 version, however, Miss Jenny's words have gained an adventitious sort of dramatic irony. That is, the reader cannot help reading into her words more than she could have meant, since he knows not only about Tommy's death but about some horrific violation Temple Drake had suffered out there. Such disconnectedness and spurious connectedness occurs repeatedly in the 1931 text.

Sanctuary as published in 1931 is decidedly an imperfect success, aesthetically speaking, not an instance of full reassertion of the authority of the author over the result of a long-past creative process. It is an example of an author's attempting to reassert control over old material, and succeeding, to a great degree, though not without extraneous new impulses (such as the one which led to the troublesome addition of Popeye's history) and certainly not without damage to the interrelationships that had been set up among the sentences and longer passages of the original version. Faulkner cannot accurately be said to have rewritten *Sanctuary* for the 1931 publication and cannot accurately be said even to have "written" the 1931 version. What he "wrote" was the original version (and the amount of reordering which went on during composition would be interesting to study). He reordered many hunks of the galleys without much rewriting within the hunks. Reordering plus minor tinkering simply is not the same thing as writing or rewriting, despite our near-compulsion to magnify the extent of Faulkner's labors on the original galleys.

The Sun Also Rises went into print as it did because Ernest Hemingway took seriously the good advice offered by F. Scott Fitzgerald and, rather than attempt a series of small excisions and modifications, simply discarded the first three galleys, which represented sixteen pages of the final typescript. For his efforts Fitzgerald has been celebrated as the second-best friendly critic of the century, a half step behind Ezra Pound. No one who has read the discarded opening of *The Sun Also Rises* has had a kind word for it, from James B. Meriwether (apparently its first academic reader), to Philip Young and Charles W.

Mann.[35] I am not going to praise "The *Sun Also Rises* Nobody Knows," either, but I do want to suggest several questions and a few possible answers.

How much worse is the original opening than a good many of the early passages in the printed version? I'd give you much of the Georgette scene of the novel as published if you would give me the discarded account of how Jake got to be European Director of the Continental Press Association. How *different* was the original opening from the rest of the novel? Well, aside from its displaying the "elephantine facetiousness" which Fitzgerald accused it of, it nowhere utilizes the novel's distinctively Hemingwayesque technique of tempering exposition with terse, noncommittal records of actions, a technique which rewards the alert, perceptive reader who is willing to be told what Jake feels but is just as willing to figure out what he feels by what he says or does. How much alteration of the subsequent galleys was made to accommodate the removal of the first three? Apparently very little was required because the opening was, as Fitzgerald argued, far too wordy to begin with. Does anything that was retained in *The Sun Also Rises* lose any of its intended effects because of the deletions? Naturally there are disruptions, some trivial, some more significant. Without the knowledge that Brett habitually sits for her portrait, various references to painters such as "the little Greek portrait-painter" Zizi are weakened; more important, without the opening sentences declaring that this is "a novel about a lady," Lady Brett Ashley, the implication is lost that Jake is also painting a portrait of a lady, a modern work to hang, perhaps, by the portrait of Isabel Archer. It matters also, matters significantly, that we know Jake is a partner of sorts in the news service he helped to start, not just an ordinary employee, that in the final typescript and the galleys he was, as readers of the book can't realize, freer financially than his colleagues Woolsey and Krum. Then at the end of

---

35. "Fitzgerald's *Sun Also Rises*: Notes and Comment," Philip Young and Charles W. Mann, *Fitzgerald/Hemingway Annual, 1970*, 1-13, the sources of the quotations from F. Scott Fitzgerald's letter to Hemingway about *Sun*. The deleted galleys are quoted from Frederic J. Svoboda's *Hemingway and "The Sun Also Rises": The Crafting of a Style* (Lawrence: University Press of Kansas, 1983), pp. 131-37, with thanks to Bern Oldsey for passing Svoboda's study to me before it was published.

Chapter 3 when Brett says to Jake, "'Oh, darling, I've been so miserable,'" it makes a difference whether or not we already know that she has been living with Mike Campbell. It even matters whether or not we have been told straightforwardly that Jake is a Catholic, since without that information two later passages are somewhat blurred. Such examples suggest that even though Fitzgerald's criticisms led Hemingway to delete some of the worst writing that had stood in the typescript and had survived into the galleys, the loss of the opening was not clear gain for the book as it was published. But for the excision to have been clear gain, of course, nothing in the first sixteen pages of the typescript could have had any significant relation to the rest of it.

Since Fitzgerald was a superb technician and a generous friend who took seriously his chance to help Hemingway improve an important book, his fumbles are as interesting as the comments which are unerringly on target. The fumbles, it seems to me, tend to occur when he is trying to say what is wrong about Hemingway's handling of his first person narrator. He singles out this paragraph as "maladroit," but not as more specifically inept:

> So my name is Jacob Barnes and I am writing the story, not as I believe is usual in these cases, from a desire for confession, because being a Roman Catholic I am spared that Protestant urge to literary production, nor to set things all out the way they happened for the good of some future generation, nor any other of the usual highly moral urges, but because I believe it is a good story.

Fitzgerald objected especially to page nine of the typescript, which included the paragraphs in which Jake described how he came to be a newspaper man living in Paris, but he was again unable to formulate the precise source of his uneasiness: "Somehow its not good. I can't quite put my hand on it—it has a ring of 'This is a true story ect.'" (The "ect" for et cetera is Fitzgerald's.) Lost in the deletion which Fitzgerald provoked were the passages which explicitly established Jake as writing "a novel about a lady" and having to grope toward the right way to tell the novel ("I did not want to tell this story in the first person but I find that I must"). Lost was Jake's sense of acting out a cliché: "Like all newspapermen I have always wanted to write a novel, and I suppose, now that I am doing it, the novel will have that awful taking-the-pen-in-hand quality that affects newspaper men when they start to write on their own book." Such passages made Fitzgerald uneasy, and his inability to put his hand on what was amiss is understandable, for he had just written a novel with a similar narrative problem, *The Great Gatsby.*

Nick Carraway's publishing his story of Gatsby was unbelievable, since it incriminated his cousin Daisy Buchanan in the death of Myrtle Wilson; his writing down the story is acceptable only if it is for his own benefit, a private way of affirming his sense of what Gatsby had come to represent to him. Fitzgerald had finessed the problem, but in the original opening pages of *Sun* Hemingway was writing himself into a moral and aesthetic corner every time he had Jake talk about writing a novel. In the book as published Jake a few times plainly is addressing the reader—and disconcertingly so, for it simply is not in character that he publish the book. Robert Cohn will betray his friends by putting them in a novel, as Frances Clyne claims: "'You know Robert is going to get material for a new book. Aren't you, Robert? That's why he's leaving me. He's decided I don't film well.'" Jake can behave badly, as when he betrays Montoya's friendship, but, to lay the finger directly on the wound, Jake is not the man to betray all his friends by writing a novel in which they figure. In writing a roman à clef to which too many people held a key, Hemingway was himself blithely betraying some of his own friends, and he seemed not to realize that he had created a hero with finer moral sensibilities than his own. Ironically, even though Hemingway took Fitzgerald's advice seriously enough to drop his opening, he at once began to lay down the defenses behind which he stood for the rest of his life, for he wrote Maxwell Perkins about the deletion as if it were his own idea, adding that "Scott agrees with me."[36] Hemingway the man was proving himself less than the best Hemingway hero; and the book as published, while the better for well-intended

36. *Selected Letters,* to Maxwell Perkins, 5 June 1926, p. 208.

advice stoutly if crudely acted upon, was left with the crucial narrative flaw still unidentified and untreated.

Conspicuously, as writers are unable to publish a work for months or a year or more after finishing it, they become willing to compromise to get it published, even if that means not getting *all* of it published. They not only become willing to change things of their own accord or to carry out someone else's instructions, they also resign themselves to letting someone else cut down a novel so that it (more precisely, *part* of it) can be published in some form, as when William Faulkner allowed Ben Wasson to reduce *Flags in the Dust* to four-fifths length for publication under the title *Sartoris*. And writers don't complain afterwards, as a rule—they make a deal and they stick with it. Naturally, the results of someone else's hacking away at a novel are apt to be ludicrous. Wasson left *Sartoris* incoherent. To name only some instances in which Byron Snopes figures, the reduced text leaves the reader not knowing the candy Byron gives Virgil Beard is stale, information which partly explains the boy's lack of enthusiasm; leaves the reader not knowing for sure that Byron has actually bought Virgil the airgun he is shown using to kill a mockingbird; not knowing that Virgil hounds Byron into moving; not knowing why Byron goes back to the bank after he injures himself escaping from Narcissa's room; and not knowing why a Negro is waiting for him in a car behind the bank. The reader of *Sartoris* may waste time over the trivial mystification of why Byron finds a car and driver mysteriously waiting for him, but from the evidence before him the reader cannot begin to perceive more serious problems, such as the fact that the sexually tormented bookkeeper had once, in *Flags in the Dust*, stood as a representative of the jealously resentful underclass just as Harry Mitchell stood as the vulgar nouveau riche, while young Bayard Sartoris and Horace Benbow stood respectively as degenerate representatives of the old aristocracy and the old professional class. In the aptly named *Sartoris* only young Bayard seems to play the full role originally assigned him, but ironically even though almost all the words about him are retained his character is imperfectly placed in relation to the post-war South, for as Faulkner designed the book, before it was cut down, he was defining Bayard through a complex set of parallels and contrasts involving one or more other males, including Horace, Byron, Harry, and Buddy MacCallum, the representative yeoman. *Sartoris* is typical of editorial condensations: little awkwardnesses are left to distract the reader momentarily, while more important aspects of the structure were so thoroughly removed that the reader cannot suspect they were ever present.

In general, writers tend to crumble when the exigencies of publication or republication come home to them. Even writers who have struck idealistic postures in defense of the sacredness of the text as they wrote it may see nothing sacred at all about a text long after they have written it. The writer who defends his every mark of punctuation against an imagined legion of prissy typesetters may very well, in another mood, allow lengthy sections of his prose to be scrapped, sacred commas right along with sacred adjectives. One such fulminator against sacrilegious typesetters, Mark Twain, agreed to take the raftsmen section out of *Huckleberry Finn* after no argument at all and very little consideration of the logistics that ought to have been involved. (Patently, writers will agree to excise something, whether the opening of *The Sun Also Rises* or Chapter 12 of *The Red Badge of Courage*, more readily than they will agree to do something which requires more work, such as writing a new section for a work the writer has already thought of as completed: look at how grudgingly Nathaniel Hawthorne agreed to add a postscript to *The Marble Faun*.)[37] With all due allowances for differences in authorial memory, character, and aesthetic acuteness, the more time passes the more likely the writer is to venture far-reaching (though readily accomplished) alterations on his own and the more likely he is to agree to alterations that someone else suggests, as when Melville not only accepted the expurgations of the Revised Edition of *Typee* but proceeded to rationalize them as giving the book more unity.[38]

37. *The Marble Faun*, ed. Fredson Bowers (Columbus: Ohio State University Press, 1968), Introduction by Claude M. Simpson, p. xxx-xxxii.

38. There was a salving basis for this rationalization, since some of the expurgated passages began as late additions to a "completed" manuscript. See Hershel Parker, "Evidences for 'Late Insertions' in Melville's Works," *Studies in the Novel* 7 (Fall 1975): 422, n. 18. In the treasure trove of Melville documents acquired by the

As editors, editorial theorists, critics, and literary theorists, we have located the sacredness of the literary art in whatever form of the verbal icon we encounter (we have, after all, to read *some* text), or else in the person of the creator (it's his work, we say, so he can do what he wants to do to it). Ignoring, for the most part, the creative process itself, we have revered the creator at the wrong time, after he has gone from creator of his own work to merchandiser or promoter of it. And we often revere the verbal icon not in the form it had when the artist was most in control of it, when it was most fully realized, but in the form which we encounter, even if that form was the result of an attempt, sometimes haphazard, sometimes systematic, to reduce some aspects of the product of the creative process. Hamlin Hill insists that to put the raftsmen passage back into Chapter 16 of *Huckleberry Finn*, right where Mark Twain wrote it to stand, would be "a literary tampering."[39] Whether it is good or bad, Hill says, the passage belongs out "because Mark Twain left it out." According to Donald Pizer, it is only "a superficial editorial romanticism which posits that an author's initial and 'instinctive' expression is of greater worth than his later critical reflection."[40] Pizer stubbornly insists on giving the writer "the last word," which in the case of the Appleton *Red Badge* means giving the editor the last word and depriving Stephen Crane of hundreds of words from his short book, precisely the words the editor sensed were most charged with strongest authorial meaning. One result of our revering the work in its familiar text instead of the product as it emerged from the creative process is that we squander time and effort explicating texts which are in part inexplicable. A result of our revering the writer as permanently all-powerful over any text he ever wrote is even worse—a hardening of our hearts toward authorial struggles and anguish,

---

New York Public Library in 1983 is manuscript of *Typee* carefully labeled by Melville (the young writer starting a professional archive) as the first draft, later much enlarged and revised.

39. From Hill's Introduction to his photofacsimile of *Huckleberry Finn* (San Francisco: Chandler, 1962), p. xii.

40. Review of the Pennsylvania Edition of *Sister Carrie*, *American Literature* 53 (January 1982): 733. The comment on giving Crane "the last word" is in "A Note on the Text" in Pizer's Norton Critical Edition of *The Red Badge of Courage* (New York: W. W. Norton Co., 1976), p. 3.

toward achievement and failure alike, a refusal to see in human terms the fact that a book can be the result of more than one creative process, one or more of which may never have been completed, or that a book can be the result of an incomplete creative process.

I hope I have worried my examples enough to warrant my pointing some morals for those long-suffering editors, editorial theorists, critics, and literary theorists whom I charged at the outset with having shied away from talking about the creative process. Rather than throwing up his hands and declaring that an author can do anything he wants to do to any of his texts, an editor should be concerned to find what degree of authority governs an author's textual decisions, early and late. Every editor and editorial theorist should test editorial theory and practice by its compatibility with the best that is known about the creative process, whether from the work of biographers, textual scholars, clinical psychiatrists, aestheticians, or others. Freed from the duty to celebrate the mystical authority of the author and the magical perfection of a literary text, critics should accept the duty of justifying their choice of text for citation and analysis and the duty to take account of the creative process as a genuine process, beginning, continuing, and ending. So freed, they may astound us more than ever with subtle analyses of the way passages functioned when they were composed and the ways they may later function, or not function, or seem to function, after the author has somehow altered the text (in these passages or elsewhere). Literary theorists should also take account of the creative process, of the way authority is worked into a literary text and can be lost, and of the possible aesthetic implications of textual and biographical (and even bibliographical) evidence.

Yet no one interested in the creative process and the authority of the author can be downcast for long at the state of scholarship, since we have lived into a time when we can be more responsible (as editors, editorial theorists, critics, and literary theorists) than ever before. As a legacy of the CEAA, we have for the first time great quantities of textual data about American literature, much of it available in forms clear enough so that we are not overwhelmed as we try to make sense of it. We have had many conscientiously prepared photofacsimiles of manuscript versions of important literary works; we have had exemplary articles and books on "the making of" American literary works; and we have seen the beginnings of sophisticated critical analysis of some of the issues raised by this new knowledge. Because of the quite extraordinary work of Rothenberg and others, we have enough empirical evidence about the creative process to let us vault past those maudlin accounts which so offended Hirsch's lucid mind. We still must approach the topic of creativity in reverence, not with impudent knowingness, but we can approach it confident that much hard data has been recorded and analyzed. We also have the chance to learn by holding an aesthetician like Krieger to account, testing his sense of how the mind works in the composing process against our empirical evidence. We have, first and last, evidence and arguments enough to tease us into tough thinking about creativity and literary authority. Once we realize that the creative process, like any other process, has bounds, beyond which no author, however fine a craftsman, is apt to intervene with impunity, we can cheerfully give up the superstition that the author is infallible and that the literary work is necessarily a perfect verbal icon. For even if an author later forgets why a work ever was as it was, we do not need to surrender our conviction that great art is as it is, or was as it was, for good and wondrously subtle reasons.

CHAPTER 3

The Authority of the Editor and His Formula:

Textual Theory and Practice since "Bibliography and the Novelistic Fallacy"

In the heyday of the New Criticism, Bruce Harkness gave a speech on "Bibliography and the Novelistic Fallacy" at the 1957 MLA and published it in the 1959 *Studies in Bibliography*, the annual edited then, as now, by its founder, Fredson Bowers.[1] The essay was hailed immediately as a classic polemic and subsequently has been reprinted three times (1966, 1969, and 1974) in collections widely assigned for introductory graduate courses in methods of research in British and American literature.[2] Harkness's title, as anyone would have recognized at the time, was a truculent takeoff on "The Intentional Fallacy" and "The Affective Fallacy," two much discussed essays by theorists of the New Criticism, W. K. Wimsatt, Jr., and Monroe C. Beardsley.[3] His point, trenchantly argued, was that under the

1. Bruce Harkness, "Bibliography and the Novelistic Fallacy," *Studies in Bibliography* 12 (1959): 59-73.
2. Lester A. Beaurline, ed., *A Mirror for Modern Scholars: Essays in Methods of Research in Literature* (New York: Odyssey Press, 1966), pp. 56-71; O. M. Brack, Jr. and Warner Barnes, eds., *Bibliography and Textual Criticism: English and American Literature 1700 to the Present* (Chicago: University of Chicago Press, 1969), pp. 23-40; and William J. Handy and Max Westbrook, eds., *Twentieth Century Criticism: The Major Statements* (New York: The Free Press, 1974), pp. 339-51.
3. W. K. Wimsatt, Jr., and Monroe C. Beardsley, "The Intentional Fallacy," and "The Affective Fallacy," originally published in *Sewanee Review* 54 (July-September 1946): 468-88, and *Sewanee Review* 57 (October-December 1949): 31-55. Both

influence of this new school of criticism, one celebrated for
close textual analysis, critics were nevertheless "apt to be
entirely indifferent to the textual problems of a novel"; they
were "all too prone to examine rigorously a faulty text." The
same critics were somewhat more apt to take notice of textual
cruxes in Elizabethan drama or in poetry of any period, but they
seemed to think that "a few mistakes" (being "swallowed up in
the vast bulk of the novel") "damage neither novel nor criticism." For his hortatory purposes Harkness seized upon *Moby-
Dick,* "our greatest novel," as an example of the way we content
ourselves with texts known to be faulty, but he concentrated on
a twentieth-century work, *The Great Gatsby,* as his "main
illustration" of the need for what he called "bibliography" or
"textual bibliography" to be applied to novels.[4]

It was disgraceful, Harkness thought, that a reviewer could
judge the Hendricks House edition of *Moby-Dick* as definitive
because it contained, by the reviewer's count, "only 108 compositor's errors and twenty silent emendations" in a work where
there was, apparently, no complicating "problem of copy-text."
Harkness demanded: "Would anyone make such a claim for a
volume of poems?"[5] As for *The Great Gatsby,* all the available
editions were replete, he found, with dozens of erroneous or
dubious readings. The posthumous *Three Novels* text, for
instance, contained many changes of words and marks of
punctuation, some perhaps authorial, perhaps not, along with
others which seemed to be outright errors, but did not include
all of the author's known corrections to the first edition.[6] As
Harrison Hayford and I were to show a few years later, the
textual situation of *Moby-Dick* was not quite so simple as everyone had thought, and the questions Harkness raised about the
texts of *Gatsby* were not as momentous, I will show, as some

---

essays are reprinted in Wimsatt's *The Verbal Icon: Studies in the Meaning of Poetry*
(Lexington: University of Kentucky Press, 1954) and the paperback reprint (New
York: The Noonday Press, 1958), pp. 3-18 and 21-39. See my Chapter 2, n. 5.
Wimsatt's "Genesis: A Fallacy Revisited," in Peter Demetz, Thomas Greene, and
Lowry Nelson, Jr., eds., *The Disciplines of Criticism* (New Haven: Yale University
Press, 1968), pp. 193-225, restates his and Beardsley's position and rather disdain-
fully surveys some of the responses to "The Intentional Fallacy."
4. Harkness, pp. 59, 59, 64, 63, 60, and 60.
5. Harkness, p. 63 (all three quotations).
6. Harkness, pp. 67-72.

questions he did not ask. But at the time, except for his apparent ignorance of W. W. Greg's "The Rationale of Copy-Text," first published in the 1950-51 *Studies in Bibliography*, Harkness was in the vanguard of textual studies. He was alert to small signs of growing interest in textual problems of British and American novels of the last two centuries, and very much aware that he was not preaching only to the converted, even when he published in *Studies in Bibliography*, for the contributors to that annual had all but ignored the novel in their zeal to study problems in drama and poetry. Ironical, whimsical, and tough throughout the essay, Harkness concluded with this appeal: "Could we not as critics pay more attention to Bibliography and we as Bibliographers to criticism? Can not we somehow insist that editing actually be done—instead of the practice of putting a fancy introduction on a poor text? Can not we have sound texts reproduced and publisher's history stated by the editor? Can not we know *what it is* we have in our hands? For it is simply a fallacy that the novel does not count."[7]

With those sweeping, timeless questions ringing in our ears, we find an odd simplicity when we look at the particular textual problems Harkness described. He pointed out that as long as both unrevised and revised texts of Henry James's novels were being reprinted with no textual identification, anyone was in danger of doing what F. R. Leavis had fatuously done —praising an early text for its "sustained maturity of theme and treatment" but quoting as evidence the text of the New York Edition, the product of James's late and unsurprisingly mature revisions. Harkness complained that rarely did editors of paperback texts of other novelists—Conrad, for example—bother to tell what the texts were set from. Sometimes an early text was silently reprinted even though the author had revised the text

---

7. Harkness, p. 73. By "bibliography" and "textual bibliography" Harkness seemed to mean primarily the study of how the texts of literary works vary in different editions, while for Bowers "bibliography" usually applied as well to the study of the book as a physical object and "textual bibliography" implied the study of textual problems in the light of physical evidence derived from his formidable knowledge of printing practices. At the same time, Bowers was employing "textual criticism" as a synonym for "textual bibliography," but ambiguities have plagued the term "textual criticism." There is still no clear, succinct term for the analysis of the aesthetic implications of textual evidence and the search for textual causes of aesthetic cruxes.

later on: Conrad's "intrusive 'philosophizing'" in *The Nigger of the "Narcissus"* was still present in *The Portable Conrad*, although the author had cut some of it out of the collected English edition. Harkness complained that an edition of *Pride and Prejudice* numbered the chapters consecutively without indication of where the three volume-breaks had come. He complained of having to go to the weekly parts to find out for himself that the serial divisions of *Great Expectations* clarify why some characters and events are treated as they are, when the divisions ought to have been noted somehow, even in a classroom paperback. In addition, Harkness pointed out the report of errors in *Moby-Dick* and listed his own discoveries of typographical errors and dubious readings in *The Great Gatsby*, as well as the the loss of four intra-chapter breaks which had been indicated in the first edition by extra white space between paragraphs.[8]

Such a flat recital of Harkness's examples of badly edited texts or badly labeled texts makes it clear that he was indeed, as he pretty clearly indicated, writing as a frustrated teacher and scholar made squeamish by a little suggestive knowledge and much intuitive suspicion, and perhaps made defensive by the prevailing skepticism, if not contempt, which many literary critics displayed toward any enterprises involving "textual bibliography." He knew from examples at hand that textual evidence could have far-reaching implications for understanding novels, but the examples he had at hand were, after all, meager. Informing the essay was Harkness's eagerness to know whatever textual scholars might be able to discover. Then, so his largely tacit argument went, we could begin to think through the evidence—might, for instance, choose to defend the reprinting of early Conrad texts, if we wanted to, once the textual situation had been explored. Harkness was aware, in short, that what editors weren't finding out, or weren't bothering to tell their readers, might be of enormous interpretive importance, but just how such information might be important he could seldom know, for the basic scholarship had not been done.

8. Harkness, pp. 59, 59-60, 61, 61, 65-66, and 73.

Rereading Harkness's essay today, or rereading other textual pronouncements and manifestos from that period such as Fredson Bowers's *Textual and Literary Criticism* (1959), or Bowers's "Textual Criticism" in the MLA *Aims and Methods* pamphlet (1963), or William M. Gibson and Edwin H. Cady's "Editions of American Writers, 1963" (published in *PMLA* then distributed in a pamphlet so would-be editors could use it in lobbying for congressional funding), what seems most striking (aside from the now-startling patriotic strategies of the Gibson-Cady manifesto) is that everyone seemed to be thinking in terms of simple textual problems, primarily single-word corruptions and pairs of variants.[9] Every one of the scholars I have cited knew that more complicated textual situations existed, of course, and Bowers, at least, had worked with textually intricate Elizabethan dramas, but they all talked as if textual problems came in the form of simple corruptions or cruxes, whether the debate was over "sullied" or "solid" flesh in *Hamlet* or "spot" or "stop" in *Gatsby*.

In the 1960s, as I mentioned in the first chapter, the routine 1920s compositorial error of "soiled fish of the sea" in the fall-from-the-mainmast scene of *White-Jacket* (where the editions printed in Melville's lifetime had the correct "coiled fish of the sea") attained an astonishing vogue in textual discussions because a prominent critic, F. O. Matthiessen, had rhapsodized for several lines upon the "twist of imagery of the sort that was

9. Fredson Bowers, *Textual and Literary Criticism* (Cambridge: Cambridge University Press, 1959), pp. 7-9; Bowers, "Textual Criticism," in *The Aims and Methods of Scholarship in Modern Languages and Literatures*, ed. James Thorpe (New York: Modern Language Association, 1963), pp. 23-42, especially pp. 23-24; and William M. Gibson and Edwin H. Cady, "Editions of American Writers, 1963: A Preliminary Survey," *PMLA* 78 (September 1963): 1-8. For the patriotic strategy, see Gibson and Cady's last paragraph: "Suppose many of the public, school, and university libraries of the United States and all the chief United States Information Service libraries abroad had on their shelves good complete editions of fifteen American literary masters. What then? We venture one prediction. American readers of these texts would know more clearly than ever before 'the curious fate' of being an American. Readers abroad would come to understand more discriminatingly and to respect more justly the country that bred such men." (Many of my readers will perceive in this quotation not only a patriotic strategy but also unthinking sexism. In this book I have not adopted extreme strategies for combating the sexism built into the language, but whenever I mean only men I say "men," and I never say "men" when I mean "men and women.")

57

to become peculiarly Melville's." Concluded Matthiessen: "The *discordia concors*, the unexpected linking of the medium of cleanliness with filth, could only have sprung from an imagination that had apprehended the terrors of the deep, of the immaterial deep as well as the physical." Bowers was typical in drawing a warning from what befell the hapless Matthiessen: "Spectacular examples can be multiplied of like unhappy results when critics have relied in vain on corrupt editions for an accurate transmission of an author's words." Yet when Bowers pointed admonishingly to the appalling record of corruption in nineteenth-century reprints of *The Scarlet Letter*, his principal example, for a time, of textual deterioration, he could adduce only routine typographical errors and casual compositorial alterations.[10]

Where American literature was concerned, no one had "spectacular examples" to point to except Harrison Hayford and Merton M. Sealts, Jr., who chose not to lecture the innocent critics who had been writing, for instance, about the function of the preface in *Billy Budd* when the piece of prose in question was merely a discarded portion of a late chapter and had never in fact been a preface until the 1920s, when its first editor made it one. As it turned out, their edition of *Billy Budd, Sailor* (1962) has still not been utilized as a potential source for major textual theorizing, and during the early 1960s, and even after the Center for Editions of American Authors was established in 1964, writers on textual matters continued to talk in terms of single-word corruptions and simple pairs of variants, which pretty much covered the complexity of textual situations most of the newly recruited editors had encountered at first hand. Almost every writer on textual matters made an obligatory nod toward the textual complexities of Henry James's novels which might lead one editor to print one text and someone else to print another, but no one thought deeply enough about the questions James's revisions might raise to say more than that in

10. F. O. Matthiessen, *American Renaissance: Art and Expression in the Age of Emerson and Whitman* (New York: Oxford University Press, 1941), p. 329. The correct reading, "coiled fish," was first pointed out in John W. Nichol, "Melville's "Soiled" Fish of the Sea,'" *American Literature* 21 (November 1949): 338-39. See Bowers, "Textual Criticism," p. 23.

any such thorough revision it would probably not be desirable to produce an eclectic text based upon the first edition although incorporating late revisions.

From the vantage point of the 1980s it is clear, as it was not in the 1960s, that the habit of thinking as if editorial problems came a word at a time was what allowed a generation of American editors to stake their reputations on the validity of the rationale of copy-text set forth by W. W. Greg. In fact, Greg's rationale worked splendidly in certain very simple textual situations. According to Greg, when the earliest form of the text is the first edition and you know the author corrected typographical errors and compositorial misreadings or made revisions in a copy of that edition or in the setting copy for some subsequent edition, or merely left some other record of the errors and revisions, you choose the first edition as copy-text because it will preserve more authorial usages, both in words and in punctuation, than a later edition will preserve, since new compositorial changes, deliberate or unintentional, will almost invariably be found in the later edition, even though it may also incorporate some authorial corrections. But you will emend the first edition with any subsequent corrections or revisions which you identify as authorial.[11] As I mentioned in Chapter 2, Greg had taken a crucial half step beyond Ronald B. McKerrow, who had realized that the first edition should be copy-text but had assumed that once you identify an author's hand in a later text you should adopt all of the verbal variants in that text except the ones which are manifestly erroneous.[12] Greg by contrast allowed for compositorial error and casual alterations: the editor would choose to adopt only those variants which seemed clearly to be authorial. Perfect in his advice on how best to incorporate authorial corrections and revisions while minimizing the risk of adopting nonauthorial changes along with the corrections, Greg simply asserted, without debating the issue, that it is not up to the editor to decide whether or not authorial

11. W. W. Greg, "The Rationale of Copy-Text," *Studies in Bibliography* 3 (1950-51): 19-36.

12. Ronald B. McKerrow, *Prolegomena for the Oxford Shakespeare* (Oxford: Oxford University Press, 1939), p. 18.

revisions are improvements but merely to decide whether or not they are authorial, and then to adopt them, once they are so identified.

Greg avoided, I now see, the basic difference between correction and revision, the former restoring an original intention and the latter embodying what may well be a new intention. The distinction was not immediately enforced upon the new American editors as an important one, for most people took for granted their agreement with Greg that an author had the right to do whatever he wanted to do to his text and that an editor's job was to present to the reader what the author's final intention was for any text. The inexperience of most of the new followers of Greg assured that no CEAA editor in the early 1960s would immediately identify the problematical nature of revisions as a major sticking point in the application of Greg's rationale; objections were voiced only hesitantly, or else were briefly raised then blurred by the confused textual arguments which accompanied them. Nor was Greg's essay intruded upon the notice of literary critics and literary theorists, for the rationale was published in the American bibliographical annual and Greg's arguments, in any case, were couched in terms of what an editor could do or might want to do, not in terms of what a literary critic or a literary theorist might do with the evidence behind the editorial decisions or with the product of such editing.

In this absence of serious discussion, Bowers acted as apostle for Greg's rationale in many speeches, essays, and editions, beginning even before he published the "Rationale" in his annual and accelerating in the 1960s around the time of the founding of the CEAA. By the time he wrote the "Textual Criticism" essay for the MLA *Aims and Methods* pamphlet, he had firmly concluded that the "duty of an editor" was to edit according to Greg, "to synthesize the authority of the revised substantives with the authority of the original accidentals"; that is, to choose the first edition as copy-text (if no manuscript survives) and emend into it any words (and even punctuation marks) from a later edition which the editor becomes convinced are authorial revisions.[13] In "Scholarship and Editing" (1976), Bowers flatly asserted the triumph of eclectic editing according to Greg:[14]

> Opposition has been voiced to such eclectic texts by a small group of students of American literature who were not brought up under the discipline of textual criticism as developed for English literature; but the idea of a single composite final text as defined by Greg's theories seems both so practical and so rational a benefit both to author and to reader as to admit of no controversy as a proposition, subject only to the caveat that a few literary texts exist in such special multiple revised forms as to resist conflation and to require either separate publication or the modified form of separate publication represented by parallel texts.

In the 1970s G. Thomas Tanselle put his own growing prestige in support of Greg's rationale—prestige built up, primarily, by his unrivaled series of magisterial essays in each year's volume of *Studies in Bibliography*. According to Tanselle in the 1975 essay, Greg's rationale of copy-text "would seem to apply to all situations," the only qualification to "its universality" being the rare problem which Bowers had identified as "radiating texts," variant texts all based on identical originals, as in the case of pieces published in various newspapers from the presumably identical proofs sent about by a newspaper syndicate. Otherwise, Tanselle said it was self-evident that Greg's "recommended procedure would serve in handling editorial problems involving manuscripts as well as printed books, arising in twentieth-century literature as well as sixteenth," and of course arising in those situations in other centuries as well.[15]

In the decade and a half after the founding of the CEAA the dominant issue was not whether or not Greg's rationale was universally applicable—it was assumed that it *was*, although Bowers as early as 1963 was quietly reverting behind Greg's

13. Bowers, "Textual Criticism," p. 39.
14. Fredson Bowers, "Scholarship and Editing," *PBSA* 70 (1976): 161-88; the quotation is from p. 184.
15. G. Thomas Tanselle, "Greg's Theory of Copy-Text and the Editing of American Literature," *Studies in Bibliography* 28 (1975): 180, 181, 182, and 182.

basic insight to McKerrow's imperfect position, incorporating compositorial and editorial changes along with authorial ones. Bowers continued to violate some of Greg's soundest principles in the Henry Fielding edition as well as in the Stephen Crane and William James editions, particularly the latter, where he elaborated a rationalization for repudiating Greg which obviated the need to transcribe the manuscripts (and thereby led to the ignoring of some authorial readings which had been misconstrued by the first compositor). The dominant issue, however, was neither Greg nor Bowers's departures from Greg. The first issue was Bowers himself, Bowers the man, who attacked in public those who were in his way, casting himself at the 1965 MLA in Chicago as the scourge of conscienceless hacks of textbook makers (with no doubt left in the audience's mind that a prime example of such a hack was Hyatt Waggoner, who well before the Ohio State Edition of *The House of the Seven Gables* was completed had conscientiously edited the same novel from manuscript for the Riverside series of paperback editions).

The second issue was Bowers the officious editor, who proclaimed that "the business of an editor is to edit. If he is unprepared to take the risks of backing his own judgment, he should peddle another line of goods."[16] Bowers cast himself at other times in the roles of forensic scientist in the laboratory and judge with the criminal text before the bench. He bravely faced "difficulty" as "one of the hazards of editing," making "painful analysis of the evidence," in some cases deciding that one "may occasionally take one's courage in his hands" and having done so may find that some variants are so "neutral, perhaps, as to require adjudication on a rather impressionistic basis." An editor should boldly "go the whole way" once he decides to produce a critical (i.e., eclectic) edition, rather "than dip his big toe in the water and then draw back in alarm lest he suddenly find himself out of his depth." Bowers made editing look like the preoccupation of a distracted precisionist, for while preaching a policy of full textual accountability in which the editor "should place all his textual cards on the table—face up," in

16. Bowers, "Scholarship and Editing," p. 184, n. 25.

practice he scanted biographical research, overlooked relevant forms of the text such as pre-publication excerpts, and sometimes simply fudged the evidence (as in not making the standard Hinman collations required by the CEAA).[17] Turning his formidable powers toward the minutiae of editing, spelling and punctuation, in many CEAA volumes he regularized yet still claimed to be presenting unmodernized critical texts (although in fact regularizing *is* a form of modernizing). His editorial excesses attracted such hostile attention that some of his wisest, most practical innovations, notably the line-end hyphenation lists (which however pedantic-looking are essential for accurate quoting), were mocked by angry and bewildered reviewers.

Most of the reviewers of the CEAA volumes ranged in a narrow belt from subservient, not to say sycophantic, praise (the "blend of astute critical judgment and technical expertise needed to effect this text of *Maggie* is awe inspiring"), up to blind faith (the "chief benefit of these volumes may be a heightened respect for the methodology needed and available to produce the authoritative text, and a firmer faith that here are stories as close as human ingenuity can bring them to what Stephen Crane meant to create"). Intimidated but unconvinced reviewers tended toward persnicketiness: "The reader may have more tolerant understanding of how deviants slip into a text if he notices that in this infinitely careful edition page cxi of Volume V has a large where a small capital belongs, and pages xvi, xx, cxxx, 328 and 332 have small where large capitals are required."[18] But the discrepancy between Bowers's work at its best (such as the brilliantly lucid original version of the "Textual Criticism" essay in the 1963 *Aims and Methods*, before he choked it in its revised form with dubious examples from Stephen Crane and others, exhaustingly argued) and his actual

17. Fredson Bowers, Textual Introduction to *Maggie*, in *Bowery Tales* by Stephen Crane (Charlottesville: University Press of Virginia, 1969), p. xciii; "The New Look in Editing," *South Atlantic Bulletin* 35 (1970): 3; *Maggie*, p. lxxiii; "Some Principles for Scholarly Editions of Nineteenth-Century American Authors," *Studies in Bibliography* 17 (1964): 223; and "Textual Criticism" (1963), p. 42.

18. These quotations are from William S. Kable, *South Atlantic Bulletin* 36 (1970): 103; William Randel, *American Literature* 42 (March 1970): 110; and Arlin Turner, *South Atlantic Quarterly* 70 (Autumn 1971): 607.

practices did not go altogether unnoticed by reviewers. He was attacked on three fronts both as editor of particular editions and as the most visible spokesman for the CEAA.

First, Bowers was challenged from within the American Literature Establishment by friends of Hyatt Waggoner who rallied to his defense against the bibliographer. In *American Literary Scholarship, 1965*, Richard Harter Fogle protested against Bowers's "insulting" dismissal of Waggoner's text of *The House of the Seven Gables* in a footnote and declared that Waggoner's edition "is greatly preferable in critical acumen and general humanity."[19] Second, Bowers was attacked by a misguided Grand Old Man of the American Cultural Establishment, Edmund Wilson, who out of a woeful mixture of vivid and imperfectly-concealed personal pique and fuzzy textual ideals blundered into the pages of the *New York Review of Books*.[20] Wilson, whose project for editing American writers had lost out to the CEAA in the competition for federal funding, launched what G. Thomas Tanselle with his customary honest cautiousness has called "an ill-tempered and incoherent attack," specifically on the Melville, Hawthorne, Howells, and Mark Twain editions, but also upon Bowers specifically as the leading spokesman of editorial theory and practice. Had Wilson's two-part attack "been written by a lesser figure," Tanselle concluded, "its obvious motivation and manifest

19. Richard Harter Fogle, "Hawthorne," *American Literary Scholarship: An Annual, 1965* (Durham: Duke University Press, 1967), pp. 24 and 26.
20. Edmund Wilson, "The Fruits of the MLA: I. "Their Wedding Journey," *The New York Review of Books* (26 September 1968): 7-10. Wilson entered the fray after another Grand Old Man had ventured out against a CEAA edition. Lewis Mumford, whose biography of Melville had been corrected at many points in William H. Gilman's book on *Redburn*, and who had japed at Gilman in a preface to a reprinting of that biography, printed in the same periodical (18 January 1968), pp. 3-5, what might temperately be called a fatuous, narrow-minded, and mean-spirited attack on the new editions of Emerson's journals and miscellaneous notebooks, of which Gilman was the chief editor, "Emerson behind Barbed Wire." Mumford was smugly content with Bliss Perry's old "heart" of Emerson's journals. Yet within a few years young scholar-critics mining the new journals and notebooks were shattering some of the most common and fervently-held beliefs about Emerson; David Hill, for example, showed that we had all misunderstood the relationship between the death of Emerson's son in 1842 and the composition of "Experience." See "Emerson's Eumenides: Textual Evidence and the Interpretation of 'Experience,'" in Joel Myerson, ed., *Emerson Centenary Essays* (Carbondale: Southern Illinois University Press, 1982), pp. 107-21 and 204-05.

confusion would have prevented its being taken seriously.''[21] As the *New York Review of Books* became ever more highly politicized, young academics of the New Left took up the causes of the Grand Old Man. Before you knew it the perpetrators of the CEAA were equated with the initiators and pursuers of the war in Vietnam, and editors were seen as pacifying the civilian population and imposing alien texts upon their unwilling subjects. Hinman Machines, unsurprisingly, were discovered to be dangerous to children and other living things, including even graduate students. But those hostile parties soon faded away, except for an occasional foray.

Finally a third group emerged—reviewers who apparently had no personal or ideological axes to grind but who had done their textual homework. Roy R. Male charged (*American Literary Scholarship, 1968*) that "the tendency discernible in the earlier volumes toward making Hawthorne merely an interesting case study for textual bibliographers has reached grotesque proportions" in *The Marble Faun*.[22] The Centenary Edition of Hawthorne is indeed monumental, Male observed, "but the monument pays tribute to Fredson Bowers, not to Hawthorne." In 1970 John Freehafer published another indictment, more devastating because much more detailed:

> The treatment of Hawthorne's text in the Centenary *Marble Faun* suffers from four major defects: (1) tendentious and narrow analysis of internal bibliographic evidence, without regard to pertinent external evidence; (2) inattention to pertinent linguistic and lexicographic evidence; (3) "normalization" of variants which often runs counter to Hawthorne's artistic and linguistic intentions; and (4) adherence to a predetermined editorial practice which is not adequate to deal successfully with the special problems in editing *The Marble Faun*.

Freehafer summed up his analysis in a terse, saddened paragraph:[23]

21. Tanselle, "Greg's Theory," pp. 198 and 199.
22. Roy R. Male, "Hawthorne," *American Literary Scholarship: An Annual, 1968* (Durham: Duke University Press, 1970), p. 21.
23. John Freehafer, "*The Marble Faun* and the Editing of Nineteenth-Century Texts," *Studies in the Novel* 2 (Winter 1970): 488 and 499.

Of the 700 emendations in the Centenary *Marble Faun*, half consist of obvious corrections and authorial changes, nearly all of which were made in the first edition. The emendations of later origin, about 250 of which first appear in the Centenary edition, are usually incorrect. A critic who tried to judge Hawthorne's linguistic habits, style and artistic intentions from the sham Briticisms, false personifications, pretentious capitals, and miscorrections in the Centenary *Marble Faun* could come to odd, erroneous, and unflattering conclusions. In the last chapter of his book, Hawthorne spoke as a true prophet when he asked his "kindly Readers" to bear in mind that *The Marble Faun* was "a fragile handiwork, more easily rent than mended."

After these unrefuted and indeed irrefutable charges it almost seemed that those critics Harkness charged with being "entirely indifferent to the textual problems of a novel" had been guilty only of benign neglect, not active mischief.[24]

Bowers was in fact producing many quite literally nonsensical texts by editing them rigidly according to Greg's notions of incorporating authorial revisions, however misguided those revisions might have been. He was also producing apparatuses from which no one could readily gain the information he would need in order to begin thinking about the history of a text, and sometimes (because the lists were misconceived or error-ridden, or both) could not possibly gain that information. And he was by his persistent teaching through precept and example identifying himself with the CEAA and identifying the CEAA with him. With my comments in the 1974 *PBSA* "Interim Assessment" of the CEAA I became, not without strong forebodings, the first critic from within the CEAA to raise serious objections to Bowers's editing. Concerned, more concerned than was good for my peace of mind, at what I found on close analysis of Bowers's edition of *Maggie*, I took a still stronger stand the next year, attempting to dissociate Bowers from editorial principles and practices in certain non-Bowersean CEAA editions and announcing that I had requested the CEAA to rescind the seal granted to *Maggie* (a step the advisory committee unanimously refused to take). In the March

24. Harkness, p. 59.

1976 *Nineteenth-Century Fiction* I exposed Bowers as having fudged some of the research required by the CEAA's *Statement of Editorial Principles and Procedures* and criticized him for having mired himself in minutiae while missing the basic evidence that Crane had cut down his manuscript in response to pressure from Ripley Hitchcock, the editor at Appleton's. As I concluded there, serious textual and critical study of *The Red Badge of Courage* had hardly begun.[25] Soon afterwards my student Henry Binder showed that Bowers had neglected textually important documents that Crane scholars had reported years before.[26] There's a law in textual scholarship—waste your time on trivialities and you'll miss some of the most significant evidence and its implications. There's another law—no editorial formula, even one as appealing as Greg's, can substitute for the expertise which comes only from years of conscientious (and preferably loving) biographical and critical study of the author whom one presumes to edit.

The CEAA and its successor the Center for Scholarly Editions closed ranks behind Bowers, ignoring the demonstrations of the magnitude of his erroneous textual decisions and procedures, and he pursued his increasingly idiosyncratic course through the 1970s and into the 1980s, while some of his students and associates followed his example into new extravagances of apparatus, as in a nineteen-page list of variants in nonauthorial texts in the Kent State edition of Charles Brockden Brown's *Arthur Mervyn.*[27] In 1978 David J. Nordloh pronounced a judgment on the Virginia Edition of Stephen Crane that constitutes a judgment on Bowers's other CEAA and CSE editions as well. Its effect on its readers was all the greater for

25. Hershel Parker with Bruce Bebb, "The CEAA: An Interim Assessment," *PBSA* 68 (1974): 129-48; Bruce Bebb and Hershel Parker, "Freehafer on Greg and the CEAA: Secure Footing and 'Substantial Shortfalls'," *Studies in the Novel* 7 (1975): 391-94; Hershel Parker, review of "Stephen Crane, *The Red Badge of Courage: A Facsimile Edition of the Manuscript*," and "Stephen Crane, *The Red Badge of Courage: An Episode of the American Civil War*," both edited by Fredson Bowers, *Nineteenth-Century Fiction* 30 (1976): 558-62.

26. Henry Binder, "Unwinding the Riddle of Four Pages Missing from the *Red Badge of Courage* Manuscript," *PBSA* 72 (First Quarter 1978): 100-06.

27. See my review of the Kent State University Press edition of Charles Brockden Brown's *Arthur Mervyn, Nineteenth-Century Fiction* 36 (September 1981): 196-98.

his not having previously embroiled himself in controversy with Bowers. The texts, Nordloh said, "are not reliable," but "are theoretically and practically a chaos," and the mere fact of their appearance in a set as the standard edition would "delay for too long the publication of a more careful edition of Stephen Crane."[28] To some of us who had, as I once lamented, staked our youthful hopes on the CEAA, it was heartbreaking to see what had become of the great national editing enterprise, and it was cold comfort to realize too late that the CEAA had doomed itself the moment it was decided that its examiners' reports would be kept secret: almost no one learned from anyone else's mistakes and triumphs. In the 1980s it is not wholly reassuring to watch the course of the Library of America, a successful resurrection of Edmund Wilson's project which frankly acknowledges that it is a publishing venture, not an editing venture which, whatever its faults, might be expected regularly to contribute to knowledge.

Meanwhile Tanselle's astonishing flow of essays continued in each volume of *Studies in Bibliography*. Committed to the defense of the universality of Greg's rationale of copy-text and always preferring to see Bowers at his best rather than looking closely at how he was editing actual volumes, whether of British or American literature, Tanselle more than anyone else gave sanction to the basic apparatus Bowers had devised, for his lucid consideration of "Some Principles for Editorial Apparatus" in effect standardized that apparatus, even though he properly warned that he was merely considering the sort of apparatus which was becoming standardized.[29] Furthermore, Tanselle through his explications of Greg simplified textual issues, reducing the "Central Questions of Editing" (1981) to three matters in two of which the author tended to fade out of the picture. The first question is whether "the aim is historical—the

28. David J. Nordloh, "On Crane Now Edited: The University of Virginia Edition of *The Works of Stephen Crane*," *Studies in the Novel* 10 (Spring 1978): 103-19.
29. G. Thomas Tanselle, "Some Principles for Editorial Apparatus," *Studies in Bibliography* 25 (1972): 45. In the most important of his essays for my book as a whole, "The Editorial Problem of Final Authorial Intention," *Studies in Bibliography* 29 (1976): 167-211, Tanselle, for the first time, anywhere, brought editorial terminology into relation with legal, philosophical, and aesthetic usage, so that editorial discussions of intention need no longer be carried on in an intellectual vacuum.

reproduction of a particular text from the past or the reconstruction of what the author intended" or whether the aim is to create an edition to fit the editor's own subjective desires. The second is the problem an editor of a critical edition may have in deciding how to handle the issue of what the author did as opposed to what the author may have expected or wanted to have done to his text. The third central question is "the problem of the so-called 'indifferent' variant: that is, how is the editor to choose among variants in those cases in which critical analysis of the evidence finds the variants equally balanced and provides no basis for the critical choice of one over another?"[30]

There is an enormous difference, I would say, between Tanselle's "Central Questions of Editing" (which I have baldly summarized in a spirit akin to his own "intentionally brief and unadorned" fashion) and some of the central questions involving the aesthetic implications of textual study which have emerged from the examination of representative American texts in the last decades. As long ago as 1960 E. D. Hirsch had asked those brilliant offhand questions I quoted in Chapter 1 ("With a revised text, composed over a long period of time . . . , how are we to construe the unrevised portions? Should we assume that they still mean what they meant originally or that they took on a new meaning when the rest of the text was altered or expanded?"),[31] and in 1962 Hayford and Sealts had asked somewhat comparable questions:[32]

> Wherein lay the difference between *Billy Budd* and the other late pieces? Did its quality of greatness emerge with one transforming major stroke somewhere in the gradual process of growth by accretion? Were all the instances of his [Melville's] minute verbal revision necessary to its greatness, or were many of them merely nervous or fussy gestures? To what extent do the revisions show a sure intuition of what was vital in the work as it stood at the end in semi-final manuscript? To what extent are many of the revisions

30. G. Thomas Tanselle, "Recent Editorial Discussion and the Central Questions of Editing," *Studies in Bibliography* 34 (1981): 60, 62, and 64.
31. E. D. Hirsch, *Validity in Interpretation* (New Haven: Yale University Press, 1967), p. 233.
32. Harrison Hayford and Merton M. Sealts, Jr., eds., *Billy Budd, Sailor (An Inside Narrative)* (Chicago: University of Chicago Press, 1962), pp. 34, 35.

purely random strokes that overlie and obscure the emerging conception? Into what categories do the stylistic revisions fall? . . . What, then, did Melville suppose was the effect of his late revisions? What attitude was he himself taking when he made them? Had he in fact completed them? And what may a reader make of them?

These questions, growing out of the most complicated American textual situation yet investigated, were simultaneously textual and aesthetic in nature as few questions were during the next two decades, during the triumph of Greg's rationale as propagated by Bowers and later as explicated and defended by Tanselle.

In preparing the Norton Critical Edition of *Moby-Dick* in the mid-1960s Hayford and I had advanced a little beyond the Hendricks House Edition.[33] Unknown to earlier editors, we found, Melville had looked over the Harper sheets before they were sent to England, so although *The Whale* was subsequently expurgated it nevertheless contained a number of authorial corrections and minor revisions. Harkness had invented a stooge, a philistine critic who did not think textual errors mattered ("'It doesn't *really* alter my interpretation'").[34] Merely by reading for sense Hayford and I found a number of errors which did make a difference in interpretation. It mattered whether Ishmael spoke the long paragraph in "The Gilder," as every critic had assumed (sometimes as crucial evidence in arguments comparing Ishmael to or contrasting him with Ahab), or whether quotation marks should go around the paragraph, making Ahab the speaker, as the structure of the chapter as well as the wording of the surrounding paragraphs argued. But our findings in the Norton *Moby-Dick* did not make any discernible difference to literary critics.

Nor, perhaps more surprisingly, have critics found any interpretive significance in Hayford's more recent speculations in "Unnecessary Duplicates" (1978), a study of Melville's compositional methods in *Moby-Dick* as derived from exceedingly

33. Harrison Hayford and Hershel Parker, eds., *Moby-Dick* (New York: W. W. Norton, 1967), especially "Textual Problems of *Moby-Dick*," pp. 471-77.
34. Harkness, p. 64.

70

close analysis of the Harper's text, but informed with knowledge of the way Melville demonstrably composed *Billy Budd, Sailor.* Hayford hypothesized "a multiple reassignment of roles" among four of his central characters, in which Melville might, for instance, insert a character "into an already-written narrative" and then spare himself "the revisional work of writing the character into further passages of that existing narrative by instead supplying some rationalization for the character's not appearing in it but in effect 'hiding out.'" Rather than assuming, as some critics had done, that Melville either lost his interest in the comradeship of Ishmael and Queequeg, or lost "his technical control of the materials," Hayford hypothesized a genetic explanation, that some of the early pages are late-written, long after some of the Ishmael-Queequeg passages in the later chapters when the *Pequod* is at sea.[35] Some of the broader ramifications of his argument Hayford left tacit—never, for instance, arguing by analogy with other writers known to have introduced late material into passages near the front of a work, never commenting on the general phenomenon by which a reader makes sense of irreconcilable elements in a book. But this 1978 essay, far more than the elaborately arranged textual apparatus of the Norton Critical Edition, suggested textual-critical questions of an importance not hinted at in Harkness's 1959 essay.

By the late 1960s and early 1970s, it seemed that the most tangible gains from the whole CEAA enterprise might be in a by-product, the establishment and enhancement of archives in libraries around the country. Another by-product seldom noticed at the time was the prolonged tutorial in biography and literary history which many young scholars received from veterans of the first generation of Americanists and from *their* students, the generation trained in the 1940s and now emerging from the shadow of the New Criticism. In many cases these scholars had passed the 1950s quietly, engaged in long-term biographical, historical, or editorial projects which kept them from frequent periodical publication. They had, as a group,

---

35. Harrison Hayford, "Unnecessary Duplicates: A Key to the Writing of *Moby-Dick*," in *New Perspectives on Melville*, ed. Faith Pullin (Edinburgh: Edinburgh University Press, 1978), pp. 145, 140 and 149.

fallen behind their flourishing New Critical colleagues in raises and promotions. Now they found themselves in charge of almost more money than they knew what to do with. They could now, with a thoroughness not dreamed of in earlier decades, accumulate and analyze documentary evidence about the composition, publication, and reception of each book they were editing, as well as copies of all known editions. During the process of preparing historical essays on many texts the older scholars found themselves aspiring to, and being held to, higher standards than they had ever known, and dozens of young people, graduate students and assistant professors for the most part, profited from that prolonged tutorial, just at the time when academic journals were bulging with purely critical essays. In the long run, this creation of a new generation of scholars may be the greatest benefit the profession gained from the CEAA. Certainly the CEAA did not immediately produce any outstanding new editorial theory or dramatic textual revelations. The textual and editorial value of the early CEAA volumes lay in the gradual accumulation of enough data for people to begin to think about; too gradual, as I have said, because the information of most potential value to editors, critics, and theorists was withheld—the so-called "vetting reports" on CEAA editions.

Evidence in the early CEAA volumes had been sufficient to set me brooding over the challenge to Greg afforded by instances where authorial second thoughts, on examination, turned out to be inferior to what the authors had originally written. In 1967 I was heartened by learning that James B. Meriwether had similar reservations about Greg, but I had little time or opportunity to test out my uneasiness with current textual and critical theory until 1972, after a blunder by an employee at Scribner's had sent the Cowley edition of *Tender is the Night* into many classrooms, including mine, in the form of the Scribner Library paperback.[36] The case was classic: Does an author have the aesthetic (as opposed to legal) authority to take apart a copy of one of his novels, reorder the sections chronologically, label it his "final version," and attempt to print that

36. Malcolm Cowley, ed., *Tender is the Night* (New York: Charles Scribner's Sons, 1951).

version in the hope that it would outsell the original version, and presumably supersede it? And does an editor have the authority to carry out those unfulfilled (and perhaps abandoned) authorial intentions, after the author's death? Harkness had backed away from this problem, merely referring to "a few well-known oddities such as *Tender is the Night*" concerning which even the most innocent critic must become bibliographer enough to know which text he is reading.[37] I found the challenge was irresistible, not only because an essay was patently waiting to be written (waiting because, presumably, the New Criticism had deterred such textual study) but also because here was obviously a chance to approach a work through textual and biographical criticism and at the same time through a study of the aesthetic experience Fitzgerald had originally set up for the reader. As I wrote the editor of *Proof* on 19 September 1972, the essay (to be written in collaboration with Brian Higgins) would start with "*textual* grounds and *biographical* grounds" then go into an "*aesthetic* argument based on careful examination of just what violence the alteration does to the experience of reading the book, examining the effects of a reader's coming to a certain section with the Rosemary section already in his mind vs the effects of coming to it cold, or coming to it after the reordering that throws the Rosemary section between it and what had just preceded it."[38] The letter was a salespitch, for I believed before starting the article that there might be no place to publish it if *Proof* did not take it. There did not then exist a journal which one could count on to welcome such a mixture of textual and aesthetic argument, pursued far beyond the conventional ten or twelve page limit.

37. Harkness, p. 64.
38. See Brian Higgins and Hershel Parker, "Sober Second Thoughts: Fitzgerald's 'Final Version' of *Tender is the Night*," *Proof* 4 (1975): 129-52. Steven Mailloux has recently asserted that my collaborator and I could not possibly have intended, as a primary goal, to demonstrate "how biographical evidence and reader-oriented analysis can be used together to determine the priority [i.e., superiority] of the one version of a work over another," but that is precisely what drew me to the project in the first place. See Mailloux's *Interpretive Conventions* (Ithaca: Cornell University Press, 1982), p. 119. Reader-response critics occasionally need reminding that there is nothing new about readers responding to what they read and critics talking of literature in terms of readers responding to what they read.

73

The Fitzgerald essay, completed in the summer of 1973, was an elaborate though far from exhaustive analysis of how the rearranging of the novel into chronological order damaged or destroyed the aesthetic effects which had been set up in the novel as originally written and as finally serialized and published as a book in 1934. Higgins and I pointed out the aesthetic implications of the simple fact that (with trivial exceptions) in this particular novel the early pages as first printed were written early, the middle pages written afterwards, and the late pages written last of all:[39]

> after the opening of the book each sentence of any length, each paragraph, certainly each extended passage and chapter, is written the way it is because of what Fitzgerald had already written and because of what he knew the reader would already have read at a given point. When control over materials is as steady as Fitzgerald's was in the Diver drafts, when the writer knows both in general outline and in a good deal of specific detail where he is going, every passage he actually writes not only fulfills but in subtle ways alters the entire scheme. What Fitzgerald was writing at any stage was written precisely the way it was because he had in mind the general way and even particular ways it was affected by what he had already written and would affect what he was yet to write.

Book II provided a perfect example. Fitzgerald had "calculated just what degree of psychological shock he wanted the reader to experience as he passed from the largely romanticized view of Dick in his maturity to the section on Dick's wartime days," where Dick's alliterative name and exemplary school career recalled the conventions of boy's fiction.[40] The example was indisputable because Fitzgerald himself had provided a precise definition of the reading experience he had set up: "it is confusing to come across a youthful photograph of some one known in a rounded maturity and gaze with a shock upon a fiery, wiry, eagle-eyed stranger." His effect achieved, Fitzgerald took pains "to be reassuring" to the bewildered reader. Years later, in considering (as he did for at least some hours on the day he took the copy apart) how to salvage *Tender is the Night*

39. Higgins and Parker, "Tender," p. 139.
40. Higgins and Parker, "Tender," pp. 139 and 139.

after it had faded out of public attention, Fitzgerald recognized that he could not retain this short definition of the reader's experience if the four Zurich pages came at the start of the book, so he excised it, although he left in the following reassurance. He could not so easily change what he had built into those pages as he wrote them. They were as they were, in incident and in style and in authorial revelations and commentaries, because he had designed them to startle, through their brevity and straightforwardness, the complacent reader who had already encountered Dick at length, in his rounded if ambiguous maturity. The effect of the four pages depended upon what had gone before. In the reordering, that effect was irretrievably lost, and unintended, uncontrolled effects were set up by the reversal of position.

For the sake of clarity in our argument, Higgins and I did not analyze the ways in which the Cowley order distorted such small aspects as the sequence of verbal echoes. Instead, we worked with some of the larger consequences of the reordering. Most obviously, the 1951 order, we argued, confused the structure. Notably, it diminished the poignance of Dick's period of collapse, "since in this edition we go from the heroic period to the Rosemary section (in which there are ominous signs of decay) then to the fall—a *steady*, fatalistic progression, with no hint that it could have been different, with no sense of a magic, poised moment when Dick could be idolized." Because Dick's attractive qualities "affect us less strongly in the Cowley edition or else are vitiated by their being put to the service of his questionable judgment," the reader cannot ultimately feel much if any tragedy in Dick's final collapse. We pointed out that in the 1934 order the reader comes gradually to see that Dick is really *like* Abe North, not greatly superior to him, where in the Cowley order there is no gradual disillusionment, since Abe from the time he enters is perceived as a character parallel to Dick. We also examined more subtle consequences of the way the reordering destroyed the original purposes of certain pairs of incidents or images by increasing or decreasing the distance between them even though the order remained the same. Besides these instances in which the effects in the Cowley edition are adventitiously different but comprehensible, we examined instances in which the Cowley edition is obviously

75

illogical or nonsensical, as when the mystery story element remains built into the novel in which there is no mystery about what really happened in the bathroom at the Villa Diana. Fitzgerald, fine critic that he was, had absolutely no sense of the great damage that would result from a reordering of the sections. The words in the Cowley edition, editorial fiddling aside, are Fitzgerald's words, but their effect often is not precisely authorial. Aesthetic effects do result—genuine frissons—and some of them are not plainly nonsensical, but they do not emerge from Fitzgerald's own careful planning. Fitzgerald himself, and later Cowley, were treating *Tender is the Night* as if a work of art were "created simultaneously in the form of disparate blocks."[41]

In "arguing that the order of composition affected the substance and style of what was composed," so that neither the author himself nor an editor could reorder the text without damaging it, Higgins and I had no textual authorities to turn to for support, and even had we been resourceful enough to consult critical theorists we would have found no help. Instead, we sought out discussions of the creative process—now the topic of the second chapter of this book but then not a field of study that had ever been brought into textual discussions in any significant way, certainly not into discussions of Greg's rationale. We found support in a work contemporaneous with *Tender is the Night, Art as Experience*, where John Dewey argued that "the artist is controlled in the process of his work by his grasp of the connection between what he has already done and what he is to do next." The artist must "at each point retain and sum up what has gone before as a whole and with reference to a whole to come"; otherwise, "there is no consistency and no security in his successive acts."[42] This was precisely what we had demonstrated through a variety of analyses of passages in that novel. Harkness had cited *Tender* as an example of "a few well-known oddities," where any critic would have to identify

---

41. Higgins and Parker, "Tender," pp. 142, 144, and 141. If we were to revise this essay now we would be careful to emphasize that Fitzgerald takes some pains to qualify the reader's admiration for Dick even in the earlier parts of the Rosemary section.
42. Higgins and Parker, "Tender," p. 140.

the text he was writing about,[43] but neither he nor Matthew J. Bruccoli (who provided the documentary evidence that the flashback structure of the original version was the only one represented in the manuscripts)[44] had brought evidence from creativity theory to the textual history.

In retrospect the article, for all of its inadequacies, still pleases me as one of the first attempts to turn the CEAA training to critical and aesthetic purposes, for Higgins and I were in fact raising questions seldom heard in American textual discussions, seeking confirmation in a field which textualists ought never have neglected, and taking, or hoping to take, textual criticism away from the puerilities of "soiled fish." (Ironically, Fredson Bowers was at this time textual advisor to the editors of the CEAA Dewey—helping to edit him according to an editorial theory which was not compatible with Dewey's description of the creative process.) Not many people noticed what we had tried to do in the article (one factor was the poor distribution of *Proof*), and in *American Literary Scholarship, 1975,* Jackson Bryer praised it, but in the category of one of the year's "bibliographical pieces," and he did not list it among the "year's four essays" on the novel.[45] The way Bryer classified the essay is worth recalling now not to continue in public a subject of private and friendly badinage but to drive home the point that in the mid-1970s even specialists who had personal experience with departmental prejudice against anything that could be labeled bibliographical were not prepared to make a new category for a bibliographical or textual essay with interpretive implications. The gap which Harkness ruefully saw as yawning between critics and mere textualists was still as wide as ever.

In the 1970s I made it my business to be the CEAA editor who would work hardest to fill that gap, once successive encounters with the textual histories of familiar American novels had pushed me into asking questions not asked by Greg or Bowers or Harkness or others of their generation, except

43. Harkness, p. 64.
44. Matthew J. Bruccoli, *The Composition of "Tender is the Night": A Study of the Manuscripts* (Pittsburgh: University of Pittsburgh Press, 1963).
45. Jackson Bryer, "Fitzgerald and Hemingway," in *American Literary Scholarship: An Annual, 1975* (Durham: Duke University Press, 1977), p. 169.

Hayford and Sealts, and still not asked by Tanselle in his 1981 survey. In a series of polemical essays I began asking (and shamelessly recycling) a shifting but gradually enlarging set of questions, all practical, even if portentously posed. These are the questions already discussed in my previous chapters: What kinds of aesthetic effects can result when an author adds previously unplanned sections to a novel after it is thought of as completed? What are the aesthetic consequences apt to be when an author excises passages just before publication or in post-publication revision? Or when an author publishes a novel in an order which is significantly different from the order in which the parts were inscribed, as in his writing the middle or the ending before the beginning? Or when an author drastically alters characterization or even invents characters midway during the composition of a novel? Or when an author attempts to give a different cast to a novel by altering only the ending? Or when an author attempts to alter any single aspect of a work without revising the rest? Or when an author attempts to improve a work by reordering its sections after completion? More and more, my examples forced me to ask questions basic to the creative process and general aesthetics: When does intentionality go into a given passage or a work as a whole? Can an author bestow or alter intentionality retroactively? What constitutes literary unity?

In trying to answer such questions, working empirically from American texts as they came to hand, I became convinced that very rarely does a writer, no matter how sophisticated in literary techniques, have much notion of the damage he can do to a book by post-completion revisions (excisions, reorderings, rewordings, additions), especially revisions made a considerable time after a work is first completed. Such revisions are susceptible to a range of non-aesthetic pressures, primarily economic, since preparation for publication is mainly a matter of marketing, not creating, and the kind of intentionality an author brings to his conferences with an editor is seldom the same as he had brought to his work on the manuscript during the process of composition. Late revisions may also spring from a belated instinct to protect oneself from what was too recklessly conveyed during the throes of composition. Revisions, from single-word changes to those excisions of philosophizing which Harkness admired as characteristic Conradian retractions, are not automatically to be prized and adopted, as Greg thought, but are automatically suspect: why were they made? Harkness's "main illustration," *The Great Gatsby*, provides an excellent example.

Harkness was concerned primarily with some dozens of readings in various texts of *Gatsby* which were of dubious authority or were altogether spurious, typos and misguided editorial corrections. It doesn't take much straining to agree with Harkness that interpretation *is* affected, cumulatively, as when someone altered Daisy's "Biloxi, Tennessee" to the geographically correct but unintended "Biloxi, Mississippi," thereby tampering with a minor aspect of her characterization. However, what Harkness was finding wrong in editions of *The Great Gatsby* is all at the level I discussed earlier—the level of single words and, rarely, a phrase; the loss of white spaces within chapters was a major flaw in reprints of the book. If we go back beyond the first edition to the manuscript we can raise some even more serious aesthetic problems about this masterpiece of twentieth-century American literature.[46] As scholars and critics have known for many years, Fitzgerald's manuscript and typescript of *The Great Gatsby* put all of Gatsby's story of his life in Chapter 8 on the occasion of Gatsby's telling it to Nick Carraway, after the quixotic vigil outside the Buchanan house. Maxwell Perkins, the editor at Scribners, urged the author to break up the longish narrative, and after puzzling for some weeks Fitzgerald moved a little of the story, the part concerning Gatsby's youth and his experiences with Dan Cody, back to Chapter 6, making other slight adjustments to his characterization of Gatsby in the process. Later critics have uniformly endorsed the breakup of Gatsby's story as an example of Fitzgerald's "craft of revision," according to the unspoken maxim, "To Revise is To Improve." Without arguing that the published text of *The Great Gatsby* is maimed to anything like the extent of other works such as the 1895 *Red Badge*, I nevertheless want to

46. See Matthew J. Bruccoli, ed., *The Great Gatsby: A Facsimile of the Manuscript* (Washington: Microcard Editions Books, 1973).

suggest that rather than rushing to celebrate Fitzgerald's crafts-manship, we might first study the manuscript in order to see what function the autobiography had when it was all in Chapter 8, as the author wrote it.

In the manuscript, the reader has been waiting since the first page for the narrator to become "privy to the secret griefs" of the wild, unknown title character. There is a long wait, but not a distracting one, for the narrator's own contempt for overeager curiosity tempers the urgency of the reader's desire to know whatever there is to know about Gatsby. The revelation of Gatsby's past comes, in the manuscript, at a time when the reader's excitement about the plot is keenest, after the show-down at the Plaza and the death of Myrtle. The reader's attentiveness is heightened not only by these dramatic events but also by a new moral awareness, for Nick has just repudiated Daisy, Tom, and Jordan by refusing to go into the Buchanan house with them, and Nick has experienced reversals of feeling toward Gatsby so that, at the start of the chapter, he cares "too much about him" to disillusion him with the knowledge that Tom and Daisy are reunited. In the manuscript, the reader responds to the history with wry nostalgia, and a surge of affection for Gatsby and for the best of what he embodies, responds yearningly, if ironically, to Gatsby's youthful conviction of his own "ineffable destiny." Then, in the manu-script, the poignance of Gatsby's death derives in large part from its occurring just after the reader has heard the full story of his life and his impossible idealism. Furthermore, Nick's later meditation on his own youthful returns to the regions north and west of Chicago links him more closely to Gatsby because Gatsby's own Minnesota youth has recently been recounted.

Still more arguments for the original order can be made by analysis of the way the reader responds as he progresses through the text. For example, the reader of the first edition does not need the Cody pages at the start of Chapter 6, however innocently happy he is to encounter them. The pages offer precisely the sort of specific information the attentive reader has already decided he can do without, since the situation Fitz-gerald has set up remains the same as it was in the manuscript: the best readers are still willing to wait till Nick is ready to tell them, superior as they are to the avid gossipmongers who appear in the early chapters. And the pages on Gatsby and Cody when put into Chapter 6 do not fulfill the expectations that had been set up by the previous pages (what would Gatsby and Daisy do after their reunion?) and do not prepare with full cogency for what will follow. My comments here are meant to be suggestive, not exhaustive; other questions, perhaps of equal or superior interest, may be asked by someone who devotes further study to the manuscript and subsequent revisions of *The Great Gatsby*.

As the examples from *The Great Gatsby* and *Tender is the Night* show (as well as from other novels referred to in this chapter and the preceding two), the complexity of the textual evidence we now have in hand takes us beyond the proposition Harkness started with: "It is a truth universally acknowledged, that a critic intent upon analysis and interpretation, must be in want of a good text."[47] We are not restricted, any more, to identifying a "soiled fish," or catching the critic out because he has based an argument on a nonauthorial (or nonauthoritative) phrase or sentence; we can go beyond that to say that *all* criticism may be flawed, if not wholly wasted, when it is lavished upon an imperfect text. Criticism really is dependent upon textual knowledge, for there are times when *only* biographical and textual evidence can lead to literary criticism of any enduring value, times when such evidence in drafts or the earliest complete version of a work may be of interest equal to that of the first (or any later) printed edition. There may not be much a textual scholar can do with the evidence (the situation may be such that a new edition is not desirable, feasible, or even possible) except teach the work to students as one problematical in nature, not susceptible of analysis for its unity, completeness, and ultimate perfection. Also, of course, a textual scholar can do as I have done—that is, try out a range of strategies designed to lead critics and theorists to take fuller account of the possible aesthetic implications of textual and biographical evidence.

What Harkness identified as the "Novelistic Fallacy" still survives, beyond doubt—look at the articles and books which

47. Harkness, p. 59.

still cite reprints derived from reprints derived from reprints even when texts are available which do in fact let the user know what text he is holding in his hand, and even reveal, sometimes, that previous texts are in gross ways "nonauthoritative." But CEAA editors were, as a group, far guiltier of the Novelistic Fallacy, the tendency to think that the words of a novel do not matter very much, than critics had been. It is unthoughtful, to be sure, when a critic quotes from the Bobbs-Merrill edition of *Moby-Dick*, a rather careless reprint of the Hendricks House edition, especially if he quotes a textually dubious passage such as "The Gilder." But it is far more questionable when a CEAA editor, with well-nigh limitless federal funds at his command, prints an edition of *Maggie* which omits the title character's climactic encounter in Chapter 17, an encounter of the highest structural importance not only to that chapter but to the whole book, or prints an edition of *The Red Badge of Courage* which omits entire pages from the final manuscript. Whenever CEAA editors have printed texts shortened according to someone's whim, suggestion, or command, they have been acting as if sentences, and even entire chapters do not matter in a novel— even when the novel happens to be so short that there is no "vast bulk" to begin with. When editors blithely apply Greg's suggestions as the proven formula for arriving at an ideal text, they are exalting editorial rules above the product of an author's attempt to put his conception onto paper, an attempt in which, to recall Murray Krieger's words, a "drive toward oneness" is felt "by the form-making writer in the throes of his give-and-take struggle that gives him his awareness of the growing monster whose demands to satisfy its own needs he must respect, even at the expense of his own original intentions."[48] From his familiarity with the writer's strategies for affecting the reader by words, passages, scenes, chapters, and larger units of the work as originally written, the true editor, the devoted textualist, will develop special alertness to the effects that any subsequent alteration, whether authorial or not, have on those intended responses. And he will, if he is this sort of editor whose loyalty is to the author, not to his own or someone else's

48. Murray Krieger, *Theory of Criticism* (Baltimore: Johns Hopkins, 1976), p. 32.

formula for editing, perhaps even decide that an editor's job is not to edit, but to edit as little as possible, bowing always to the authority of the author—whenever (to recur to Chapter 2) the author knows what he is doing.

CHAPTER 4

The Authority of the Revised Text and the Disappearance of the Author:
What Critics of Henry James Did with Textual Evidence in the Heyday of the New Criticism

In the previous chapter I examined what people who thought of themselves as textual scholars or "textual bibliographers" actually said in recent decades about what constituted textual problems and about the implications those problems held for literary criticism. In this chapter I look at what some ninety literary critics, contemporaries of Harkness, Gibson, Cady, Bowers, Tanselle, and the other writers on textual issues, had to say about Henry James's revisions of his fiction. I assembled these hundred or so items (several critics wrote more than one essay) from standard sources (Lewis Leary's various editions of *Articles on American Literature*, the two editions of *Eight American Authors*, and *American Literary Scholarship* up through the 1981 volume), aiming at comprehensiveness. I read them in order of their date of publication, analyzing them not for relevance of evidence or cogency of argument but solely for their stated or unstated assumptions about the nature and effects of James's revisions.

I undertook this chapter only after a skeptic objected to my bumptiousness in claiming that some of us American textualists had begun to talk about the aesthetic implications of textual evidence in ways critics had not talked before: critics of Henry

James, he declared, had been dealing with precisely such matters all along, during the very period when the modern critic, according to Harkness, was "apt to be entirely indifferent to the textual problems of a novel."[1] I had to take the skeptic seriously because essays on James's revisions do make up a lavish sample of critics at work: no critic wanting to write about revisions of American literary works could avoid James, any more than the textualists cited in my first chapter could avoid referring to the fact that his texts would surely present special problems, whatever those problems might be. As it turns out, the skeptic was wrong. The writers of these essays were mainly critics who remained critics, manifesting no ambition to retool themselves as identifiable textual critics or textual bibliographers and never claiming to be operating under an editorial theory (they never mentioned Greg or Bowers) or a critical theory (they never cited any literary theorists or aestheticians, not even those we regard as New Critical spokesmen, such as Cleanth Brooks and Robert Penn Warren or W.K. Wimsatt, Jr., and Monroe C. Beardsley). They focused briefly upon the process of composition and revision only as a means for celebrating one or another finished (or re-finished) product. They were, to judge from their words, practitioners of the New Criticism without knowing it.[2]

James had in fact proved irresistible to the original New Critics who defined themselves in the 1930s and 1940s and

1. Bruce Harkness, "Bibliography and the Novelistic Fallacy," *Studies in Bibliography* 12 (1959): 59-73; the quotation is from p. 59. To keep in good conscience I have not made much use of a number of essays which seem to be derivative or somewhat duplicative, especially if they do not take account of all the documentary evidence already presented and do not adequately acknowledge the extent to which earlier essays cover the same ground. To avoid distorting my history I do not use the discussion of "Four Meetings" in Steven Mailloux's *Interpretive Conventions* (Ithaca: Cornell University Press, 1982), pp. 116-17; Mailloux was self-consciously exploring and qualifying my approach to the study of authorial revisions.
2. In their response to the respondents to "Against Theory" Steven Knapp and Walter Benn Michaels declare that theory "will continue to have no consequences for the practice of literary criticism"—*Critical Inquiry* 9 (June 1983): 800. As this chapter will demonstrate, theory has the most momentous consequences for the practice of literary criticism, whether or not the individual critic is aware of the extent to which he is working under a particular theory. In "The Practice of Theory," *Profession 83* (New York: Modern Language Association of America, 1983), pp. 21-28, Lawrence I. Lipking sums up the views of those who think theory cannot be kept out of the classroom (or out of any writing a critic does): "literary historians

gained control of many academic journals in the late 1940s and early 1950s—control which they and their followers have retained through several later fashions of criticism. In the 1920s, Robert Spiller remembered, those Southerners known as the Fugitives began "to call attention to the need for better means of analyzing the meaning of a work of art without reference to the extrinsic circumstances of its creation or to the personality of its creator, and to demand firmer standards and surer methods in literary art, as well as in religion and politics."[3] The Fugitives and others with similar aims[4]

> found in T. S. Eliot their perfect example and leader for poetry and criticism, but there was no living American or British novelist who satisfied their needs in intrinsic greatness and in devotion to the cause of art. Henry James was a ready-made "modern," and his work was complete and obviously distinguished. The "New Critics" therefore turned the full force of their talents upon him— together with Proust, Joyce, Kafka, and other European "moderns"—and, as their influence grew in academic circles, they brought to the study of James not only a new angle of vision but a good deal of basic and factual research, particularly into semantic problems approached through psychology. As a result, James received for the first time a critical evaluation which was sympathetic as well as thorough, and many of the old paradoxes in the interpretation of his life and work disappeared in the enthusiasm and the bickerings of critics who worshipped together at the altar of the master, differing only in the fine points of ritualistic observance.

The "basic and factual research" which Spiller alluded to did not often consist of biographical and textual study, one must say, and most of the new analyses of James were "explications of the text"—in the sense of close readings of the text of one printed edition or another, with no comparison of editions and

---

and critics who consider their work unrelated to theory, on this analysis, are self-deluded; they obey principles all the more dogmatic for never being brought out in the open" (p. 21).

3. Robert Spiller, in *Eight American Authors: A Review of Research and Criticism*, ed. Floyd Stovall (New York: Modern Language Association of America, 1956), pp. 364-418; the quotation is from p. 395.

4. Spiller, pp. 395-96.

no mention of possible aesthetic implications of James's revisions. There had been an early rush to pronounce preferences for or against James as a reviser of his own fiction (the novelist Robert Herrick's advocacy of the early text of *The American* was both brilliant and passionate), but critics of James after the mid-1940s so seldom excited themselves as to their preference for unrevised texts or revised texts that the critic who labeled the parties as "revisionists" and "anti-revisionists" a few years later was exaggerating the focus and strength of recent commentary.[5] In this climate Spiller was quite justified in his summation: "It would seem that the larger problem of the significance of textual variations has scarcely been touched"—and no more than the critics did he try to define the nature of that larger problem, or those larger problems.[6]

By the time Robert Gale updated the James chapter for the revised edition of *Eight American Authors*,[7] a horde of practitioners of the New Criticism, at least in its diluted academic form, had published their analyses of "the structure of" and "the time scheme in" a given story or novel, or their essays on "the unity of" and "the imagery in" (match imagery in this story, abyss imagery in another, candlestick-and-snuffers imagery, witchcraft imagery, furniture imagery, bolted-door imagery, and pagoda imagery in still others). The critics had discovered symbolism (Edenic symbolism, money symbolism, height symbolism) and had reveled in distinctions between metaphor and symbolism, appearance and reality, grammar and style, imagery and symbolism, irony and paradox; they had pondered the curiosities of operative irony, ironic imagery and symbolism, narrative irony, metaphor in the plot, and structural irony; they had analyzed the relationship between style and subject, structure and theme, punctuation and point of view, imagery and theme, form and substance, and even form and structure. Amid this New Critical maelstrom the critics I study in

5. Robert Herrick, "A Visit to Henry James," *Yale Review* n.s. 12 (1923): 724-41. On revisionists and anti-revisionists see S. P. Rosenbaum, "*The Spoils of Poynton*: Revisions and Editions," *Studies in Bibliography* 19 (1966): 161-74, especially pp. 161-62.
6. Spiller, p. 401.
7. Robert Gale, in *Eight American Authors: A Review of Research and Criticism*, ed. James Woodress (New York: W. W. Norton, 1971), pp. 321-75.

this chapter might seem to be quite anomalous in their use of what was disdainfully called "extrinsic evidence." They sometimes even made a point of the unfashionableness and ill repute of their textual work, as in this preemptive strike by a pair of collaborators:[8]

> Nowadays the study of textual niceties is not popular in many circles. The usual practice seems to be to leave such drudgery as collation to the pedant who may be good for little else and thus free one's self to engage the energies, critical faculties, and imagination in pursuing images, allegories, paradoxes, symbols, ambiguities, theological implications—what not.

But, the collaborators continued, "is it safe to overlook" textual revisions?[9] Their pleas were a little disingenuous, for in fact by the late 1950s there was a vogue for essays on James's revisions, which had come to be yet another sort of chic essay to be written on the Master, though leading, more often than not, to predictably New Critical conclusions. All but divorcing textual revisions from biography, from the historical circumstances of James's composing and revising, these critics almost managed to convert their extrinsic evidence into intrinsic evidence. The situation is more complicated, and more interesting, than the plaintive collaborators suggested.

These writers on James's revisions did not perform the basic chores of scholarship, did not, for instance, painstakingly relate James's biography during the composition of *Portrait of a Lady* to the novel as serialized and as published in book form, and did not relate the revisions for the New York Edition to the circumstances under which James made the revisions. It may be objected that for biographical research James is a special case, a major writer on whom the biographical materials were, to an extraordinary degree, monopolized by one man, Leon Edel. The inherent danger in the decision of James's heirs to invest exclusive privilege in one person was infinitely compounded when the man so privileged came to be jealous of his territory and

---

8. Thomas M. Cranfill and Robert L. Clark, Jr., "James's Revisions of 'The Turn of the Screw,'" *Nineteenth-Century Fiction* 19 (March 1965): 394-98; the quotation is from p. 394.
9. Cranfill and Clark, p. 394.

rather idiosyncratic in his literary judgments. Millicent Bell has at length, and with admirable restraint, stated the case for thinking that the exclusivity not only harmed other investigators and the cause of James biography but also harmed Edel, since it allowed him to indulge his opinions without having to consider the opinions others might have formed from the same evidence, had they been allowed to consider it.[10] So we have an extraordinary situation, bone-chilling to a Melvillean long accustomed to cozy shared messes among a mutually solicitous joint-stock company of fellow workers, a situation which might seem to invalidate my sample of the way critics behaved with textual evidence. In fact, I don't think the sample is particularly tainted. Plainly, there were people, presumably including Bell herself, who chafed at not being allowed to work with manuscript materials of the highest interest, at being forbidden access decade after decade, but in these dozens of essays on James's revisions I have found very little indication that the writers were rebelling against their restraints. S. P. Rosenbaum quite plainly would have preferred to quote letters from manuscript in his 1964 Norton Critical Edition of *The Ambassadors* as well as in one of his 1966 essays on *The Spoils of Poynton* rather than having to paraphrase from them or allude to some of their contents without quotation, but he is a remarkable exception.[11] (Emily K. Izsak, almost simultaneously with Rosenbaum, published a study of the composition of *Spoils* in which she not only used the notebook entries but somehow gained special dispensation "to quote and otherwise make reference" to some of the same unpublished correspondence which Rosenbaum was denied permission to quote.)[12]

A way of testing my conviction that the writers of these essays, far from resenting being deprived of access to archives, probably seldom realized they *were* excluded, is simply to look at what use they made of the documentary evidence which was

10. Millicent Bell, "Henry James: The Man Who Lived," *Massachusetts Review* 14 (Spring 1973): 391-414.
11. S. P. Rosenbaum, ed., *The Ambassadors* (New York: W. W. Norton, 1964), p. 353; and "*The Spoils of Poynton*: Revisions and Editions," *Studies in Bibliography* 19 (1966): 161-74; see pp. 163-64, n. 8.
12. Emily K. Izsak, "The Composition of *The Spoils of Poynton*," *Texas Studies in Literature and Language* 6 (Winter 1965): 460-71.

available. The *Notebooks* had been open to everyone since 1947, and yet were rarely used. Ward S. Worden in 1953, before the full dominance of the New Criticism, used them in a study of a condensed version of *What Maisie Knew*, but his very interesting analysis rested upon an unproven assumption that James himself made the cuts.[13] Rosenbaum complained in one of his admirable studies of revisions and editions of *The Spoils of Poynton* (1966) that critics had not used the relevant passages in the *Notebooks* despite what seemed to him their obvious importance to study of the novel (as it happened, Izsak's essay on the same book, making use of the *Notebooks*, appeared just before the first of Rosenbaum's two 1966 essays on *Spoils*).[14] Conspicuously, even when a few critics began to cite the notebook passages on a particular work they were slow to couple those passages with any comments in James's prefaces to the New York Edition, and almost none of them thought of using *Notebooks* and prefaces along with whatever other materials were readily available in collections of letters or biographies, including Edel's earlier volumes in the five-part life, published in 1953, 1962, 1962, 1969, and 1972. Biographical and historical comment in these essays tended to be rudimentary, as when Isadore Traschen referred in 1956 to James's "deficient masculinity" as if it were a matter of demonstrable fact, or when Dominic J. Bazzanella (1969) sampled contemporary reviews for a remote clue as to why James revised the ending of *Portrait* as he did, late in life, for the New York Edition, or when Nina Baym (1976) briefly tried to set *The Portrait of a Lady* in the context of the "fictional and essayistic treatments of the new American girl" in the *Atlantic Monthly* while the novel was being serialized during 1880-81.[15]

13. Ward S. Worden, "A Cut Version of *What Maisie Knew*," *American Literature* 24 (January 1953): 493-504.
14. S. P. Rosenbaum, "Henry James and Creativity: 'The Logic of the Particular Case,'" *Criticism* 8 (Winter 1966): 44-52; see pp. 47 and 48.
15. Isadore Traschen, "James's Revisions of the Love Affair in *The American*," *New England Quarterly* 29 (March 1956): 43-62 (the quotation is from p. 62); Dominic Bazzanella, "The Conclusion to *The Portrait of a Lady* Re-examined," *American Literature* 41 (March 1969): 55-63; Nina Baym, "Revision and Thematic Change in *The Portrait of a Lady*," *Modern Fiction Studies* 22 (Summer 1976): 183-200 (the quotation is from p. 194).

Nor was bibliographical research definitive, despite the appearance of Leon Edel and Dan H. Laurence's *A Bibliography of Henry James* (1957, revised 1961 and 1982).[16] Mistaking one text for another had been very common since the 1920s when Hélène Harvitt quoted a text of *Roderick Hudson* which she wrongly assumed to be identical to the first edition, and such blunders continued, as when F. R. Leavis quoted the late James as an example of stylistic maturity while thinking he was quoting early James.[17] Through the 1950s and thereafter critics discussing textual variants routinely cited some cheap paperback or other (such as the Rinehart edition of *The American*) as if it were a perfect substitute for "the" nineteenth-century version of the text (the possibility of significant variation in the early forms of the text being generally ignored). After Robert Young discovered the now-notorious reversed chapters in *The Ambassadors* a needless contretemps ensued. Edel (reacting possessively where gratitude might have been in order) corrected Young on a bibliographical point and was corrected in turn; later one publisher proudly advertised an edition as containing the chapters in the correct order but perpetuated the blunder.[18] Even Ian Watt in the wake of his brilliant and universally admired essay on the opening paragraph of *The Ambassadors* was drawn into trivial and inconclusive disputation over textual

16. Leon Edel and Dan H. Laurence, *A Bibliography of Henry James* (London: R. Hart-Davis, 1957); third edition, revised with the assistance of James Rambeau (Oxford: Clarendon Press, 1982).

17. Hélène Harvitt, "How Henry James Revised *Roderick Hudson*: A Study in Style," *PMLA* 39 (1924): 203-27. On Leavis's blunder, see Gordon N. Ray, "The Importance of Original Editions," in *Nineteenth-Century English Books*, by Gordon N. Ray, Carl Weber, and John Carter (Urbana: University of Illinois Press, 1952), p. 22.

18. Robert E. Young, "An Error in *The Ambassadors*," *American Literature* 22 (November 1950): 245-53; Leon Edel, "A Further Note on 'An Error in *The Ambassadors*,'" *American Literature* 23 (March 1951): 128-30; Robert E. Young, "A Final Note on *The Ambassadors*," *American Literature* 23 (January 1952): 487-90. Edel then claimed that Young's "final" reply had contained "certain serious bibliographical errors": "A Letter to the Editors," *American Literature* 24 (November 1952): 370-72; the quotation is from p. 370. The Harper and Brothers 1955 reprinting was advertised as correcting the reversed chapters when the erroneous order was retained.

minutiae.[19] As late as 1968 Maqbool Aziz felt it necessary to issue a warning against making literary judgments without knowing the effects of James's revisions: "few writers on James appear to realise the full critical implications of the textual difficulty: that here lie traps deadlier than those one meets in the ambiguities of James's narrative techniques and style." Critics' "suicidal manner of arriving at their particular conclusions" about textual matters provoked Aziz into an urgent attempt to save them from themselves.[20] The warning was ignored and the pattern continued: almost nobody did anything right once for all; everything was half right, at best, and if it was done over again, it was done over inaccurately. Even today anyone wanting to speak with assurance of the genealogical relationship of one edition of, say, *The Portrait of a Lady* to another edition would do best to check out everything himself, from scratch.

Nor was the particular rigorous textual chore of collation of the texts ever done once for all, unless one can except the Norton Critical Edition of *The Wings of the Dove*, edited by J. Donald Crowley and Richard A. Hocks (1978), which includes what purports to be a complete list of variants between the English and American editions of 1902 and the New York Edition of 1909. (The editor of the Norton *The Ambassadors* included only a partial collation, while the editor of the Norton *The Portrait of a Lady* included a collation of the 1881 American edition and the New York Edition of 1908 but not variants between these texts and other editions, such as the two periodical publications which preceded book publication.) The prevailing standards of academic journals was such that essays were accepted when the writer admittedly was basing broad arguments on only a sample collation—Brian Birch's 1965 essay on *The Ambassadors*, for example, or most astonishingly, H. K. Girling's 1975 essay on *The Princess Casamassima*, which was based on the variants in a single paragraph and was, I would add, weakened by the assumption that all punctuation in the

19. Ian Watt, "The First Paragraph of *The Ambassadors*: An Explication," *Essays in Criticism* 10 (July 1960): 250-274; see J. C. Maxwell, "The Text of *The Ambassadors* I," *Essays in Criticism* 11 (April 1961): 116; Ian Watt, "The Text of *The Ambassadors* II," *Essays in Criticism* 11 (April 1961): 116-19.

20. Maqbool Aziz, "'Four Meetings': A Caveat for James Critics," *Essays in Criticism* 18 (July 1968): 258-74; the quotations are from pp. 258 and 264.

New York Edition is unquestionably James's own.[21] The great majority of the writers on textual revisions in James's texts did not attempt any such elaborate analysis even of sample passages, and it is curiously hard to determine just how much real textual work any of them did. How did they make their collations, these critics who presumed to write textual studies in which their page references often were to Rinehart paperbacks? What did their collations look like? What procedures did they use for ensuring completeness and accuracy of collations? What procedures did they use for ensuring that they were recording variants in a form they could readily work from? Did any of them think of recording variants in a form others could use? If so, why did no critic announce that his collation was available for others' use at one library or another or (after the arrival of cheap photocopying) available at cost on request? Is it merely coincidental that some of the same examples of textual variants tended to recur from essay to essay? Why is it that the essays on James's revisions of *The American* do not prepare one for the minuteness of the revisions now open to readers in the facsimile of James's working pages mounted from two copies? Is it possible that some essays—on *The American*, say—were built from information in earlier essays? Except for those few who were in fact editing one of the novels, these critics of textual revisions were not hampered by any need to claim that their research had been extensive, much less exhaustive, and they displayed no unseemly urge to report their findings in pedantic detail.

To a remarkable degree the pattern of this academic criticism on James's revisions was set by F. O. Matthiessen's essay on James's revisions of *Portrait*, first published in a journal in 1944 then reprinted in his book on James later the same year. Matthiessen was singled out by Spiller as the foremost spokesman for the New Criticism as applied to James:[22]

---

21. Brian Birch, "Henry James: Some Bibliographical and Textual Matters," *Library* 20 (June 1965): 208-23; H. K. Girling, "On Editing a Paragraph of *The Princess Casamassima*," *Language and Style* 8 (Fall 1975): 243-63. The printers were in fact enjoined not to insert what James called death-dealing commas (James to the Scribner firm, 12 May 1906, in the Scribner Archive at the University of Princeton Library).

22. Spiller, *Eight American Authors* (1956), p. 409.

Using Edith Wharton's text, "for him [James] every great novel must first of all be based on a profound sense of moral values and then constructed with a classical unity and economy of means," he [Matthiessen] concludes that the traditional misconceptions have arisen from the attempt to divorce content from form as well as from the mistaken notion that James's devotion to art was an alienation from life. This is the point from which the new criticism takes its start, and it was made emphatically clear by Matthiessen's analysis of the four later novels. . . .

What Matthiessen actually said about textual revisions tends to be banal. James revised, Matthiessen said approvingly, to show a "more mature sense of a dramatic scene," to "sharpen the reader's impression" of something, to tone down something, to take the reader "right into the action," to make something "much more explicit." As if that was not riches enough to achieve through revisions, James also did "an expert job" of heightening an effect, he drew "a far more telling portrait," he wove "the texture of his style more complexly," he made "his later statement stronger," he exploited "dramatic possibilities" to "the full," he paid "much subtle attention" to something, and he gave something else "the final twist to the knife."[23] This sample of vacuous praise is characteristic of the essay, which is notable for containing few graspable ideas about the nature of James's revisions in particular or literary revision in general. Although Matthiessen's place in the New Criticism seemed clear to a literary historian like Spiller, his discussion of *Portrait* does not show any sense of being built upon any theoretical framework more sturdy than the imperfect analogy between revising a novel and retouching a painting. The writers of later essays (who once or twice were admittedly taking Matthiessen's hint that an essay like his might be written on *The American*) likewise failed to put their own essays into a theoretical framework. Yet it is easy enough now to identify New Critical assumptions underlying almost all of these essays, from Matthiessen's onward.

23. F. O. Matthiessen, "The Painter's Sponge and Varnish Bottle: Henry James' Revision of *The Portrait of a Lady*," *American Bookman* 1 (1944): 49-68 (the quotations are from pp. 50, 51, 51, 52, 53, 56, 58, 59, 60, 62, 62, and 63); reprinted in *James: The Major Phase* (New York: Oxford University Press, 1944), pp. 152-86.

Perhaps the most widespread assumption among these critics is ultimately platonic but may be derived more immediately from Wimsatt and Beardsley's "The Intentional Fallacy" (1946), one of the essays which, as we have seen in Chapter 3, Bruce Harkness parodied in the term "Novelistic Fallacy." Commenting on the apparent change of intention whenever an author revised a later edition, Wimsatt and Beardsley said brusquely (in the passage discussed in Chapter 2, n. 5): "If there is any sense in which an author, by revision, has better achieved his original intention, it is only the very abstract, tautological, sense that he intended to write a better book and now has done it."[24] Maqbool Aziz (1973) by using the word "archetype" seemed to be taking an explicitly platonic view of the problem: what the revision of "The Pension Beaurepas" "finally achieves is that, by using a variety of the right 'brush-strokes,' it brings the final version closer to the archetype of the intention in the author's mind."[25] In this view, James was able, with the benefits of age and experience, to fulfill his original intentions in a superior way—not to fulfill new intentions but the same intentions he had earlier tried to fulfill and, apparently, had failed to achieve. As in so much else Matthiessen provided the model by saying that the fictional character Caspar Goodwood in *Portrait* had always possessed his "energetic drive" but that the later James was able to convey much more of that drive to the reader. James had become able, according to Matthiessen, to make "unmistakably explicit what he had always meant to imply."[26] Viola Dunbar (1950) similarly spoke of James's becoming able "to bring out more clearly the meaning" of a situation—presumably the original meaning.[27] Royal A. Gettmann (1945) thought the revisions of *The American* did "justice to Newman as James

24. *Sewanee Review* 54 (July-September 1946): 470. See Chapter 2, n. 5 for the slightly revised version of this sentence in Wimsatt's *The Verbal Icon* (1954 and 1958); more James critics may well have encountered the revised version than the original.

25. Maqbool Aziz, "Revisiting 'The Pension Beaurepas': The Tale and Its Texts," *Essays in Criticism* 23 (July 1973): 268-82; the quotation is from p. 281.

26. F. O. Matthiessen, "The Painter's Sponge," pp. 53 and 65.

27. Viola Dunbar, "The Revision of *Daisy Miller*," *Modern Language Notes* 65 (1950): 311-17; the quotation is from p. 316.

originally conceived him."[28] Dominic J. Bazzanella (1969) echoed Matthiessen in saying that the revision of *Portrait* makes "'unmistakably explicit'" what James had intended all along; revision "removes any possible ambiguity," removes any "unintentional ambiguity."[29] Sydney J. Krause (1958) did not plainly discriminate as to old or new meanings when he commented on James's effort "to make his style explicit enough for the meaning it had to express," but he seems to have had in mind the meaning which is both the original one and the final one.[30] Vincent Tartella (1960) said some touches "define the narrator's personality more certainly" in "Four Meetings," presumably meaning the man's personality was basically the same before and after revisions.[31] Thomas M. Cranfill and Robert L. Clark, Jr. (1965) said that revisions of *The Turn of the Screw* "tell us something" about James's "intentions regarding. . .the governess's reactions"—again apparently meaning first and continuing intentions.[32] Adaline R. Tintner (1973) said that in *The American* Mme. de Bellegarde's adultery (like her murder of her husband) "appears to have been James's intention from the start," so in adding some incriminating words to the New York Edition James was restoring or renewing "an original feature of the crime."[33] Similarly, Robert D. Bamberg (1975) said a comparison of the texts of *Portrait* "can offer the reader real guidance toward the elucidation of the author's meaning," apparently a single meaning.[34]

Herbert F. Smith and Michael Peinovich edged onto a slightly different terrain when they said (1969) that changes in *The Bostonians* (made soon after the original publication, the

28. Royal A. Gettmann, "Henry James's Revision of *The American*," *American Literature* 16 (January 1945): 279-95; the quotation is from p. 288.

29. Dominic J. Bazzanella, pp. 59, 58, and 59.

30. Sydney J. Krause, "James's Revisions of the Style of *The Portrait of a Lady*," *American Literature* 30 (March 1958): 67-88; the quotation is from p. 82.

31. Vincent Tartella, "James's 'Four Meetings': Two Texts Compared," *Nineteenth-Century Fiction* 15 (June 1960): 17-28; the quotation is from p. 18.

32. Cranfill and Clark; the quotation is from p. 395.

33. Adaline R. Tintner, "The House of Atreus and Mme de Bellegarde's Crime," *Notes and Queries* 218 (March 1973): 98-99; the quotations are from pp. 99 and 98.

34. Robert D. Bamberg, ed., *The Portrait of a Lady* (New York: W. W. Norton, 1975), p. viii.

novel not having been included in the New York Edition) "reflect second thoughts and elaboration upon the characters" and "help the reader to see James's intentions" (presumably the original intentions despite the second thoughts) then went on to say that some changes "present the fillip that makes the character come to life."[35] Such comments on second thoughts which can make a character come to life (for the first time?) move toward comments on James's ability to identify serious flaws in his novels and repair the damage belatedly. Taking their hint from James's preface, Max F. Schulz (1955) writes of James's late attempt "to mask" the "central artistic problem" of *The American,* the "falsely romantic conception of denouement," and Isadore Traschen (1956) writes of James's attempt "to correct his failure adequately to represent his lovers' intimacy" in the same book.[36] Such critics see James not as working over all the novel with equal diligence but as having "consistently revised certain parts"—to use Schulz's example—in an effort toward "deepening Newman's consciousness."[37] Sydney Krause more explicitly said that James's revisions usually "improve the prose of specific passages without ramifying their meaning for a more comprehensive or symbolic effect," improve the part without affecting the whole.[38]

Yet Krause also said that sometimes an "adjustment in meaning has a clarifying effect which goes beyond the individual passage in question and embraces basic matters of theme and structure."[39] Krause was still focusing on revisions as "clarifying" something which was already present, but he seemed uneasily aware that local changes or larger patterns of changes might affect something more than the passages being altered. Although Krause was beginning to think of the revised parts not merely in isolation from other passages, to sense that any

35. Herbert F. Smith and Michael Peinovich, "*The Bostonians*: Creation and Revision," *Bulletin of the New York Public Library* 73 (May 1969): 298-308; the quotations are from p. 306.
36. Max F. Schulz, "The Bellegardes' Feud with Christopher Newman: A Study of Henry James's Revision of *The American*," *American Literature* 27 (March 1955): 42-55 (the quotation is from p. 42); Isadore Traschen, "James's Revisions of the Love Affair in *The American*," p. 43.
37. Schulz, pp. 43 and 48.
38. Krause, p. 72.
39. Krause, p. 69.

change might affect other parts of the book or even the book as a whole, the typical comment on the relationship between part and whole in revised editions was vague, as in Sacvan Bercovitch's 1969 claim that in the revised *Roderick Hudson* certain "heightened reactions presuppose a good deal less open-mindedness on Rowland's part than has been claimed for him."[40] Bercovitch's idea seems to collapse distinctions between the response of modern critics to the 1875 text and the response of presumably other modern critics to the 1907 text; it also seems to take a fluid view of relationships between the texts such that what one identifies as "less open-mindedness on Rowland's part" in the 1875 text applies to Rowland in the 1907 text.[41] His presupposition seems to be that the character inhabits both texts equally so that evidence can be drawn from either to identify, perhaps, the archetypal Rowland. A couple of critics noticed that revision created new local awkwardnesses (Isadore Traschen [1956] mentioned one spot in *The American* and Charles Vandersee [1968] another one in "Pandora"),[42] but no one advanced the notion that intentionality might be so thoroughly built into a piece of fiction as originally written that local revisions would disrupt larger patterns and that original intentions would persist in particular unrevised passages (or even in revised passages), although some of the clues to the meanings of the passages might be obscured.

In its clearest form the question of the degree of change made by James's revisions was whether or not the changes worked a "transformation." Gettmann had said that meaning was not fundamentally changed by the revisions, which "refine and expand and comment upon the original ideas" but make "no essential changes in the characters."[43] Schulz said that James had "no intention in his revision . . . 'to retouch the *substance* of the thing.'"[44] Krause found "no changes in the themes

---

40. Sacvan Bercovitch, "The Revision of Rowland Mallet," *Nineteenth-Century Fiction* 24 (September 1969): 210-21; the quotation is from p. 218.
41. Bercovitch, p. 218.
42. Traschen, "James's Revisions of the Love Affair in *The American*," p. 54; Charles Vandersee, "James's 'Pandora': The Mixed Consequences of Revision," *Studies in Bibliography* 21 (1968): 93-108; see p. 95.
43. Gettmann, pp. 285 and 286.
44. Schulz, p. 54.

or in the essential structure," and Bamberg partially confirmed James's own view that "changes did not substantially alter the outlines of the Portrait or its essential statement," while Charles Fish (1967) said that although James "could not completely recast the story" (*Watch and Ward*) "here and there he could make changes."[45] Yet some of the same critics leapt over into the notion of the miraculous revision, the transformation, as when Schulz said that Newman is "transformed into a vociferous lover of America," or when Traschen (1956) said that in "reimagining" Newman's relation with the Bellegardes, James "unfortunately transformed his first-rate study of international manners into second-rate melodrama," then went on to comment upon the effect of the "transformation."[46] Nina Baym bluntly declared that the revisions of *Portrait* "transform" Madame Merle and Osmond into "empty shells," making the version of 1881 "a different work."[47] According to Anthony J. Mazzella, the revised text is indeed transformed: "we are responding in a new way to new characters in a new work."[48] There would seem to be a quantum difference between this notion of magical transformation and the more common notion of revision as merely heightening an effect, yet the notion of transformation was latent in less aggressive claims that a revision made a character "come to life."

Although several of these critics seem to have felt inklings of unexplored complications, their conclusions tended to be tamely couched in popular New Critical formulas like those in the article titles I cited from Gale's survey of criticism on James. Traschen said that "If style is the form that meaning takes, then a study of meaning would seem to be a study of the primary

---

45. Krause, p. 68; Bamberg, p. vii; Charles Fish, "Form and Revision: The Example of *Watch and Ward*," *Nineteenth-Century Fiction* 22 (September 1967): 173-90 (the quotation is from p. 190).

46. Schulz, p. 47; Isadore Traschen, "Henry James and the Art of Revision," *Philological Quarterly* 35 (January 1956): 39-47; the quotation is from p. 46.

47. Baym, pp. 190, 190, and 184.

48. Anthony J. Mazzella, "The New Isabel," in the Norton Critical Edition of *The Portrait of a Lady* (1975), pp. 597-619. This essay is printed from Mazzella's 1970 Columbia dissertation, which was the source of Edel's comments on James's revisions of *Portrait* in *Henry James: The Master: 1901-1916* (Philadelphia: J. Lippincott Company, 1972), pp. 326-29.

motivation of James's revisions."[49] Others said James was trying "consciously to impart to the meanings of his images a consistency with theme" (Schulz), or said he "wanted to correct his style, as such, and he wanted to intensify the symbolic texture of his language for the purposes of thematic motivation," or to "make his style explicit enough for the meaning it had to express," or said that revision had a "clarifying effect" on "theme and structure" and that in revising James was "maintaining connotative clarity" or "connotative precision and thematic clarity" (Krause).[50] The critics had indeed succeeded in converting an essentially extrinsic kind of study into a near-intrinsic kind by ignoring the way the part and the whole of the literary work functioned as it was first written; rather, with a few exceptions such as Izsak and, most notably, Rosenbaum,[51] they hurried to discuss how it functioned in the final platonic verbal icon, ignoring biographical evidence in their haste and making "James" a fiction-producing machine rather than a human being living and working in particular late nineteenth- and early twentieth-century milieux. Parallel developments in literary theory and textual theory had directed concern toward an ultimate product, not toward the processes by which a work achieves its completed form, or forms, and not toward the author's intentions as embodied in the first form or any intermediate forms of a work.

The major exception to all these generalizations is Sister Stephanie Vincec's 1976 essay on *The Wings of the Dove*. Vincec started, quite heretically, with a problem in reading:[52]

49. Traschen, "Henry James and the Art of Revision," p. 39.
50. Schulz, p. 44; Krause, pp. 67, 82, 69, 69, 70, and 71.
51. I have refrained from discussing Nina Baym's "Fleda Vetch and the Plot of *The Spoils of Poynton*," *PMLA* 84 (January 1969): 102-11, because she does not describe how extensive and complex the earlier essays by Izsak and Rosenbaum were, does not, for instance, mention the Scudder letters Izsak was able to quote from and otherwise refer to, and does not mention Rosenbaum's *Studies in Bibliography* essay.
52. Sister Stephanie Vincec, "'Poor Flopping *Wings*': The Making of Henry James's *The Wings of the Dove*," *Harvard Library Bulletin* 24 (January 1976): 60-93; the quotation is from p. 60, as is the one which follows. Vincec's essay is not mentioned in the Norton Critical Edition of *Wings* (New York: W. W. Norton, 1978) and the editors, J. Donald Crowley and Richard A. Hocks, tell an incomplete story of

I hardly expected easy going: the book is long, full of Jamesian contours, labyrinthine metaphors and ethereal dialogue. I was just congratulating myself on my success in following this very demanding author through the first volume of the novel when I lost my way. Up to this point James had presented a fiction made up of definite elements with clear connections and proportions, but in the second volume he seemed to ignore these connections and, without any guidance for the reader, to arrange his elements in a quite different manner. A second and third reading of the novel did not reveal any artistic reason, if one existed, for the shift. Were the two parts of the total composition unified by some subtle relationship which I had not grasped?

One of the joys in Vincec's account is her sense of where she was in her academic training and where her quest for knowledge drove her. She was a student, she says, from "the ascendancy of objective criticism," the New Criticism, according to which she ought to be able to read a James novel by reading a James novel. Her personal experience was revolutionary: she found she could not read a James novel merely by reading the James novel, for she located a problem in the book which she could not solve, with all good will and repeated readings. Vincec illustrates a point Brian Higgins and I have made, that a new kind of literary scholarship is emerging which is "distinguished not only by fresh vigor in the pursuit and analysis of historical, biographical, textual, and bibliographical evidence but also by the alert sophistication with which such evidence is probed for its aesthetic implications; or the trajectory of research can go in the other direction, as when a study begins with the recognition of an aesthetic problem which turns out to be resolvable only by external evidence."[53] Vincec's work is a perfect example of the second kind of trajectory, a study which begins with an intuitive uneasiness with the text and tries to explain it by finding and analyzing documentary evidence.

---

the composition and publication in "Notes on the Text," pp. 407-21, apparently because they relied on the Yale archive to the exclusion of the other major archives Vincec consulted, those at Princeton and Harvard.

53. Hershel Parker and Brian Higgins, "The Chaotic Legacy of the New Criticism and the Fair Augury of the New Scholarship," in *Ruined Eden of the Present*, edited by G. R. Thompson and Virgil L. Lokke (West Lafayette: Purdue University Press, 1981), pp. 27-45; the quotation is from p. 28.

Vincec gives a wry account of herself as a child of the New Criticism in search of answers to questions a seemly New Critic was not supposed to ask. She began with the *Notebooks*, available since 1947 but, as we have seen, rarely used by those writing on James's revisions. Rather than resolving for her "the problem of structural disparity," the notebook entries "raised some new questions." In turn, she found that James's preface to the novel "evades the issue instead of providing a real answer."[54] Neither of these sources, she decided, "describes the entire work as it stands": "The late Preface seems to be based on what James thought he had written rather than on the actual novel, and the notes were recorded long before the novel was a reality. Could I choose between the backward-glancing Preface of 1908 and the anticipatory notes of 1894?" Not our heroine: "I turned to other primary sources"[55] (published letters). The more she found, the more there was to do: "My initial aim of accounting for the oddities of structure of *The Wings of the Dove* was set aside; I needed to discover more about the genesis of the novel, its course of composition, and its immediate pre-publication history before I could evaluate the concrete results. I began to search for unpublished letters in the hope that they would yield additional facts. I found that scores of such letters existed."[56]

Availing herself of documents just released from Edel's exclusive use, Vincec ended up writing a history of the genesis of the novel, its course of composition, and its pre- and post-publication history. She concluded that the vicissitudes of composition had prevented James from exerting full control over the two conflicting subjects of the novel:[57]

> Prior to and during most of the dictation of the novel, James focused on one of his "historic bricks," namely the relationship of the engaged couple; during another phase he was carried away by the sick girl's situation and produced another brick large enough to distort the effect of the first but not large enough to assert beyond doubt, its own centrality. A "free and independent" mode of treatment aggravated the results of this division of attention.

54. Vincec, p. 10.
55. Vincec, p. 61.
56. Vincec, p. 62
57. Vincec, p. 93.

Finally, James's failure to apply that effective antidote, compression, left on his hands a too-lengthy novel with structural imbalances that no mere verbal revision could correct. One thing is clear. The author's subtlety has no bearing on the structure of this novel.

In her last paragraph Vincec glanced at criticism of *Wings*, suggesting that the more New Critical the reading, the more subjective; the more the critic pays attention to the biographical circumstances of its composition, the more likely he is to write truly objective, and presumably enduring, criticism. A sufficient indictment of the state of scholarship and criticism is that when the article was briefly mentioned in *American Literary Scholarship*, the writer of the James chapter devoted three of his six lines to censuring Vincec for her temerity in alleging that ignorance of the circumstances of the composition might lead a critic to subjective conclusions.[58]

Vincec's is an epochal article, the only one on James revisions of his novels which I can imagine myself reading two or three more times after this book is published, an absolutely essential document in the understanding of late James. Yet she does not tie the whole problem up, does not fully justify her impressions about the crucial flaw in *The Wings of the Dove* by internal evidence matched to the brilliantly assembled external evidence. She names the problem but does not fully analyze it by a "reading" of the novel. This is a small inadequacy in the only one of these James essays which plainly began with a critic's attempt to solve a genuine aesthetic puzzle and resulted in the critic's finding that the problem was in James's biography and the solution was in biographical scholarship; Vincec's is the only one of these essays which, rather than seeming to some extent make-work, a take-home assignment from Matthiessen, resulted from the fact that the problem and the solution proved so fascinating that the investigator was driven to share them with the world.

Criticism on James's revisions of his novels is, despite the hundred and more items, startlingly limited. We have one

---

58. "James," by William T. Stafford, in *American Literary Scholarship: An Annual, 1976* (Durham: Duke University Press, 1978), p. 106.

superb study of the compositional history and publication history of a major novel, a study which reveals alertness to the aesthetic implications though not a detailed exploration of those implications. Aside from Vincec, very few critics have attempted to recognize the importance of the writer at work, Emily K. Izsak and S. P. Rosenbaum being among the best of these few. Otherwise, we have a string of more or less mechanical studies in which James is found to be a good reviser or, very seldom, is found to have revised incautiously, a string of more or less mechanical essays with interchangeable New Critical assumptions and interchangeable New Critical conclusions. No one besides Vincec even tried to answer such a general question as how long and how intense were James's work rhythms. No one else tried to find out, more or less systematically, all that can be known about the way James wrote—what he did in preparing to write, what he did between the time he thought of writing and the time he began to write, how systematically he actually worked, once he started, and what he did to part or all of a novel between the time he thought it was finished and the time it was set in type (often for one magazine serialization, or two) and the time it was reset in book form (often reset both in England and the United States). No one tried to find out how thoroughly he ever planned out his works in advance and how often any advance planning was designed to accommodate later insertions. No one tried to identify the stage or stages at which James characteristically arrived at what Melville called the pervading thought which impels a book. No one else asked seriously about how interruptions might have affected James's progress, whether or not he typically discarded or drastically recast large sections of his manuscripts, or how much late backtracking and local tinkering was part of his usual process of tidying up a manuscript. Very curiously, critics did not consider the relation of the part to the whole: if James transformed Madame Merle and Osmond, what did that do to Isabel and the other characters: did they continue to react the same way to different characters? Did the alteration of Christopher Newman's characterization have any effect on the other characterizations? Were other characterizations altered to fit into new interrelationships, which were presumably now rendered dynamic in different ways? No one asked how successful an

105

author is apt to be when he tries to give a different cast to a novel by making his ending more explicit or how successful James (and any other author) is apt to be when he attempts to alter any one aspect of a work without revising the rest. Perhaps oddest of all, no one exhaustively analyzed James's letters or his prefaces to work out a full theory of how he regarded after-thoughts, or more important how he regarded revisions made much later—as casual elaborations or improvements on the original plan, for instance, or as essential corrections or even transformations.

As we saw, no critic of James seized the opportunity to explore seriously the possible difference between a first intention and a much later intention. The enduring appeal of the old notion of achieving the archetype is obvious from the number of critics who espoused it, but it turns out under examination to be very curious indeed. Some psychologists, psycholinguists, and philosophers would tell us that such a platonic notion of creativity cannot be taken seriously since no writer can have fully thought something if he cannot then and there express it —no writer can intend to mean something before he is able to state that meaning in words.[59] The notion also runs counter to descriptions of the creative process such as those by John Dewey, who would hold that what an author writes at a given moment not only fulfills what he has already written but allows or compels him to write what he is yet to write in the particular way that he actually writes it. Therefore if the author is unable to realize his intentions in a particular passage of a novel, as he composes that passage, the failure will affect what is yet to come, and any revision that alters the site of one failure without redoing what follows (if not also what comes before) will intro-duce something anomalous to the surrounding prose and per-haps anomalous to prose remoter still from the site of the revision.

Just as the "textual bibliographers" or "textualists" of my third chapter had felt free to mention the concept of "versions"

---

59. To be fair to James critics, we should remember that no one else was saying anything better about versions. James Thorpe's comments (1972) were quite con-fused, and even G. Thomas Tanselle in his important 1976 essay said with uncharacteristic recklessness that the 1893 and 1896 *Maggie* are "discrete works."

without analyzing it very thoroughly, so most of these James critics failed to explore ideas they had about what constitutes a version. They left an abundance of unasked questions. What does it take, the critics might have wondered, for revisions to constitute a different "version," and then what more does it take for revision to push a text beyond the status of a new version into the status of a different literary work, "a new work"?[60] Is a work new when even in something so thoroughly, not to say compulsively, revised as the 1907 *The American*, a good many lines at a stretch, occasionally, are wholly unrevised, while some other revisions respect the structure of a long paragraph while altering it stylistically sentence by sentence? Nor did critics raise some very interesting side-questions, such as whether or not James ever felt he had to suppress in an early "version" some aspect of an intended characterization, notably the erotic fears felt by Isabel Archer in 1907, if not 1880 and 1881. Did he work out the novel to completion with those fears in his mind as motivation, then years later see that he could fill out passages to convey explicitly what he had formerly dared only to hint at, for fear of censorship, implied or direct? This is the sort of question one might have asked in trying to work with Mazzella's evidence of numerous touches, all fairly small if undeniably powerful, rather than leaping into discussion of not merely two versions but two different works of art. With the exception of Aziz, who in 1968 attempted to argue out a partial theory of versions, such questions were almost never raised. Almost without exception, the critics' own assumptions bearing the greatest theoretical implications were left unexplored.

In their zeal to avoid the taint of extrinsic evidence, critics ignored even the simplest biographical questions, such as what order James worked in. No critic bothered to ask what the chronological relationships were between James's revising of his works and his writing of the prefaces for the volumes in which those works appeared. Did he, for instance, write the preface to *The American* after rereading it but before revising it? The preface is an evocative celebration of the still-youthful

60. See John R. Searle's application of this idea to his own prose in *Intentionality: An Essay in the Philosophy of Mind* (Cambridge: Cambridge University Press, 1983), p. x: "if you can't say it clearly you don't understand it yourself."

period in which he composed the book with "the free play of so much unchallenged instinct," during "such hours of fine precipitation," when he was riding hard his realistic hobby, obsessed with the notion that his hero must be wrongly used, when he was not yet a famous writer, certainly not a Master.[61] Was most or all of the preface written before he began what must have been many hours, many days, perhaps many weeks of arduous labor over the revisions for the New York Edition—toil over a book whose plot he could not believe? I see only one reference in the entire preface, at the beginning of the last paragraph, to the revisions. Was the preface drafted before he revised the book, then touched up afterwards? If James wrote the preface in the flush of rereading the book, during the first nostalgic memories of Paris and other locations where he worked on the manuscript during its hazardous serialized composition, does it, to evoke the specter of Harkness's stooge from my previous chapter, really matter? Would we think differently about James's defining the novel as a romance pretending to be a realistic work if we knew he was writing on the basis of a rereading of the original version rather than on the basis of his having so torturously revised it?

(I had intended to luxuriate in asking provocative questions in this history of James's critics at work, but since writing it I have answered some of the questions in *Nineteenth-Century Fiction* 38 [March 1984], the special issue honoring its former editor, Blake Nevius; see "Henry James 'In the Wood': Sequence and Significances of his Literary Labors, 1905-1907." I was wrong, it turns out, to suspect that the tone of the Preface to *The American* was due to its being composed before James revised the book. There is, however, a special reason for the ebullience of James's tone—the fact that he was immensely touched and gratified by the praise he had just received from his editor at Scribner's for the first two prefaces he had written, those for *Roderick Hudson* and *The Portrait of a Lady*. My establishment of the sequence of James's early labors on the New York Edition culminates, you will not be surprised to

61. Henry James in his Preface to *The American* in the New York Edition, as printed in *The Art of the Novel*, Introduction by Richard P. Blackmur (New York: Scribner, 1934), p. 25.

learn, in a set of new questions we can now ask for the first time about, for instance, the possible relationships between James's revisions and his work on particular portions of *The American Scene.*)

To pursue the topic with skeptical questions, would we think differently about *The American* if we studied the discrepancy between the evocative celebration of the creative process, however self-deluded, as we see it in the preface, and the thoroughness with which James altered that product of his younger days?—a brutality of sacrifice, one might almost say, that imposed his later self upon a younger conception and execution, upon a work which he would never have conceived and executed at the time he was revising but which he drastically altered from that estranged point of view. The estrangement extends even to commentary on the passage of time, as in altering "a cafe which projects" to "a cafe which projects, or then projected," shifting the events into a past time instead of letting them endure in a timeless contemporaneity.[62] James estranged himself by an equal distance in intellectuality and emotionality as he compared, for instance, the hero of his history to a dry specimen in a museum. He made his bluff strong hero vaguely overformal if not effete, having him say "I should like to converse with elegance" instead of "I should like to learn French," turning him self-consciously self-correcting, as when his laconic "I have been my own master all my life" became "I've enjoyed that blessing, or that curse, all my life."[63] James made his hero speak more elegantly at times, more slangily at other times, and while retaining the assertion that Newman was not in the habit of expressing himself in poetic figures nevertheless endowed him with figures, such as a comparison of knotty problems to knots of ribbon. He overwhelmed Valentin's direct

---

62. *Henry James, "The American": The Version of 1877 Revised in Autograph and Typescript for the New York Edition of 1907,* Houghton Library Manuscript Facsimiles I (London: Scolar Press, 1976), p. 18. In the "Introduction," Rodney G. Dennis mistakenly describes the document being reproduced as James's setting copy for the New York Edition of *The American.* In fact, what James supplied the printers was copy completely typed from this document, and of course further revised on the typescript; smaller changes were made in proofs.

63. Scolar Press Facsimile of *The American,* pp. 20, 12, 16.

observation that he "was too short" to afford a belly, superimposing an old man's heavy whimsy by making him say that he "was too short a story" to afford "an important digression."[64] After paging through the revisions visible in the facsimile of the first working copy for the New York Edition (further changes followed on typescript and in proofs), I would say that James's shame at what he saw as the raggedness and vulgarity of his earlier prose led him into lavishing an appalling outlay of human ingenuity and determination upon an impossible dream of successfully renovating something which had been beautifully of its original time and place. I also think that in human terms we cannot blame him. He did what was right for him, and we can go on reading the 1877 version.

The matter of the platonic conception which James was at first unable to bring fully into reality then years later was able to achieve also calls for some skeptical questioning. Once critics began seriously comparing the notebook entries and the prefaces with the text (any version of the text) it became obvious that after James jotted down the germ of a piece of fiction he usually did not go on to do precisely what he thought he was going to do, and it became obvious also that he did not in the prefaces always recollect what he actually had done, in the original version or in the revision, or else did not tell the truth about what he recollected. (All this is muddied by the failure of critics to define the chronological relationship of preface and revision.) The most critics did (and this occurred only two or three times) was to say that the discovery of such discrepancies would have significance for anyone interested in the creative process. They never brought up a related question which seems well worth anyone's time to answer: If James was unwilling or unable to *do* what he planned to do, and unable or unwilling to *recall* accurately what he had actually achieved (regardless of what he had thought he was achieving before or during composition), then how can we trust him to achieve at last what he had meant to do from the beginning but had been unable to do? How can we trust him to attain that poor platonic archetype if he

64. Scolar Press Facsimile of *The American*, pp. 37, 101.

intuited it as early as the 1870s and was able to realize it trium-
phantly only after three decades had passed? The unreliability
of both the *Notebooks* and the prefaces as guides to the finished
works (finished in one or more versions) strikes me as strong
evidence against James's having wanted to do something while
he first composed and not having been able to achieve his
meaning (his single meaning, original and final) until long
afterwards, even thirty years or more afterwards.

Just as no critic during this third of a century placed James's
work in the context of the dominant literary theory and none
showed any awareness that such a thing as editorial theory
existed, so did the critics ignore the possible relevance of
experimentation concerning memory and of theories about
memory. Even aside from the *Notebooks* and prefaces, what do
James's autobiographical writings reveal about the vagaries or
tenacity of his memory? How reliable was his memory for, say,
his own plots or those of other writers? Did he habitually get the
plots right when he reviewed novels? Did he recall other people's plots accurately years after he had read their novels? How
reliable, in particular, was his memory as to what piece of fiction he was engaged upon in a given year, in a given city? He
rather coyly declines to assert whether or not he finished *The
American* in Paris or carried it to England to finish there. Would
it not be simply human of James to have forgotten, at times,
which manuscript had been on his work table in Rome or Paris
or London? Cognitive psychologists studying memory tell us
what we all know from our own experiences, that the multiply-
ing of similar events makes it less easy to recall any particular
one of them.[65] Some events will stand out in one's memory, such
as the first time one dares to attempt serial publication without a
completed manuscript in hand before the first installment is
published, but even such a memory is subject to confusion and
loss.

Again using our sense of how our own memories function,
as well as some suggestive if not directly applicable research
into memory, we can ask if it is possible that in James's memory

65. Marigold Linton, "Transformations of Memory in Everyday Life," in *Memory Observed: Remembering in Natural Contexts*, ed. Ulric Neisser (San Francisco:
W. H. Freeman, 1982), pp. 77-91.

while he reread and revised there was not only the composing and proofreading of *The American* but also rejected plans, subsequent reactions of reviewers, his responses to public and private comments, and so on? We can also imagine that James's memory may have been thronged not only with the characterization he achieved for Newman in *The American* but also by any partial characterizations he had projected before finally settling upon one, and had never expunged from his mind; if there were a living model or a literary source for Newman, then that source might also hover in James's mind along with his own tentative and his own achieved characterization. Furthermore, all the Americans abroad whom he had created before Christopher Newman and during the years after the publication of *The American* may have remained in his mind, overlaying his specific memories of what he put into *The American*. How did James's later writing—the fact, for instance, of his having written another story of an American man in Paris, *The Ambassadors*—affect the way he remembered Newman as he thought about or as he reread the earlier book, and as he revised it? Are there not ways that *The American* and all the memories of it and associated with it interacted with the composition and publication of later similar, and partially superseding conceptions, such as *The Ambassadors*? Is it not potentially relevant that the revision of *The American* was performed by the man who had lived to write *The Ambassadors* and then had lived years beyond the writing of *The Ambassadors*? Since, as students of memory tell us, doing something similar to something already done tends to lead us to confuse the events in our memories, might not James's having written the at least slightly similar characterization of Lambert Strether have influenced the way he revised the characterization of Newman a few years later? My notion of the thronging and overlapping conceptions—characters brought into fictional reality in completed and published works, characters rejected before they came into the real life of print—may seem merely a fanciful encumbrance to the argument, but I think such presences are attested to by the survival in James's published writings not only of overlapping characterizations, from story to story, but also of characterizations which go in different directions at different points of the same story, in the work as initially published, as in some novels which were serialized during composition. Critics insist that James changed his characterization of Miss Birdseye in mid-composition of *The Bostonians*, for instance; and beyond question he changed the status of Fleda Vetch as orphan during the serialization of *Spoils*.

Provocative questions involving memory might be asked about something as sacred to the New Criticism as imagery, such as what may happen when a writer more or less systematically adds certain patterns of imagery to books written long before. Thinking in images can be hazardous, as in the extreme case of "S," the Russian mnemonist who recalled images so frequently and so vividly that he could not read a novel without importing settings and characters from other stories or from his own life, and had to stop reading because of the welter of images which involuntarily thronged his head, most of them irrelevant to what he was trying to read.[66] James was no such mnemonist, but might not some minor sort of thronging of images, and blurring of characterizations, have occurred when, to take merely one example, he began to delineate more and more of his female characters by bird imagery, defining Maria Gostrey by it while he wrote *The Ambassadors*, for instance, then a few years later putting it retroactively into the portrait of Countess Gemini when he revised *The Portrait of a Lady?* Did he contaminate such already-achieved characterizations with such imported imagery? At the very least, as when James more or less systematically added images of wine to his portrayal of the Bellegardes, did he not disrupt the ecology of the early version by importing into its fabric associations formed or elaborated late in life? Should we be asking questions not about the effect of added images to the text (early and late) of one novel but the relationship of the images James added to *Roderick Hudson* to those he added to *The Portrait of a Lady* and *The American?* That is, should his late revisions be studied in relation to each other as well as to the earlier texts?

To James a vivid memory is a moral capacity and forgetfulness is an outward manifestation of selfishness: we need to

66. A. R. Luria, "The Mind of a Mnemonist," in Neisser, *Memory Observed*, pp. 382-89.

think only of May Bartram in "The Beast in the Jungle" remembering and for a while letting John Marcher pretend to remember "the Sorrento day," or of Marcher's perverse care, in later years, not to forget her birthday. Yet revision was also a moral act for James, and when the opportunity came for his monument to his art to be erected, his respect for, and memory of, his past achievements collapsed before his compulsion to reshape his immature works for an ultimate, ideal audience indistinguishable from his later self. What James did as he revised *The American*, for instance, was of the highest importance to him, worth his lavishing upon it what must have been many days, or weeks, of the uncertain span of working life left to him. Misguided it may all have been, but the impulse was profound, and as much moral as aesthetic. Little of this high comedy and high seriousness, tragicomedy but also tragedy, was remotely sensed by the pack of academics whom the New Criticism loosed upon the words of the disembodied Master, Henry James in name only, a phantom who shared few points of resemblance with the Henry James who wrote the arrantly romantic *The American* then insisted stoutly that readers who objected to the ending really didn't know the world and couldn't measure the merit of a novel by the degree to which it realistically corresponded to the world, the Henry James who could alter characterization as he went along without revising what he had already written, the Henry James who when stymied could pigeonhole a novel for months, the Henry James who could elaborate one part of a novel in a way disproportionate to his treatment of another part, who could behave, at times, almost as if he were as much akin to as alien from his American contemporary, Mark Twain.

CHAPTER 5

Pudd'nhead Wilson:
Jack-leg Author, Unreadable Text, and Sense-Making Critics

In the remarks he wrote during 1894 to introduce *Those Extraordinary Twins* Mark Twain declared that the reader had "been told many a time how the born-and-trained novelist works"; now he was going to complete the reader's knowledge "by telling him how the jack-leg does it." He claimed to have found himself in a difficult situation once his story of the Italian freaks Angelo and Luigi (Siamese twins with two heads, four arms, one trunk, and two legs) was usurped by the story of the changeling Tom Driscoll, one thirty-second black and a slave. He was left, he said, with "not one story, but two stories tangled together; and they obstructed and interrupted each other at every turn and created no end of confusion and annoyance."[1]

---

1. See *The Tragedy of "Pudd'nhead Wilson" And the Comedy "Those Extraordinary Twins"* (Hartford: American Publishing Company, 1894), p. 311; the quotations later in the paragraph are from p. 310. I draw most of my evidence about composition from the manuscript at the Pierpont Morgan Library (in the form of a Xerox copy supplied by the late Frederick Anderson for my preliminary work on the California Edition), and I cite material which will be in Volume 4 of the California *Notebooks & Journals* as well as letters at the Bancroft Library, some unpublished and others printed in collections such as Hamlin Hill, ed., *Mark Twain's Letters to His Publishers, 1867-1894* (Berkeley: University of California Press, 1967), but all of which will appear in the forthcoming collections edited by Robert H. Hirst and his associates at the Mark Twain Papers. Since so much of my evidence is from unpublished material, I avoid footnotes as often as I decently can. Quotations from

This situation existed much as Mark Twain described it, but the evidence suggests that he did not see the tangle as a problem at the time he was creating it, at the end of 1892. In these same introductory comments Mark Twain moved from distorted recollection to outright untruth: "I could not offer the book for publication, for I was afraid it would unseat the reader's reason," he said, so he "pulled one of the stories out by the roots, and left the other one—a kind of literary Caesarean operation." In fact, he *had* tried to get the two stories into print, still "tangled together," but his cautious and overburdened employee-publisher Fred Hall had deterred him. For *months*, beginning in December 1892, when he completed the enormous manuscript, Mark Twain expected to get it published. He needed the money and didn't seem to recognize any great problem in the literary work itself—it was a book manuscript like any other. Then by early February 1893 it was a typescript ready to publish, and the acknowledged deterrent to publication (perhaps in some degree a strategy on Hall's part) was the confused state of the Charles L. Webster & Company finances, a confusion which involved Mark Twain's capital. Mark Twain was also entangled in the Paige Typesetter disaster, and the nation was going into the Panic of 1893, but the problem with the book, before the book was the *Pudd'nhead Wilson* we know, was that Hall had geared the company to sell trade books while the big money had been possible only under the subscription system, which was then dying out.[2]

unpublished material are used with the permission of the University of California Press and the Mark Twain Foundation, and may not be further reprinted without new permission.

Three members of the staff of the Papers, Victor Fischer, Michael B. Frank, and Kenneth M. Sanderson, and my former student Philip Cohen, all tried to help me avoid errors, and I thank them. The material truly is enough to "unseat" one's reason, and it would be miraculous if I have not gotten some things wrong.

Hardly a day passes that I do not mourn Frederick Anderson a little, and I guarantee you if he were alive to read this he would find something acerbic to say about it.

2. See the letter to Hall from Florence on 24 January 1893 in Hill's collection, p. 333. Hall wrote Clemens on 10 March 1893 that he had received "the Ms of 'Those Extraordinary Twins'" but had "not yet looked it over." He continued: "While I have not read 'Those Extraordinary Twins' I am sure, judging from the condition of the book trade in all its branches, that to get the book up in handsome style, as you

Pudd'nhead Wilson

I am not going to lie to you, as Mark Twain did, but I am going to describe situations that at worst might indeed unseat anyone's reason and at middling bad might make you stop reading before you get to the parts of the story which will intrigue you with their implications for literary criticism and aesthetic theory. I'll have to describe complicated situations which have been ignored by most critics of *Pudd'nhead Wilson* and more or less wildly misunderstood by almost all of the few who have made any attempt to talk about the history of composition and publication.[3] Although I have eased you into this story in some of the earlier chapters, I think we need a set of groundrules.

Groundrule #1: If you remember anything of what Mark Twain said in *Twins* about how he wrote the manuscript, forget it. He would have you think that he created "a woman named Roxana" before he had a function for her, that he created her and her son Tom before he thought of Pudd'nhead, and so on. Wait till you have read all of what I say before you start trying to reconcile it with what he says. You have to be cautious because part of what he says in *Twins* is true.

Groundrule #2: You can pretty much believe Arlin Turner's brief description of the process of composition and what I have recently said in various places and what my former student

---

suggest, illustrating it fully and putting a high price on it, would merely mean to sink money in it. I doubt if we could get our money back out of it." This was five weeks before the start of the Panic.

3. There were two good early studies, Anne P. Wigger, "The Composition of Mark Twain's *"Pudd'nhead Wilson" and "Those Extraordinary Twins"*: Chronology and Development," *Modern Philology* 55 (November 1957): 93-102, and Daniel Morley McKeithan, "The Morgan Manuscript of Mark Twain's *Pudd'nhead Wilson*," *Essays and Studies on American Language and Literature*, No. 12 (Cambridge: Harvard University Press, 1961), pp. 1-64. Wigger tells, with considerable accuracy, something I do not tell in this chapter—how Mark Twain seized upon fingerprinting as a plot device and what some of his preliminary plans were once he thought of the changeling plot. Despite her title, Wigger did not attempt to establish the sequence of the composition, although she recognized that it had begun with the arrival of the Twins. McKeithan printed for the first time many passages from the manuscript which were in neither *Pudd'nhead* nor *Twins*. The interpretive implications of these two studies were all but ignored by later critics, and now, ironically, there is not much point consulting either since I am telling here, or will soon be telling in the California Edition, a fuller and more accurate story.

Philip Cohen says, but until you have finished this chapter don't believe anything that anybody else has said. Do not, I warn you, read what Sidney E. Berger says in the Norton Critical Edition.[4]

Groundrule #3: Remember that the big manuscript which Mark Twain completed in Florence in December 1892 survives, intact, at the Pierpont Morgan Library. While he was composing it Mark Twain alternately called it *Those Extraordinary Twins* and *Pudd'nhead Wilson*, and for months he referred by either title to the typescript which was made in January 1893 and was completed by the third of February, at the latest. (The typescript ultimately provided almost all the printer's copy for what Mark Twain serialized as *Pudd'nhead Wilson* and, a year later, printed as *Those Extraordinary Twins*. Not a page of it is extant, so far as we know.) When I say *Pudd'nhead Wilson* (or *Pudd'nhead*, for short), I will always mean what Mark Twain extracted from the typescript in July 1893, augmented slightly with new bridge passages, serialized in the *Century* from December 1893 through June 1894, then reprinted twice with only slight variations—first in England (London: Chatto & Windus, 1894) and then in *The Tragedy of "Pudd'nhead Wilson" And the Comedy "Those Extraordinary Twins"* (Hartford: American Publishing Company, 1894). When I refer to *Those Extraordinary Twins* (*Twins*, for short), I will mean what was on some (not all) of the typescript pages left over after the

---

4. For a version of this chapter in the form of an extended review of Sidney E. Berger's Norton Critical Edition of *"Pudd'nhead Wilson" and "Those Extraordinary Twins"* (New York: W. W. Norton, 1980), see "The Lowdown on *Pudd'nhead Wilson*: Jack-leg Novelist, Unreadable Text, Sense-Making Critics, and Basic Issues in Aesthetics," *Resources for American Literary Study* 9 (Autumn 1981): 215-40 (published late in 1983), especially pp. 228-30 (not reprinted here) on Berger's confusing and erroneous history of the composition and publication and on his quite chaotic apparatus. See Arlin Turner, "Mark Twain and the South: An Affair of Love and Anger," *Southern Review* 4 (April 1968): 493-519; Parker and Henry Binder, "Exigencies of Composition and Publication: *Billy Budd, Sailor* and *Pudd'nhead Wilson*," *Nineteenth-Century Fiction* 33 (June 1978): 131-43; Parker, "Aesthetic Implications of Authorial Excisions: Examples from Nathaniel Hawthorne, Mark Twain and Stephen Crane," in *Editing Nineteenth-Century Fiction*, ed. Jane Millgate (New York: Garland, 1978), pp. 99-119; Parker, "The 'New Scholarship': Textual Evidence and Its Implications for Criticism, Literary Theory, and Aesthetics," *Studies in American Fiction* 9 (Autumn 1981): 181-97; and Philip Cohen, "Aesthetic Anomalies in *Pudd'nhead Wilson*," *Studies in American Fiction* 10 (Spring 1982): 55-69.

extraction of *Pudd'nhead Wilson* as combined with Mark Twain's new running commentary in the 1894 American Publishing Company volume.

Groundrule #4: Remember that in the manuscript which Mark Twain completed in Florence in December 1892 the story of the freaks and Pudd'nhead and Tom Driscoll (lily-white, as I explained in the first chapter) was all mixed in with the later-written Pudd'nhead-Roxy-Tom story in which Tom is part black. Mark Twain continued planning and actually writing some of the farcical Twins pages even after he started the Roxy-Tom plot shift. On 2 January 1893 he wrote Laurence Hutton: "I've finished that book & revised it. The book didn't cost me any fatigue, but revising it nearly killed me. Revising books is a mistake." He was lying. What nearly killed him, if anything, was writing the new beginning of the book and tying it up to the old start and old middle of the book. He did *not* revise what he had written before he invented Roxy and the changeling plot. The typescript made in January 1893 was of this big version. Comparison of the manuscript with the first printings of *Pudd'nhead* and *Twins* shows that the (nonextant) typescript must have been accurate enough, despite some eye-skips by the typist and a few failures to turn "OVER" to pick up little additions on the backs of pages. You can forget about the manuscript for now. Mark Twain put it off somewhere out of the way as soon as the typescript was made, although he dragged it out in March or later to stick in the new holograph pages about the weather signs and the "Note Concerning the Legal Points" (later called "Whisper to the Reader") once he had typescript (or cleaner manuscript) for those new pages. The manuscript does not figure at all in the early publishing history. In 1909 Mark Twain dug it out and sold it to J. Pierpont Morgan for his new library.

Groundrule #5: Remember also that once he sent Hall the pages of the typescript which were used for the serialization, Mark Twain was rid of *Pudd'nhead* except for frothing to his wife over the punctuation of the early *Century* proofs (in a letter of 21 September 1893).[5] On those typescript pages was

---

5. The letter described the "fine fury" he had been in since seeing the first magazine proofs of *Pudd'nhead*, the criminal being "De Vinne's peerless imported proof-reader, from Oxford University."

whatever local tinkering Mark Twain had done between February and the time he started the extraction process in July, as well as the bridge passages and other small changes made *during* that process. After mid-August 1893 he was left with a pile of typescript pages—all of what we know as *Those Extraordinary Twins* (except for the commentary he added in 1894), plus a good deal more. Daniel Morley McKeithan published many of the scraps in 1961 and Sidney E. Berger reprinted some, in a curious disorder, in the Norton Critical Edition; there's still some which has not been published and won't be until the California Edition comes out in a few years.[6]

Groundrule #6: Remember that the mere fact that something in *Pudd'nhead* or *Twins* differs from something in the manuscript does not necessarily mean that the change was made as part of the July 1893 *Pudd'nhead* salvage process or the 1894 scavenging of the typescript remnants for *Twins*. Most of the minor authorial revisions found (mixed in with compositorial changes) in the *Century* serialization of *Pudd'nhead* were not made for what we know as *Pudd'nhead Wilson* and most of the minor authorial revisions found (mixed in with compositorial changes) in the 1894 publication of *Twins* (I don't mean the new commentary) were not made for what we know as *Twins*. Instead, most of these minor authorial revisions were made on the big typescript during the first half of 1893, while it was all one literary work. Very likely many of them were made on shipboard, for Mark Twain seems to have carried the typescript back with him from New York to Florence in May 1893, after Hall discouraged him from printing it.[7] That is, to belabor a simple point because critics and textual scholars have never recognized it, don't assume that *every* authorial revision on the nonextant typescript was made as a part of the process of salvaging *Pudd'nhead Wilson* in July 1893, which involved rejecting many episodes where the Twins played the dominant

6. Just for the hell of it I may edit the whole monstrous thing and, for good scholarly and commercial reasons, Robert H. Hirst may publish it that way, as well as the usual way.

7. In the preliminary remarks in *Twins* Mark Twain said that he "carried the manuscript back and forth across the Atlantic two or three times, and read it and studied over it on shipboard." More likely, he carried the typescript back from New York to Italy, once, in May.

roles and which involved an effort to separate them into two non-freakish brothers when they were present in scenes which were retained; and don't assume that all authorial variants in *Twins* (that is, variants from the manuscript) were introduced as Mark Twain prepared printer's copy for *Twins* in 1894. Mark Twain's scattered minor revisions on the typescript were mainly his intermittent efforts over the first half of 1893 to polish various spots in the big typescript, when it was thought of as a single literary work.

Groundrule #7: Remember that there was only one manuscript, the one at the Morgan Library. Some thirty pages of the manuscript (which ends with the page numbered 633½) are typed. Mark Twain started the story in Bad-Nauheim, Germany, with a version of the description of Dawson's Landing, the sensational arrival of the Twins and their conversations with their landlady, and the anecdote about how David Wilson made a fool of himself to the townspeople and became a lawyer who never had a client. Mark Twain left the pages there to be typed and forwarded to him in Florence. When he received the typescript he stuck it up against manuscript pages he had written in the interval. The typist in Bad-Nauheim returned 124 pages of manuscript with the corresponding 30 typed pages, and this batch of early manuscript survives in the Berg Collection at New York Public Library. I will have to refer to the manuscript pages at the Berg and will have to refer to some pages of the manuscript at the Morgan as being typed. (All but the first page of the Bad-Nauheim partial typescript survives in the Morgan manuscript, but in different order and placement: the anecdote about how Wilson got his nickname comes in the Morgan manuscript long before the arrival of the *Twins*.) But there is only one manuscript, the one at the Morgan, which has twenty-nine typed pages in among the early sections. The pages of manuscript now at the Berg were superseded (as far as Mark Twain was concerned) once he received the typescript made in Bad-Nauheim. The only full typescript was the one made in Florence in January 1893 (and there is no reason to think any carbon copies were made).

With these groundrules to rely on, I will now outline, in some detail, the sequence in which Mark Twain inscribed the manuscript. I won't describe his preliminary notes, many of which dealt with misadventures of the Twins, or his later, *new*, preliminary notes made after he thought of having Tom be part black. Nor will I describe the passages in the manuscript where Mark Twain would start off on one plot-line then change his mind at once (as when he first had Pudd'nhead realize right away that the "girl" over in Tom's room was Tom, then crossed that out before writing any further and proceeded to make Pudd'nhead wonder who the girl was). Nor will I try to identify all the sections which were interpolated into sections already written, much less try to show the earliest possible time an interpolation *could* have been made and the latest time by which it *must* have been made. I am not talking about the final order of the manuscript which Mark Twain sent to the typist in Florence and which is preserved in the Morgan Library: that's in the next section of this chapter. Some of the scenes I mention will be unfamiliar to you, even if you have read *Twins* recently. I go into this much detail now because I want to remind you of the comic element which enlivened several scenes we encounter in *Pudd'nhead* in lifeless versions and because I want to prepare you to see what discontinuities riddle the novel *Pudd'nhead Wilson* as you have always known it.

The earliest surviving pages are those in the Berg. In them Mark Twain describes Dawson's Landing, downriver from St. Louis, and introduces Aunt Patsy Cooper, who receives a letter from the Italian brothers, Count Angelo and Count Luigi, applying to rent the room she has been advertising. The brothers, due late Thursday, arrive after midnight, and arrive spectacularly, for they have two heads, four arms, and two legs, and occasion a great deal of confusion as to how to refer to him, or them, or it. The selection of incidents that follow is governed by one principle—that what is not funny when two ordinary twins are involved becomes hilarious when the twins are freaks endowed as Angelo and Luigi are. The Twins bicker at considerable length, for they differ in almost every possible taste and opinion and inflict their excesses on each other—as when Luigi's smoking makes Angelo nauseated and his drinking gives Angelo a hangover. Aunt Patsy's daughter is smitten with Angelo—just what you'd expect from a girl so devoted to Sir Walter Scott that she has rechristened herself Rowena. The Twins regale their hostess with tales of Europe and their own habits, and the Coopers have a formal reception the next day to show the boarders off. Judge Driscoll wins the honor of showing them around town, his friend Pudd'nhead Wilson is introduced as his fellow Freethinker, and we are given the anecdote about how he got his nickname and became a lawyer who had never tried a case. What saves the situations from sadism is that the Twins are unabashedly proud of their uniqueness and that almost everyone who sees them admires them (after the initial shock passes).

Then the Berg pages and the typescript pages made from them run out, and in holograph pages (all the rest is only at the Morgan and is only in holograph) the brothers attend a meeting of the Freethinkers' Society (which consists of the Judge and Pudd'nhead) then the Baptist Bible Society. (Luigi is the Freethinker and Angelo wants to become a Baptist.) The Twins both take a liking to Pudd'nhead—a rare instance of their agreeing on anything. Later at his house Pudd'nhead wonders about the "girl" he saw that morning in Tom Driscoll's room across the yards. (Before or soon after writing this passage Mark Twain interpolated Tom into the story a few pages earlier, as a local boy, the Judge's nephew, a suitor to Rowena, and a love-rival for Angelo; he is not described as being all white because there was not any thought that he would be anything *but* all white.) The Twins arrive and chat with Pudd'nhead. Tom drops in and they all talk about Pudd'nhead's hobbies of palmistry and fingerprinting; after Pudd'nhead's uncanny success at reading Luigi's palm, Angelo tells how Luigi had saved his life by killing a man. The Twins and Tom go to the Sons of Liberty anti-Temperance meeting (the teetotaler Angelo goes under compulsion, Luigi being in charge of their legs that week, their system being to trade control at midnight Sunday), and Luigi kicks Tom when he gets tipsy and insults them. Tom is tossed about by the crowd and the next day sues the Twins for assault. There is a trial, very lengthily described (Pudd'nhead for the defense—his first case), and a very lengthy commentary by the presiding judge (not Judge Driscoll, who is off fishing). The legal question, of course, is which Twin kicked Tom, since the brothers have only two legs all told. Pudd'nhead scores a great victory. Judge Driscoll belatedly hears about the trial and is so shamed that Tom brought a lawsuit instead of challenging his

123

attacker to a duel that he disinherits him. Tom mournfully visits Pudd'nhead, where they talk about the theft raid that took place during the reception and about Luigi's stolen dagger in particular. (Tom is the thief. No theft scene had been described because it was an afterthought which Mark Twain could cover for by having characters talk about it.) A delegation of Democrats calls upon the newly popular Pudd'nhead to offer to support him for any civic office in the upcoming election—a great triumph for the lonely man. Pembroke Howard reports to the Judge on his call to challenge the Twins (Luigi wants to fight and Angelo doesn't), then the Judge and Howard (after a casuistical argument about the propriety of killing off the innocent Twin with the guilty) prepare for the duel next Sunday, in which the Judge will try to kill Luigi. The Judge redraws his will, making Tom his heir again. Tom overhears them, then reads the will and in self-satisfaction tortures two spiders while the two spiders are themselves torturing a grasshopper which Tom keeps calling "unky"—"Uncle." (These four sadistic pages were taken out, possibly before the manuscript was typed, and survive in the Bancroft Library.) The duel takes place, at great length, Luigi, who is in charge of the legs, keeping Angelo on the scene greatly against his wishes until at midnight he gains control and flees, taking the reluctant Luigi along. The outcome of the duel is that the principals are fine but the seconds and most of the bystanders are injured a little. Doctor Claypool goes to Aunt Patsy's to treat Angelo for his wound (the medicine works on Angelo only if Luigi takes it) then Angelo insists on being baptized (amid great public interest) and Luigi, of course, gets the bad cold from the submersion. The Twins get well, but only after the doctor leaves town. The Democrats nominate Wilson for mayor and the Whigs respect his popularity too much to nominate anyone against him. In their new celebrity the Twins are candidates also, the Democrats running Luigi for alderman and the Whigs opposing him with Angelo. On Saturday Constable Blake, Pudd'nhead, and Tom discuss the theft, and Pudd'nhead confides unwarily that he has a secret scheme to catch the thief. Tom is concerned, since he needs to dispose of the gems in the dagger he has stolen from Luigi.

Then comes a startling passage: "Tom had tried for several days to guess out the secret. . . but had failed. Then it occurred to him to give Roxana's smarter head a chance at it." Rowena we had met, but this is the first mention of any Roxana. When Roxy is brought into the action a few pages later, she enters in style. The first thing she does is to smash a whiskey bottle to emphasize that her son Tom is going to have to straighten up. In these pages Tom is a changeling, abruptly, with no retrospective account of how he came to be one. The only stumble Mark Twain made in this part of the surviving manuscript was in having Tom uncertain of how to address his mother—a result of Mark Twain's having invented Roxy and having thought of the changeling history for Tom just before he wrote them into his ongoing plot, rather than pausing to describe their histories and their recent reunion. Then Tom takes a steamboat for St. Louis and is robbed of his plunder (but not of Luigi's knife). To save him from being disinherited, Roxy offers to be sold as a slave— in humane Missouri, of course. Tom sells her down the river instead. The campaign continues with the Twins dragging each other to inappropriate gatherings, depending on who has control of their legs; in the last such adventure Luigi drinks so his Baptist brother will be drunk at the teetotalers' meeting, after which Rowena petulantly breaks with Angelo because of his drunkenness. Pudd'nhead is elected mayor, and Luigi is elected alderman but can't take his seat on the board because he would have to bring along an unauthorized person. Roxy confronts Tom in St. Louis after escaping from her brutal "owner." Looking out for herself now, she demands that he ask his "uncle" for money to buy her freedom. Luigi challenges the Judge to a new duel for the insults he made during the campaign (while believing Tom's lies), but the Judge will not fight an "assassin." During this public exchange of insults Tom returns, planning to rob the Judge rather than ask for money, but when the Judge comes in during the robbery Tom kills him —with Luigi's dagger. The Twins happen by and are arrested. Pudd'nhead defends them at the trial. Things look bad for the Twins, but Pudd'nhead makes a great discovery, thanks to an overconfident visit from Tom, and dazzles the court with his fingerprinting display which proves that Tom is a murderer and a slave and that "Valet de Chambre," in what may be the earliest surviving mention of him, is the real Tom.

Only then, after writing the ending, did Mark Twain go back to write the early history of the new main characters, a longer version of what we know as the first chapters of *Pudd'nhead Wilson*. He threw away the first typescript page (which contained what was on the first four pages of the manuscript at the Berg) and wrote an expanded version of his description of Dawson's Landing and its citizens, setting the period back two decades so when "Tom" reached twenty-two the time would be around 1850, the time that had originally been specified as the period of the Twins' arrival and the subsequent events. He salvaged the two typed pages on Pudd'nhead's arrival in town and his settling there, and expanded them with an account of his taking up the hobby of fingerprinting. He wrote a brand-new account of the slave Roxy and the coincidence of her bearing a son on the same day as her mistress, and went on to write about Wilson's fingerprinting the children, Roxy's fear of being sold down the river, her plan to kill herself and her baby whose fancy name is shortened to "Chambers," her changing her baby for her master, the children's growing up, the false Tom's vicious behavior toward the real Tom, who is being raised as the slave Chambers, and his viciousness toward Roxy, whom he thinks of only as a slave. In this new section, Tom's master, Percy Driscoll (invented as a brother of the Judge) frees Roxy on his deathbed, and she engages in extensive theological banter with a black man, Jasper, who has been set free for saving his master's daughter from a runaway carriage. Judge Driscoll and his wife take in the worthless Tom and the Judge sends him to Yale for two years. The Judge tries to rehabilitate Pudd'nhead Wilson's reputation but fails. Then Mark Twain ran in the twenty-seven remaining pages of the typescript, those dealing with the arrival and reception of the Twins. After the pages in which Aunt Patsy and her neighbor Aunt Betsy discuss the effects of Angelo's arrival on the romance between Rowena and Tom (pages retained in apparent unawareness that the romance would now seem interracial), Mark Twain wrote new pages to explain that Roxy had gone steamboating after she was freed and then traced her subsequent history through success as a chambermaid to the crash of her bank and her return to Dawson's Landing, broke except for her fund of worldly experience and the possible value of her secret relationship to young Tom. Then Mark Twain wrote her confrontation with Tom and her revelation of who he really is and the passages in which Tom agonizes over the news and becomes a little less distressed as he projects a new theft raid on the village. (Before finishing the big manuscript Mark Twain cut out some mystery about who Tom's father was and Tom's desire to kill that white man, whoever he is. He left in more of Tom's speculations about the possible effects of "nigger blood" and social training on his being a coward than he kept in the book, and more of Tom's reflections on his bastardy.) Having brought the new material back around to some of the pages written long before, Mark Twain wrote a triumphant linkage: "After this long digression we have now arrived, once more, at the point where Pudd'nhead Wilson, while waiting for the arrival of the Twins from the Bible Society on the same Friday evening, sat puzzling over the strange apparition of that morning—a girl in young Tom Driscoll's bedroom; fretting, & guessing, & puzzling over it, & wondering who the brazen huzzy might be." This is the last bit of writing Mark Twain did on the manuscript, with the probable exception of one or more short interpolations.

Such, in outline, was the sequence of composition. Now I will describe, still more tersely, the final order of the manuscript, after Mark Twain had moved the hunks around, in December 1892, apparently without throwing anything away. He put the six hundred or so pages together (perhaps he had not yet prefaced the chapters with quotations from Pudd'nhead Wilson's Calendar) so that the story began with his newly written description of Dawson's Landing in 1830 and its inhabitants, including Roxy and Pudd'nhead. Then followed the Roxy scenes: her master's threat to sell his slaves down the river, her thoughts of suicide, her changing the babies, their boyhood, their growing up, her master's setting her free at his death, and her banter with Jasper. Then Judge Driscoll takes charge of his "nephew" and "Chambers" and sends "Tom" off for two years at Yale; Tom returns and drinks and gambles. The Judge tries to rehabilitate Pudd'nhead's reputation. The Twins arrive and settle in. After the reception for them the Judge takes Luigi to the meeting of the Freethinkers, then Angelo makes Luigi stay for the meeting of the Baptist Bible class. While waiting for the Twins to come to his house Pudd'nhead puzzles over the "girl" he saw in Tom's room. "It is necessary, now, to hunt up Roxy," Mark Twain says, and tells of her eight years of chambermaiding, her bankruptcy, her return, her appeal to Tom, her revelation, Tom's distress, and his settling back into his old ways. The Twins arrive at Pudd'nhead's and Tom joins them. Pudd'nhead elicits the story of Luigi's killing a man. Tom and the Twins accompany the pro-Rum group to a rally, where Tom gets tipsy and insults the Twins. Luigi kicks Tom into the crowd. Then comes the kick trial (Pudd'nhead winning the case), Judge Driscoll's learning the news, his disinheriting Tom, and Tom's visit to Pudd'nhead, where they talk about the theft raid. The Democratic delegation calls on Pudd'nhead. Howard reports on Luigi's acceptance of the challenge from the Judge, who remakes the will, which Tom then reads. The farcical duel takes place, Tom worries about how to dispose of Luigi's dagger, Roxy tells Tom about the duel, and Tom promises to reform. Dr. Claypool treats Angelo's wound by prescribing for Luigi, Angelo insists on being baptized, Luigi catches cold, the Democrats nominate Pudd'nhead for mayor and Luigi for alderman, and the Whigs run Angelo against Luigi. Pudd'nhead tells Tom and the constable about his scheme to catch the thief. Tom consults Roxy, who understands his plight and offers to save him by letting him sell her as a slave. He sells her down the river. The campaign continues, with the Twins having farcical misadventures and the Judge slurring them. The election takes place. Pudd'nhead becomes mayor, but Luigi can't take the office he has won. Roxy confronts Tom in St. Louis and demands that he get money from the Judge to buy her freedom. Luigi challenges the Judge. Tom robs his "uncle" then kills him. The Twins are accused, and Pudd'nhead defends them. Pudd'nhead proves that Tom is a murderer and a slave and that Chambers is the real Tom.

This is the final order of the episodes in the manuscript and the order of the typescript made from it in January 1893. This is the "old book" which Leslie Fiedler, apparently without paying a visit to the Morgan Library, romanticized as "a living unity that could not be split without irreparable harm."[8] In fact, during

8. Leslie Fiedler, "As Free as Any Cretur," first published in the *New Republic* 133 (15 and 22 August 1955), as reprinted in the Norton Critical Edition, p. 221.

the great expansion of the manuscript in December 1892, Mark Twain had perpetrated not a "living unity" but some serious anomalies involving vestigial functions for characters. Back *then*, Mark Twain went through his first retro-wishing process. Tom's original role (as an afterthought) had been as a love-rival to Angelo for Rowena's affection, but once Mark Twain made Tom part black he could not be a serious rival without making present drama from the theme of miscegenation rather than keeping that theme safely in the past. He stopped developing Tom as a suitor, but during the December expansions he never removed all the vestiges of that earlier plot; indeed, it survives in Chapter 13 of the published *Pudd'nhead*,[9] although he dropped out of *Pudd'nhead* other parts of it, such as Aunt Patsy's and Aunt Betsy's gossip about Tom and Rowena, which he had interpolated just after inventing Tom, and which survived into the typescript. Furthermore, already in the December expansion certain scenes seemed to gain adventitious meanings, as in the example I used in Chapter 1, Tom's snatching away his hand because he is afraid that Pudd'nhead will guess that he is a thief; once Mark Twain had written the passages in which Tom is part-black and worried about being found out and had placed those passages ahead of the earlier-written hand-snatching scene, the reader cannot avoid assuming that Tom snatches away his hand lest Pudd'nhead perceive *that* secret. In the material which was published as Chapter 12, Tom's cowardice in not challenging Luigi dates from the time he was all white, although in the full typescript it would have struck any reader as a symptom of his black blood, since the late-written passage about being a "nigger" and a "coward" closely preceded what we know as Chapter 12, and in the published *Pudd'nhead Wilson* (which lacks the section on blackness and cowardice) it seems to gain the implication that it has something to do with his role as a changeling. In what was later numbered Chapter 13 Tom was left worrying about the wrong thing—how to sell Luigi's knife rather than how to avoid being exposed as an impostor. In Chapter 14 he is still worried about being exposed only as the thief, not as impostor and

9. Philip Cohen discusses this in some detail in the article cited in n. 4.

slave. Nowhere in the manuscript is there any indication that Mark Twain tried to create these effects which I have called adventitious, no indication that he tried to exploit them, and indeed no indication that he was aware of them either during the months he tried to publish the big version or afterwards.

All these anomalies were created in December 1892 and survived Mark Twain's tinkering on shipboard a few months later. Almost all of them survived his salvage job, when in July 1893, half a year after completing the manuscript and having it typed and three months after learning that his publisher would not print it, he saw a way to make a salable little book out of part of the typescript, probably not realizing then that he could use some of the scraps too, later on. Since he had the typescript to work with, his job was simple. Whether he put it to himself in such explicit terms or not, he had two obvious options. First, he could discard the freakish Twins. Many sizable segments of the typescript involved only the Twins in their interminable bickering or else involved only the Twins and minor characters such as the Coopers, so Mark Twain could simply have lifted out these episodes. The trouble with this option was that it would have required a little new writing. If he were to minimize the new writing by holding to the same basic plot involving an insult, a lawsuit, a challenge, a duel, a robbery, and a murder, he would have to create a new character who would insult Tom and thereby bring about his evasion of a duel so that his "uncle" would disinherit him and issue the challenge in his stead; and this new character would have to be the one suspected of murder and put on trial. As far as we know, Mark Twain dismissed this option out of hand, if he thought of it as a serious possibility: the little work it would have taken was more than he was willing to perform. Instead, he chose a second option: to discard the scenes involving the Twins where he could and to separate and minimize the Twins where he kept them. He could accomplish a great deal of the work in a few minutes: all he had to do was to go through pulling out the pages of typescript which primarily concerned the Twins' wranglings and misadventures in private or around characters other than Pudd'nhead and Tom. They had no scenes with Roxy, although in December 1892 Mark Twain had interpolated a long passage in which she tells Tom of witnessing the duel and getting wounded herself.

All the main characters are present at the murder trial, technically speaking, but the Twins and Roxy are not more than minimally aware of each other. Mark Twain laid the unneeded Twins pages aside (he did not have to tinker with them, of course, because they were not going to be used). Then he reduced their remaining scenes whenever he saw a chance to do so without much trouble, shortening, for instance, the account of their arrival and reception.[10]

Mark Twain was then left with a smaller pile of typed pages, but probably not an untidy pile, for the farcical material he had put aside was mainly discrete—hunks consisting of many pages which he could remove without taking anything else along. On the rare occasions when he wanted to salvage something on a page and reject the rest, he could take the page and cross out on it anything he did not want to keep. At the improbable worst, if he was thinking ahead to use of the rejected material, he could do a tiny bit of recopying so he could leave the reject pile comprising everything not put into *Pudd'nhead Wilson* rather than, for instance, lacking a passage involving the Twins which he pulled out in order to get something else on the page involving Tom. Afterwards he had to write a few transitional passages for the salvaged material—a non-conjoined version of the electioneering, for instance. Then, only then, most likely, when it would require the least possible effort, did he look at the pile of typed pages he was going to use for *Pudd'nhead* and change any references he saw to the Twins as conjoined. He did not do a conscientious job—that would have taken half an hour or so, far more time than he was willing to expend. (Remember, he did not need to check very many pages—just those few salvaged pages where the separated twins [I will change to lower case in my references to them] appeared, not the many pages about the Twins which were in the reject pile.) Last of all, probably, judging from the sacrificial tone of his comments to

10. In *Mark Twain: The Fate of Humor* (Princeton: Princeton University Press, 1966), James M. Cox points out the peculiarity of Mark Twain's describing the novel *Pudd'nhead Wilson* "not as the child of the farce but as the *mother* from whom the child—the farce—is forcibly extracted" (p. 227). Maybe the image can be explained as Mark Twain's remembering having pulled the farce pages out of the big typescript and leaving on the table the pages he was going to use for *Pudd'nhead Wilson.*

Fred Hall, he went back through trying to streamline what remained and in the process cut down Roxy's scenes with Jasper (if he had not cut them down a little earlier in the salvage job) and discarded his prized description of Roxy's first view of a floating palace, a Mississippi steamboat. In any case, to think up a solution to his problem of a typescript incongruously containing both the freaks and the changeling story and to bring that solution into actuality need have taken only a matter of a few hours or a day or two from his travel schedule. And it was a relatively neat solution. To be sure, it retained the twins, separated whenever Mark Twain noticed that they needed to be taken apart, in a story where they had no business, but it did not create anything he recognized as requiring drastic alteration. The process was pretty much just pull out a batch of pages here and there, keep the remaining pages in the same order, and do a little bridging when it was absolutely essential.

Full of virtuous triumph, Mark Twain wrote Fred Hall from Krankenheil on 30 July 1893:[11]

> *This* time "Pudd'nhead Wilson" is a success! Even Mrs. Clemens, the most difficult of critics, confesses it, and without reserves or qualifications. Formerly she would not consent that it be published either before or after my death. I have pulled the twins apart and made two individuals of them; I have sunk them out of sight, they are mere flitting shadows, now, and of no importance; *their* story has disappeared from the book. Aunt Betsy Hale has vanished wholly, leaving not a trace behind; aunt Patsy Cooper and her daughter Rowena have almost disappeared—they scarcely walk across the stage. The whole story is centred on the murder and the trial; from the first chapter the movement is straight ahead without divergence or side-play to the murder and the trial; everything that is done or said or that happens is a preparation for those events. Therefore, 3 people stand up high, from beginning to end, and only 3—Pudd'nhead, 'Tom' Driscoll and his nigger mother Roxana; none of the others are important, or get in the way of the story or require the reader's attention. Consequently, the scenes and episodes which were the strength of the book formerly are stronger than ever, now.

11. In Hill's collection, pp. 354-56.

In the next paragraph he bragged that he had "knocked out everything that delayed the march of the story—even the description of a Mississippi steamboat"; the story was "stripped for flight!"

What Mark Twain did to salvage something salable from the typescript is clear enough, and we can pretty well chart the stages in which he did it. We can pretty well guess at what he said to himself, too, for we not only have the letter crowing about his achievement to Hall but we also know what he said, for instance, when he let Charles Webster cut the raftsmen episode out of *Huckleberry Finn*:[12]

> Yes, I think that raft chapter can be left wholly out, by heaving in a paragraph to say Huck visited the raft to find out how far it might be to Cairo, but got no satisfaction. Even *this* is not necessary unless that raft-visit is referred to later in the book. I think it is, but am not certain.

As Peter G. Beidler has shown, Mark Twain had no idea that in obliging Webster he was leaving "a curious narrative gap in the novel." (You will recall from Chapter 1 that Huck's decision "to paddle ashore the first time they see a light and ask how far ahead Cairo is" immediately precedes his conclusion that "There warn't nothing to do now but look out sharp for the town and not pass it without seeing it.") In what Mark Twain wrote, as opposed to what he so cavalierly agreed to have printed, the reader understood that Cairo was already passed from the way the raftsmen scoff at Huck's lie about his Pap's wanting a message taken down to Cairo. Furthermore, as Beidler points out, it was the raftsmen's talk that gave Huck the knowledge that the Ohio and Mississippi don't like to mix, knowledge that he displays at the end of Chapter 16. What Mark Twain said to himself when he had taken out what we know as *Pudd'nhead Wilson* was something like, "Now it'll do fine. Nobody will know how this book got the way it is." As we saw, Mark Twain

12. "The Raft Episode in *Huckleberry Finn*," *Modern Fiction Studies* 14 (Spring 1968): 11-20, conveniently reprinted in the Second Edition of the Norton Critical Edition of *Adventures of Huckleberry Finn*, eds. Sculley Bradley, Richmond Croom Beatty, E. Hudson Long, and Thomas Cooley (New York: W. W. Norton, 1977), pp. 241-50.

did not require of himself a serious effort to locate all the places in the salvaged pages where the twins were referred to as if they were conjoined, although he was aware of the problem and took care of those instances which he noticed.[13] Worse, he did not ask himself a series of other questions about the way the parts of the salvaged material had originally functioned and how they would function (or seem to function) in their new positionings. Instead, he contented himself with a tiny bit of retro-fitting and a great quantity of nebulous retro-wishing.

Almost all the anomalies which were created in December persisted intact into the published *Pudd'nhead*, and still other anomalies were created by the July salvage operation. (The December anomalies primarily involved Tom, not the Twins.) Whatever residual function there was for the Twins being conjoined when Mark Twain finished the manuscript in December (at least their scenes were comical), there was no function for their being conjoined in *Pudd'nhead* and indeed no need for their being twins at all. The surviving vestiges of their status as Siamese twins are a distracting embarrassment, but so is their very presence. And their having separate bodies in *Pudd'nhead* (except in those places which Mark Twain overlooked) deprives several scenes of any reason for being. *Pudd'nhead* in these instances is stuck with once-hilarious situations (Mark Twain certainly thought so) which have been robbed of the one element which made them comical. They make sense now but in a most pallid way. The twins still play duets in *Pudd'nhead*, but any set of twins can play duets. What made Angelo and Luigi wonderful to watch, as I said in the first chapter, was their having four hands on the keyboard and only one bottom on the piano stool. The point of the kick scene, which occasioned dozens of pages of raucous humor in the manuscript, was that responsibility was hard to assign—which Twin did the kicking? And sometimes humor is not involved but sense is missing nevertheless as when the delegation calls on Pudd'nhead and asks him to run for office with no reason at all for liking him better than the day before (when he is now said to have lost his first case—the outcome of the kick trial being altered from the

13. See George Feinstein, "Vestigia in *Pudd'nhead Wilson*" *Twainian* 1 (May 1942): 1-3.

manuscript, where Pudd'nhead was victorious), and no reason for thinking the town fool has a better chance of winning than he would have had any time in the past two decades.[14]

When Mark Twain (probably not until 1894) saw the chance to make an extra $1500 by scavenging some of the rejected material as *Those Extraordinary Twins* he had only to write a humorously boastful confession as an introduction then run in hunks of the leftover typescript pages (still in the same order after his new removals of still more hunks) and intersperse them with an occasional summary of omitted material or a comment on the July 1893 salvage process. (He didn't, of course, have to try to separate the Twins this time.) Getting *Twins* ready for print required the writing of only a few pages of commentary, perhaps a day's work, allowing for billiard breaks, but not more than a few days' at worst.

What with the anomalies created by the compositional process in December 1892 and the new anomalies created by the salvage process in July 1893, the published *Pudd'nhead Wilson* is strange indeed. Philip Cohen, in a paper written under my direction, has described some of the aesthetic anomalies. They include minor structural anomalies which I will not rehearse here. More important, they include serious awkwardnesses in the characterizations. Roxy sounds like a comical darky in some of the early (and late written) scenes and like a heroine of a tragedy in some of the late ones (written soon after she was invented). Chambers is a figure of some interest in the early (late-written) scenes and becomes a mere plot device in the last ones (written before Mark Twain had thought much about what his role would be in the unwritten new opening). Tom in one scene is weighed down by the knowledge that he is a slave and in later ones (written while he was still white) is oppressed by nothing weightier than his fear of being found out for gambling, drinking, and stealing, and his recurrent fear of being disinherited. In Chapter 9 Tom learns he is a slave and in Chapter 11 he participates mindlessly in the riot scene at the Rum Party

14. Stuart A. Lewis points out this awkwardness in "Pudd'nhead Wilson's Election," *Mark Twain Journal* 15 (Winter 1970): 21; displaying resourcefulness unusual among critics, Lewis explained the anomaly by using the evidence in *Those Extraordinary Twins.*

meeting (which has been rendered all but meaningless by the separation of the Twins into ordinary twins). It appears to the reader that Mark Twain built Tom up into serious status (his emotional upheaval in Chapter 10 is impressive) then lost interest in him, while in fact Chapter 10 was written very late, and Mark Twain was making Tom a more impressive figure as he came near to finishing his work. As Cohen shows, major themes such as "the evil effects of slavery and the effects of heredity and environment in the determination of character" were also rendered peculiar by being placed, for the most part, early in the book, then to all appearances neglected or dropped later on.[15]

While the published *Pudd'nhead Wilson* is thus patently unreadable, anyone who knows literary critics will know that a simple fact like that has not deterred them from trying to read the book and bragging about having done so. It would be easy enough to spend many pages indicting critics for writing articles riddled with errors growing out of such ignorance of facts and the implications of those facts. I'm not going to do that, but there's a reason to mention some egregious conclusions reached on the basis of this thrown-together text: most people still think that F. O. Matthiessen's little blunder with the single-word error in *White-Jacket* ("'soiled' fish") is about as far wrong as a faulty text can lead you.[16] *Pudd'nhead* leads critics into far more ludicrous conclusions. Clark Griffith darkly says that through the book "move" both the "false-Tom Driscoll, in his total corruption, and (always just off-stage, yet always the object of our very considerable interest), the true Tom Driscoll, in his sad vulnerability."[17] The most curious part of this formulation has Chambers moving through our minds in chapters written before he was invented and in other chapters written before he was anything but a plot device thought of but not yet developed at all. In another quite breathtaking passage Griffith exclaims sympathetically, thinking of some of the middle chapters

15. Cohen, p. 66.
16. See Chapter 3, paragraph 6.
17. Clark Griffith, "*Pudd'nhead Wilson* as Dark Comedy," *English Language Notes* 43 (Summer 1976): 209-26; the quotation is from 212 and the following ones are from p. 220.

written when Tom was a white scamp, "What incredible diffi-
culties Mark Twain must have faced in portraying false-Tom
Driscoll as he did." Griffith's analysis of Mark Twain's
"consummate irony" includes this statement about a passage
written when Tom was white and the Twins were conjoined:

> But such is the degree of his iniquity that it occasions the novel's
> one really important recognition scene. This occurs in Chapter XI,
> when Luigi, meeting false-Tom for the first time, remarks privately
> on his "veiled" and "sly" look, his disagreeable manner of
> speaking and behaving. The point seems to me Twain's quite
> conscious attempt to relate source to tributary, to draw closer a
> bond between the symbolized principle of darkness and the social
> incarnation. Thus the comments of Angelo come in revealing
> counterpoint, as he too looks at the stranger and pronounces false-
> Tom "good...pleasant...a sufficiently nice young man." We
> need only add that the qualities Luigi here discerns—and Angelo
> misses—could be applied to every other major citizen of the
> village, save one. With a single exception, they are all Luigi's
> familiars, occupants of a dark-dominated world where, often in
> secret and always in action, each lives out the predestined course
> of a "native viciousness."

This passage praises an innocuous scene, written to introduce
young white Tom to the freaks, as the only really important
recognition scene in the novel—more important, for instance,
than Tom's acknowledgment that Roxy is his mother or the
town's acknowledgment that Chambers is the real Tom
Driscoll.

Malcolm Bradbury, with equal zeal but less melodrama,
praises Mark Twain for the way he modulated Tom's agitation
over the news that he is part black and a slave. Here the praise is
at least slightly deserved, for Mark Twain did go to the trouble
of mentioning that Tom's agitation soon diminished, but Bradbury assumes a remarkably complex narrative control:[18]

> Twain constantly strains at the probabilities he has created, the
> rules of narration he has laid down, to develop his plot. Yet the

18. Bradbury, Introduction to *Pudd'nhead Wilson* (Harmondsworth: Penguin,
1969), p. 29.

elliptical quality of the telling does have the effect of making the ironies much more final. When Roxy reveals the facts of his true ancestry to Tom, Twain carefully analyses Tom's response—there is a 'gigantic irruption' which changes his 'moral landscape'. But Twain cannot afford to have us too long concerned with him at that inward level; so Tom gradually drops back 'into his old frivolous and easy-going ways'. Twain must protect his right to distance and irony. And he does this by self-evidently neglecting an artistic opportunity; the imbroglios must develop, the farces of human behaviour continue to operate, the characters must keep coming back for more.

Another critic, James W. Gargano, elaborates upon Bradbury's justification of the center chapters written when Tom was white: "Twain's consistent ironic-comic posture is preserved by a strategy of reticence and avoidance. As Malcolm Bradbury has brilliantly shown, *Pudd'nhead Wilson* avoids psychological analysis and ideological commitment through a plot constructed of 'inexorable life in events.' Whenever a character's inner problems threaten to become too 'serious' and thus undermine the author's poise, the novel escapes into a new twist of plot or of tonal incongruity. Twain briefly explores the psychological change wrought by Tom's discovery of his blackness; but after an intense flurry of thought and self-doubt, Tom soon returns to his 'frivolous and easy-going ways.'"[19] There is almost nothing so bad that you can't get one critic to praise it and another to praise the first one for having praised it.

I have taken some satiric glee in quoting Griffith and Bradbury, in particular, because of their tone of High Seriousness about *Pudd'nhead Wilson*. Comparable examples from less portentous critics could readily be mustered, since as in Chapter 4, for which I read everything in the standard bibliographies on James's revisions, I have taken notes on everything I could find on *Pudd'nhead Wilson*. I hope I have made my point, without quoting other critics, that Matthiessen's blunder should be dropped forthwith out of the active clichés of textual lore. Its value is historical only, now that such more significant critical pratfalls can be assembled. Rather than belabor the game of

19. James W. Gargano, "*Pudd'nhead Wilson*: Mark Twain as Genial Satan," *South Atlantic Quarterly* 74 (Summer 1975): 365-75; the quotation is from p. 373.

catching the individual critic out, I want to look at what the critics think they are doing as critics. In the case of *Pudd'nhead Wilson* this is not difficult to ascertain, for Mark Twain's own calling attention to some peculiarities in the creation of the novel had the effect of flushing the critics' assumptions out of hiding. Most of them plainly approach the text as the most trusting of New Critics, and what they find is unity. They find the book "a far more unified, more balanced novel than many of its critics have been willing to grant," they find a "unity of theme and general organization," unity from themes and images, unity from "the concern with property," "artistic and philosophical unity," "unity of vision," and unity from "metaphors."[20]

Only the rarest of curmudgeonly critics complained of any lack of unity. Robert A. Wiggins in criticizing, to his own surprise, the "technical flaws" in the book rightly declares that Mark Twain was "a butcher rather than a surgeon in performing his literary Caesarean operation," and he pointed out something I have also made a great point of: "By his surgery Twain removed the original comic function of the twins, but he appears not to have inquired into what remaining function they performed. It is not a useful one so far as the main plot and theme are concerned. Indeed the presence of the twins is more than just irrelevant to the central concerns of the book; their behavior is actually distracting."[21] Elsewhere Wiggins failed to

20. These quotations are from Edgar T. Schell, " 'Pears' and 'Is' in *Pudd'nhead Wilson*," *Mark Twain Journal* 12 (1963-65): 12-15 (p. 15); John Freimarck, "*Pudd'nhead Wilson*: A Tale of Blood and Brotherhood," *University Review* 34 (June 1968): 303-06 (p. 302); Robert Rowlette, *Mark Twain's "Pudd'nhead Wilson": The Development and Design* (Bowling Green: Bowling Green University Popular Press, 1971), p. 85; Eberhard Alsen, "Pudd'nhead Wilson's Fight for Popularity and Power," *Western American Literature* 7 (Summer 1972): 135-43 (p. 135); Stanley Brodwin, "Blackness and the Adamic Myth in Mark Twain's *Pudd'nhead Wilson*," *Texas Studies in Literature and Language* 15 (Spring 1973): 167-76 (p. 169); Michael L. Ross, "Mark Twain's *Pudd'nhead Wilson*: Dawson's Landing and the Ladder of Nobility," *Novel* 6 (Spring 1973): 244-56 (p. 256); and Earl F. Briden, "Idiots First, Then Juries: Legal Metaphors in Mark Twain's *Pudd'nhead Wilson*," *Texas Studies in Literature and Language* 20 (Summer 1978): 169-80 (pp. 169-71).

21. Robert A. Wiggins, "*Pudd'nhead Wilson*: 'A Literary Caesarean Operation,'" *College English* 25 (December 1963): 182-86; the quotations are from p. 184.

think in terms of an explanation from the compositional process, and he did not make use of Anne P. Wigger's essay which
might have spurred him into doing so, since she did mention, as
a matter obvious to anyone who looks at the manuscript, that the
arrival of the Twins was the first event inscribed. Philip Butcher
also briefly acknowledges weaknesses in the characterization of
Roxy which add up to a failure to create "artistic unity."
Confused in many details, Butcher nevertheless guessed right
about "careless excision" and hasty composition, and he concluded accurately that Mark Twain's "need for money made him
more interested in selling the manuscript than in creating a
work of high quality."[22] These two, operating partly on what
Mark Twain bragged about in *Those Extraordinary Twins* and
partly on tough personal responses to an unsatisfying text, were
the anomalous grousers.

Wiggins's and Butcher's New Critical colleagues defined
their procedural problem quite explicitly. Where ordinarily
they could have taken artistic unity for granted, here they were
confronted with a text about which the author had told a story
which threatened their very right to treat the book as a verbal
icon. Undaunted, and indeed rising bravely to the challenge,
they defined their job as that of taking up a book which has
been regarded as problematical in one way or another (it is
known to be problematical because the author happened to
reveal something of the peculiar way it came into being) and
then demonstrating that it is in reality perfect or nearly perfect,
not problematical at all, once the right approach is taken and
the right reading is arrived at. Edgar T. Schell typically sets out
to reveal a "complex and coherent design" in what were
"apparently disparate elements." According to George M.
Spangler, the "striking lack of agreement about the merits" of
the book "is unquestionably related to the equally striking
disagreements over interpretation." Observing that "all the thematic analyses so far presented leave important aspects of the
novel unaccounted for," Spangler steps in to save the situation:
"Clearly what is necessary is a thematic analysis that can
answer" charges against "Twain's uncertain artistry" by a

22. Philip Butcher, "Mark Twain Sells Roxy Down the River," *CLA Journal* 8
(March 1965): 225-33; the quotation is from p. 232.

reading which will "demonstrate a coherence" that "has too often been denied." Robert Rowlette acknowledges the trouble that information about the compositional process has posed for readers, as well as the problem of complex themes and plots, and even argues that F. R. Leavis, Leslie Fiedler, and James M. Cox have, by focusing on the book's greatness in spite of flaws in plot and characterization, through "their very authority discouraged any systematic analysis of the principles of the novel's structure and unity." Rowlette then produces just that analysis in order to show that "*Pudd'nhead Wilson* is more artfully constructed and unified than critics have heretofore indicated":

> More than a memorable and unassimilated assemblage of discrete plots and modes, it is a complex (though by no means flawless) unity, a symmetrical pattern of interwoven, interdependent themes and of finely interlaced imagery. In no previous work of Twain's has theme been more influential on form, or form a more discernible epitome of his larger fictional world.

Eberhard Alsen acknowledges Spangler's efforts to refute the usual charge that the novel lacks coherence and agrees with Spangler that unity derives from the pervasive concern with a particular theme; however, rather than Spangler's theme of "property" Alsen proposes that the unifying theme "evolves out of David Wilson's twenty-three year fight for popularity and power." Stanley Brodwin likewise acknowledges the "standard criticism" that the fingerprinting plot was "never quite integrated with the tragedy of Roxy and her son," but insists that there is "some fundamental thematic connection," namely, "the necessity of the fall of man." Michael L. Ross surveys some critical comments which indicate that the feeling remains widespread that the book "is a partial or even a total failure as a work of art" because of Mark Twain's "uncertainty in handling his major theme," Negro slavery; then Ross argues that despite the "*a priori*" cause for doubts about the book's coherence, given Mark Twain's "eccentric habits of composition," he did exercise "suprising control" throughout the novel: "when given a sufficiently attentive and unbiased reading, *Pudd'nhead Wilson* reveals a cogency and power that distinguish it as a classic American fable." The "real subject of the novel" is the presence in the New World of a form of feudalism. Karen Mann likewise pulls "formal structure" out of apparent disparity. Declaring that criticism on the book "seems to have come to a dead end," John C. Gerber proposes a solution: we should read *Pudd'nhead* not as a novel but as a "fabulation" which may ignore the realism of both the "subject matter and its presentation."[23] In all of these, and many others, the critics define their role as bringing order out of a chaos which they insist is only apparent, not real. The order *must* be there, awaiting the sufficiently attentive and unbiased reading which the present critic is always the first to supply. I emphasize again that the critics speak so specifically about their purpose to demonstrate unity only because Mark Twain had supplied a sensational revelation of how the book came to be. Usually the critic would take unity for granted, as critics of *An American Dream* have done.

Shameless author that he was, Mark Twain would rejoice in such tributes just as he rejoiced in the praise of a professor from Pennsylvania in 1894.[24] But, as he bragged, he was a jack-leg novelist, and these are born-and-trained critics, surely, who ought to be raising serious aesthetic questions rather than racking their brains for new gimmicks which might demonstrate coherence, unity, and tragic structure.[25]

To supply the vacancy, I again offer some questions in basic aesthetics which critics might begin to ponder; not one of them is raised in the most convenient collection of criticism, Sidney E. Berger's Norton Critical Edition (1980). Can a writer infuse intentionality into a passage or a chapter or a group of chapters

23. Schell (p. 12); George M. Spangler, "*Pudd'nhead Wilson*: A Parable of Property," *American Literature* 42 (March 1970): 28-37 (pp. 28-29); Rowlette (p. 85); Alsen (p. 136); Brodwin (p. 171); Ross (pp. 244-45); Karen B. Mann, "Pudd'nhead Wilson: One Man or Two?" *Research Studies* 42 (September 1974): 175-81 (p. 175); John C. Gerber, "*Pudd'nhead Wilson* as Fabulation," *Studies in American Humor* 2 (April 1975): 21-31 (22).

24. On 12 January 1894 Clemens wrote his wife about the sensation *Pudd'nhead Wilson* was making in New York City and quoted the praise of the characterization of the hero by Professor Powell of the University of Pennsylvania in a talk on 11 January 1894, as reported by Fred Hall, who had heard the lecture.

25. What D. N. Perkins says in Chapter 6 of *The Mind's Best Work* (Cambridge: Harvard University Press, 1981), p. 178, applies to the New Criticism and its practitioners: "In many ways, the established paradigm is the enemy of discovery. An anomaly may not be perceived for what it is, precisely because it is not expected."

by an act of will, or of wishing, after the passage is composed? or can he do so by a new placement of passages? How can the slavery theme or the heredity *vs.* training theme inform brief passages or longer units of the book which were written before Mark Twain introduced those themes into the manuscript (and which were not later revised to contain those themes)? How can a thematic study be valid when it ignores the fact that the theme was not present when certain parts of the work were written? or when the theme was originally written into not only the parts which survive in the printed text but also (in stronger form) into parts which were discarded? How can anything sensible be said about Mark Twain's attitudes toward training and heredity on the basis only of the published *Pudd'nhead*, which omits the strongest of Tom's ruminations on race? How can we talk sensibly about characterization "throughout" a novel when chapters survive from stages when a character was white and a stage when he was part black? How can we talk sensibly about characterization "throughout" a novel when chapters in it date from a stage when that character had not been invented? How can passages written as extravagant farce gain profound social significance merely because Mark Twain placed in front of them later-written passages imbued with such significance? How can an image study be valid when the document being analyzed consists of pieces of a larger document which was composed in another order than its final one, while the parts of the shorter document also stand in another order than the one in which they were composed? How can the cynical sayings in Pudd'nhead Wilson's Calendar, the "affyisms" which Mark Twain took huge delight in creating (apparently with no specific contexts in mind for them), and which he later placed at the chapter heads more or less casually, function as major structural device? How can the same ending close plots as different as those in the full manuscript and the published *Pudd'nhead Wilson*? How could the ending (when it was written, and the way it was written) round out the many farcical pages in which the Twins figured most prominently? Since it followed hard upon a major shift in the plot, how can the ending somehow round out the twins passages in the published *Pudd'nhead Wilson*, where the brothers are, most of the time, separate people and not very important to the plot? How can the ending be said to close the Roxy-Tom plot satisfactorily, when it was written before any of the Roxy-Tom pages at the start of the novel were written, before Mark Twain had more than a general plan for the pages he had yet to write?—and when what he did go on to write was not precisely what he later put into *Pudd'nhead Wilson*? What light can this textual situation shed on the psychology and the physiology of the sense-making reader? Such questions are preliminary, to be answered before elaborating any interpretation—or even before deciding that any interpretation can legitimately be elaborated on such a "work of art."

The splendor of Mark Twain's best prose blinds us all to the large measure of truth in his self-satisfied admission that he was only a jack-leg novelist. We should take this admission as seriously as his assertion in *Old Times on the Mississippi*, Chapter 6, that he loved the profession of piloting far better than any he had followed since. He gives this as the reason: "a pilot, in those days, was the only unfettered and entirely independent human being that lived in the earth." By comparison, writing was paltry: "We write frankly and fearlessly, but then we 'modify' before we print." There's more to the difference between the two occupations than the caution a writer imposes on himself or lets others impose on him. Piloting demanded a fierce alertness. You could not with impunity fake being a pilot when you were at the wheel, but you could, if you were skillful enough or merely bold enough, fake part of your way along the production of a literary work, dropping out an essential episode of *Huckleberry Finn* in order to accommodate the publisher, padding out the wonderful fragment *Old Times* to make up the lumbering *Life on the Mississippi*, slapping parts of the big novel together to make *Pudd'nhead Wilson*, anomalies be damned. The Mississippi, ready to take advantage of any laxness, kept pilots on their guard, but the human mind is designed to smooth out anomalies, in order not to be overwhelmed by them. As Ralph W. Rader says, drawing on the work of cognitive psychologists, the mind is a "meaning-seeking faculty"; by its nature the mind "actively seeks to impose meaning and to eliminate ambiguity in its encounters with the world, and so it must certainly be with language." In responding to an utterance,

Rader goes on, the mind "scans and interprets it so as to discover that meaning which renders the whole coherent and significant, to the exclusion of partial and incomplete meanings."[26] It is this order-imposing instinct, finally (however much it manifests itself in the guise of a mere literary approach such as the New Criticism) which impels readers to celebrate a text containing passages of indubitable interest and power but faked, palmed off as a genuine novel like another good novel, one where early scenes prepare for the middle and the later scenes, where patterns established at the outset are fulfilled in subsequent pages, where all the aspects really do work together in a transcendent unity.

26. Ralph W. Rader, "The Concept of Genre and Eighteenth-Century Studies," *New Approaches to Eighteenth-Century Literature*, ed. Phillip Harth (New York: Columbia University Press, 1974), pp. 79-115; the quotations are from pp. 84-85. Rader (p. 84, n. 7) cites James J. Gibson, *The Senses Considered as Perceptual Systems* (Boston: Houghton Mifflin, 1966) for the demonstration that the tendency of the mind to impose meaning and eliminate ambiguity holds true "even at the level of sensory experience." See especially Gibson's Chapter 12, "The Pickup of Ambient Information-Scanning"; Chapter 13, "The Theory of Information Pickup"; and Chapter 14, "The Causes of Deficient Perception."

CHAPTER 6

The Red Badge of Courage:
The Private History of a Campaign that —Succeeded?

Ringing an ironic change on a title of Mark Twain's, "The Private History of a Campaign that Failed," I have cast this chapter as a personal narrative of how I came to have the idea of reconstructing *The Red Badge of Courage* as Crane wrote it, what I did with the idea, and what the fate of the reconstructed text is apt to be. An arbitrary starting point of the story is December 1972, when I reacted skeptically to Joseph Katz's assertiveness about the text of *Red Badge*: "the only authoritative source of its text is the first edition published by Appleton in 1895," he declared; and "there is no evidence that he did anything more to the book once the first edition appeared. So there is one authoritative source of the text: the first edition. Simple."[1] About that time, Blake Nevius gave me a copy of Fredson Bowers's Virginia Edition of *Bowery Tales* (that is, *Maggie* and *George's Mother*) unfit to offer to a reviewer for *Nineteenth-Century Fiction*—unfit because it was cased upside down and backwards.[2] When I finally worked through the volume during

---

1. Joseph Katz, "Practical Editions: Stephen Crane's *The Red Badge of Courage*," *Proof* 2 (1972): 301-11; the quotations are from p. 303.
2. *Bowery Tales*, ed. Fredson Bowers, Introduction by James B. Colvert (Charlottesville: University Press of Virginia, 1969).

my Guggenheim year (1974-75) I found the textual introduction to be argued with bewilderingly specious pedantry and found the editorial apparatus so badly conceived and error-ridden as to be quite unusable: anyone seriously interested in the text would have to collate the 1893 and 1896 editions from scratch, as I ultimately did. In the course of those months, when I was drawn (and in turn drew Brian Higgins) into spending far too much time on *Maggie* rather than the project I had promised Gordon Ray I would work on, I came to attribute the state of my copy, as I later said, to an outbreak of symbolic bookbinding at Kingsport Press, the printer of the Virginia Edition.

My embroilment with *Maggie* was painful then, and is painful to remember. The pain and the excessive embroilment both sprang from a sense of betrayal, for I had just spent three years on the advisory board of the CEAA, had been examiner for many volumes in various editions, and was frequently writing reviews of CEAA volumes, often defending the CEAA from the misguided attacks of Edmund Wilson and others while admitting the weaknesses of particular volumes. I had staked to the CEAA not only many youthful hopes from the mid-1960s but many months of work through the next decade. My quixotic notion was to save the honor of the CEAA by having it publicly rescind the seal it had awarded to *Maggie*, but the committee voted unanimously to allow the seal to remain. Among the overt and covert consequences of my agitations against *Maggie* was my being blackballed from the Center for Scholarly Editions, the successor organization to the CEAA: in his private and confidential view, wrote an eminent bibliographer, the only person he thought ought never to be considered for the committee or chairman was Hershel Parker, who had shown himself lately to be temperamentally unfit for responsibility.[3] (When I showed the letter to Leon Howard as one of the wonders of the Age of Xerox, he scoffed: everything you wrote about anybody had always ended up on that person's desk.) Ultimately, the bibliographical and textual annual which was to have published the Higgins-Parker essay on *Maggie* did not publish it, and it was far

3. This advice was a postscript to commentary on a draft of a proposed report recommending the setting up of the Center for Scholarly Editions.

too long to publish anywhere else. I had done myself professional harm, had led my friend into an appalling waste of time
(even allowing for our learning much from our work), and had
done damage to my peace of mind and body. But the interlude
had at least one remarkable and mainly happy by-product, the
result of my asking Alan Roper, in the midst of the hubbub over
Maggie, if I could review the Virginia *Red Badge* for *Nineteenth-
Century Fiction*, along with Bowers's *Facsimile* of the *Red
Badge* manuscript.[4]

These were not easy volumes to review, for nowhere did
Bowers (or J. C. Levenson, the author of the introduction to the
Virginia Edition) lay out in precise chronological order all of
the available facts about composition, preparation of typescript,
negotiations for publication, partial newspaper publication,
magazine excerpting, and so on. One decision of Bowers's, in
particular, made it formidably difficult to think about the novel
in terms of its composition and completion. In the *Facsimile*
Bowers defined the "manuscript" as the document which Crane
gave a friend early in 1896 and which survives, bound, in the
Clifton Waller Barrett Collection at the University of Virginia.
That is, Bowers did not conceive his purpose as being to present
a facsimile of the manuscript as Crane wrote and completed it,
insofar as that was recoverable. Instead, he printed the facsimile
of only the Barrett pages as "THE FINAL MANUSCRIPT / *Text*"
and followed it with (as a new half-title announced): "THE
FINAL MANUSCRIPT / *Discarded Chapter XII* / *False Starts* /
Computations." In the first of these subsections, "*Discarded
Chapter XII*," Bowers printed, in numerical order, the surviving
leaves of Chapter 12, regardless of their present locations.
Finally, in another section, he offered "THE DRAFT MANU-
SCRIPT / *Preserved Text*"—a facsimile, in proper sequence, of
the surviving pages of the draft manuscript (pages which sur-
vive only because they happened to be reused, on the other side
of the leaves, in the composition of the final manuscript). The
Virginia Edition likewise erected a rampart of bibliographical

4. *The Red Badge of Courage*, ed. Fredson Bowers, Introduction by J. C.
Levenson (Charlottesville: University Press of Virginia, 1975) and *The Red Badge of
Courage: A Facsimile Edition of the Manuscript*, ed. Fredson Bowers (Washington,
D.C.: NCR / Microcard Editions, 1972 and 1973).

argument and apparatus against the possibility of thinking of the text as Crane wrote it. In particular, the section "The Text: History and Analysis" (pp. 181-252) is all but overwhelming in its mustering of extraordinarily detailed hypotheses and analyses, the sort of textual guessing and arguing that all but requires the reader not only to accept the editor's conclusions but also to agree with the editor's emphases, pushing the user, for instance, to accept the editor's sense of the relative importance of hypotheses about typescripts and carbons and his hypotheses about the system of regularizing attributed to Crane as well as to accept the justifications of the editor's own systems of regularizing and modernizing. The review took more thought than any I had ever written, but after I submitted it in the fall of 1975 I still had to drive over to UCLA and retrieve it.

I had to retrieve it because at last I backed away from the well-nigh impenetrable detail of the two editions and focused on a thought which had been nagging at me for years, at least since 1972, when I had jotted down a note on reconstructing the original text and then had forgotten about it. People had been reading, ever since 1895, when *Red Badge* was first published, a truncated version (three chapter endings removed, the whole of Chapter 12 removed, the last chapter snipped down), a version which did not make sense. For years I had been aware that on the level of syntax the Appleton edition did not make sense —toward the end of the last chapter you can't tell what "conviction" is referred to in "With this conviction came a store of assurance," and so on. I knew it did not make sense on that level but had not realized before that the truncations were not attempts to shorten, to speed up the pace, but were just like changes the same Appleton editor, Ripley Hitchcock, insisted on a few months later when he determined to salvage the "obscene" *Maggie*, which Crane had privately printed in 1893, as an Appleton book—daring in style and subject but not pornographic, a strong dose but one which could be assimilated profitably under the aegis of realism.

Once I decided we had been reading an editorially censored text, I scanned the facsimile of the manuscript, where parts of the deleted endings of Chapters 7, 10, and 15 (the original 15) are preserved, although crossed out, then when I got to the end of Chapter 11, I scanned the surviving pages of

150

Chapter 12, which the editor had printed not in the place where Crane wrote them to stand, but separately, in the back. When portions were irretrievably lost from the final manuscript I looked for equivalent portions which fortuitously survived in the pages of the rough draft which Crane reused for the final draft, and continued on through the last chapter, where the full version survives in manuscript, although the Appleton version had several segments snipped out. My earlier experience in flipping through the two different orders of *Tender is the Night* came in handy as I tried to purge my mind of the Appleton version I had always known so I could follow the manuscript almost as Crane wrote it. There was no question: what Crane wrote was coherent, immensely more powerful, still more of a masterpiece. I went back into my undergraduate class the next day and told them I was going to teach the book again, the way Crane wrote it. Then I got on the phone to James B. Meriwether, who was receptive at once: "Let's have a conference on it!" I also called Joseph Katz, who had come down so hard in favor of the finality of the Appleton edition. Katz said he remembered something at the Berg Collection that might be useful. Then I drove to UCLA to retrieve my manuscript of the review from the editor of *Nineteenth-Century Fiction* and wrote a new ending. The ending published the next March was, as it turned out, rewritten yet again to include new information found early in the year.

I had begun the review dashingly: "Here is riches running wild. First the riches, then the running wild."[5] The editor was not happy with my notions of agreement of subject and verb, so it started this way in print: "In these two editions Fredson Bowers offers the Crane scholar riches running wild. First the riches, then the running wild." Here I summarize the review and quote sections from it. Both editions, I said, present themselves impressively with the CEAA seal, although only the volume in the *Works* was funded by the federal government through NEH. The *Facsimile* consists of a boxed set, Volume I the "Introduction and Apparatus" and Volume II the photographic reproductions. The introduction traces the composition and early history

5. Review of the NCR / Microcard Editions *Facsimile* and the Virginia *Red Badge*, *Nineteenth-Century Fiction* 30 (March 1976): 558-62.

of *Red Badge*, describes the final manuscript and extant parts of the draft manuscript, discusses the revision of the final manuscript and its publication, and explains the apparatus, which consists mainly of lists of alterations in the final manuscript (divided according to the stages at which the editor thinks they were made) and alterations in the draft. The volume labeled "Facsimile" contains (in slightly reduced but sharply legible photographic reproductions) the final manuscript, together with the surviving pages of a discarded chapter, false starts, certain computations and the preserved pages from the draft manuscript, as well as a single-page fragment called here "Gustave and Marie." The second *Red Badge*, the stout one-volume Virginia edition, runs to 516 pages. Somewhere inside are 133 pages taken up by Crane's little book, as heavily emended by Bowers. A printed rendering of the surviving draft manuscript takes up 36 pages and the discarded chapter takes up 4, while 75 pages are devoted to lists of alterations in the draft and the final manuscript.

I then complained of a large amount of duplication between the *Facsimile* and the Virginia Edition and certain perturbing omissions, "most conspicuously a chart in the NCR edition keying manuscript pages to Virginia pages and a comparable key in the Virginia edition showing from what parts of the manuscript its own pages derive." Such waste and such omissions are lamentable enough, I concluded, "but where the Virginia *Red Badge* runs wild (aside from many of the editorial emendations found in the text of the novel) is in J.C. Levenson's eighty-page introduction, in Bowers's seventy-page history and analysis of the text, and in some of Bowers's textual notes."

After making a few observations on the editorial intrusiveness in the Virginia volumes, particularly *Bowery Tales*, Volume I, and on the failure of Levenson and Bowers to tell a straightforward story about how Crane wrote and published his masterpiece, I offered some strictures on Levenson's indulgence in highly debatable literary criticism and some speculative biographical sections, among other matters. Then I continued:

"Whatever one feels about Levenson's essay is of little importance: the Virginia *Red Badge* stands or falls by Bowers's work. . . . The most damaging faults of commission are Bowers's misleading account of Crane's revisions and his related decisions to emend the novel excessively. In a major discovery, Bowers identified Hamlin Garland's as the hand in the manuscript challenging Crane's dialect spellings. (The crucial marginal annotation by Garland, one which contains an undeciphered word, is prominently discussed in both editions: strangely, the *Facsimile* slices it half off, denying the reader the chance to see the word in context and making him dread that *authorial* writing in the margins might frequently have eluded the camera, as seems to have happened at MS pp. 111 and 131.) But Bowers manages to turn his discovery into a liability. Even though Crane's attempts to comply with Garland's criticism were halfhearted, contradictory, and soon abandoned altogether, Bowers interprets them as culminating in a complex 'system' which Crane supposedly conceived but did not come close to carrying out: imposing standard English for Henry Fleming but retaining dialect for the other characters. Eager to fulfill what he has decided were the final intentions of his author, Bowers relentlessly emends in order to impose the 'system' which he thinks he has discovered. How few or how many consistently interrelated elements make a 'system,' the reader finally asks, and what proportion of 'exceptions' invalidate one? Crane botched up his manuscript a little in response to Garland's criticism, but nothing like the Virginia botching, which creates a ludicrous discrepancy between Henry Fleming's normal speech and the dialect used by other characters (try sampling the Virginia version of the dialogue in the first two chapters). Imposing this 'system,' in which many words are erratically taken out of dialect and many others put into dialect, requires not only an unconscionable number of new editorial emendations but also frenetic picking and choosing of dialect and non dialect forms from the draft manuscript and various stages of the final manuscript. The result strikes me as one of the most disheartening mishmashes in textual history.

"The Virginia textual decisions in general, even aside from the wholesale emending of dialect words and casting of other words into dialect forms, are open to the same objections brought against many textual decisions in the Bowers Ohio State Hawthorne volumes and the other Crane volumes. Once again Bowers reveals a tendency to shelter himself under outdated McKerrowean dogma where Greg offers sounder policy; indeed, Bowers sometimes shows a curious antipathy toward the very rationale he

has proselytized for. Once again some of Bowers's aesthetic arguments in justification of his emendations are woefully unconvincing. Once again he rigorously regularizes accidentals in violation
of his claim to print an unmodernized critical text—even to the
point of sticking a prissy apostrophe into every 'aint' that Crane
wrote. The upshot is that the Virginia text, once again, is not one
you would want your students to read. More vigorous than anyone
else in defending the theoretical utility of eclectic texts, Bowers
by his actual example is forcing responsible textual scholars to
challenge indiscriminate eclecticism and to consider afresh for
every work just what form of the text (and just what kind of apparatus) will best serve scholars, critics, and students. In reaction to
Bowers's Hawthorne and Crane texts, a consensus is also emerging that no editor who is driven by an urge to impose regularity
upon a text is apt to produce a definitive edition of anything. The
Hawthorne and Crane editions are a heavy price to pay for belated
wisdom, but their faults seem apt to prove the means by which
American scholars will educate themselves, at long last, about
textual criticism.

"Serious as they are, Bowers's editorial sins of commission
may be venial compared with the sins of omission, his failures to
consider the full range of textual and critical evidence. The textual
situation of *Red Badge* which emerges from study of all the evidence now available, including the Charles E. Merrill facsimile of
the first edition, especially,[6] as well as Bowers's two new editions,
suggests important questions that have not yet been asked, much
less answered. First, should Crane's post-Garland dialect tinker-
ings be rejected on the ground that the older man had intimidated
him, pushing him into blind alleys of attempted placation? A more
significant question is whether or not Crane's hasty large-scale late
excisions might have been made under pressure from the publisher. The latest excisions of all (those where the manuscript
contains passages, not crossed out, which do not appear in the first
edition) drastically alter the meaning of the novel: in the manuscript Crane at the end is ironically and blasphemously mocking
Henry Fleming's self-delusions (as in the paraphrasing of such a
biblical passage as Matthew 10.29), while in the printed book
Henry's opinion of himself seems to have sudden and anomalous
support from the author. Was the new upbeat religiosity of the

6. *The Red Badge of Courage*, Introduction by Joseph Katz (Columbus, Ohio:
Charles E. Merrill, 1969), an enlarged facsimile of the first impression of the 1895
edition.

ending designed to appease the Appleton editor, Ripley Hitchcock, who was so soon to wipe the rouge off *Maggie*? Levenson
and Bowers refer to other instances in which Crane proved
remarkably impressionable to criticism, but they never focus on
the degree to which the differences between the final manuscript
as first inscribed and the first edition of the book may be due to
various outside pressures.

"We need to know, for careful scrutiny of the evidence suggests an absolutely paramount theoretical and practical problem.
Is it possible that Crane had the fullest sense of his 'intentions' for
the book very early, perhaps at the time of his first revision of his
newly inscribed final manuscript (the rather thoroughgoing
weeding out of proper names, where 'Fleming' became 'the
youth,' and so on), before he submitted the manuscript to Garland's criticism? After that, did Crane yield halfheartedly first to
one advisor then another, gradually losing his sense of the work as
an aesthetic unity and relinquishing his practical control of it in
order to get it (or part of it) into print, however maimed? If so, we
need to acknowledge that no literary critic will ever hold in his
hand the 'ideal' text Crane had created, for during the post-Garland revisions the original chapter 12 was discarded (and part of it
lost, then or later) and other pages were discarded from the ends
of certain chapters. One can more or less reconstruct almost all of
what stood in the manuscript prior to Garland's reading it: doing
so simply requires reinserting the surviving pages of chapter 12,
restoring passages in the manuscript which are legible although
crossed out, and eking out these restorations with any fortuitously
surviving passages from the rough draft (as when p. 86 of the draft
contains the original form of part of what must have been on the
final p. 100, now missing from the discarded chapter). This rather
motley and slightly incomplete reconstruction, I wager, would be
the best possible basis for New Critical demonstration of the unity
of the novel—the sort of essays which have been lavished upon
mere reprints (or reprints of reprints) of the Appleton text, a text
which reached its final form as the result of omissions so hasty and
ill-conceived that several passages still depend for their meaning
upon passages which were excised. We owe Bowers a debt for
putting much documentary evidence before us, however
restricted the circulation of the $60 set will be; but we must also
recognize that the elaborate textual arguments in these two editions do not touch on the most significant issue of precisely when
Crane's 'intentions' were most fully embodied forth. Furthermore,
the documentary evidence is far from exhausted. When I outlined

155

the possibility of editorial pressure on Crane, Joseph Katz called my attention to a contemporary Appleton list of corrections, unused by Bowers, which turns out to have complex biographical and textual significance.[7] This list has led to demonstration that the Appleton plates were altered in 1896, with Crane's knowledge, although Bowers asserts that the plates were 'invariant during Crane's lifetime.' (Bowers apparently failed to make the one indispensable Hinman collation, first printing against last. See Henry Binder, 'Alterations in the Appleton Plates of *The Red Badge of Courage*,' forthcoming in *Editorial Quarterly*, No. 3.) Saying this sounds strange even to my own ears, but the fact is that conscientious textual and critical study of *The Red Badge of Courage* has hardly begun."

Through the last months of 1975 and the first three months of 1976 I felt no strong uneasiness: the review was coming out, and I would be on record as advocating a reconstruction of the manuscript. Yet the problem remained: how could I get the best hearing for the evidence? Ordinarily, I would have written an essay on the *Red Badge* as Crane wrote it, but I was struggling to finish my section of *The Norton Anthology of American Literature* and knew I could not, under the circumstances, do the project justice. It seemed for a few days that a solution had presented itself. My colleague Ronald Gottesman had been approached by one of the W. W. Norton editors to do a report on the manuscript of Donald Pizer's revision of the first Norton Critical Edition of *The Red Badge of Courage*. I asked to handle the job instead, and on 8 December 1975 wrote a letter to Peter Phelps at the Norton office in New York. Here I clarify some of my sentences and change the page numbers from those on Pizer's manuscript to those in the printed Norton Critical Edition (1976):

"Dear Peter,
I am not quite setting up shop as a Crane expert yet, but my interest has been growing for the last year. Don has seen a very

7. This page in the Berg collection lists changes to be made in the Appleton *Red Badge*, changes which were in fact made in an early printing, contrary to Bowers's declaration that the text of the American plates were "invariant during Crane's lifetime" (Virginia edition, p. 248). David J. Nordloh identified the stationery as that of Thomas Wentworth Higginson and the hand as Higginson's.

thorough exposé Brian Higgins and I have done on Bowers's *Maggie*; it's unpublished but forthcoming in Proof 5. [It was not, as it turned out, printed there.] I have this fall reviewed the Bowers Facsimile and the Bowers Va. edition for the March 1976 *Nineteenth-Century Fiction*, and I've taught *RBofC* this fall in both my graduate and undergraduate classes. Even the undergraduates, I will say, reacted with great interest to the textual points I was making, to my showing the way sound interpretation depends upon knowledge of the textual history.

"What I say in the *RB* review is that the Va. edition is all wrong because it fails to lay out the textual history clearly, emends erratically, etc., but that these usual Bowersean sins (of the sort Don has been pointing out for years) are really beside the point, which is that he failed to ask all the genuinely profound questions about when the book existed as the fullest embodiment of Crane's artistic intentions.

"For years I have been using the information in the NCE to point out to classes the damage done by those late excisions, clearly *hasty* excisions, especially those in the last chapter. But now after finally understanding that Bowers had not asked any of the right questions I slowly am realizing that no critic has ever written about the book on the basis of a reliable text. It seems to me that the text I will always want my students to read does not yet exist, and will never exist, although it can be very closely approximated. I think the time Crane had the fullest sense of what he wanted to do and what he actually had done was just before he presented the MS for Hamlin Garland's criticism. Garland had just been bawled out by Richard Gilder for using dialect which would subvert the speech of American boys, so Garland in turn attacked Crane, telling him to get the dialect out.[8] Poor Crane had asked for advice so he tried to take it, but his efforts at getting rid of the dialect were erratic, unwilling, and soon abandoned altogether. (Bowers interprets these efforts quite oddly—thinking he sees a *system*, as he calls it, whereby Henry speaks standard English and everyone else speaks dialect!) It was then that Crane began to lose his sense of keeping the thing as he wanted it. A few months after he mucked up the dialect, I bet, he began getting pressure from Ripley Hitchcock, Appleton's editor, and then mucked it up in much more important ways. Judging from the similarity between

8. Herbert F. Smith, *Richard Watson Gilder* (New York: Twayne Publishers, 1970), pp. 95-99, especially Gilder's letter to Garland of 5 April, 1890 (p. 95).

the excisions in RB and those in *Maggie* (performed under Hitch-cock's thumb only a few months later), Appleton's probably leaned hard on Crane to make him take out the blasphemy. Blas-phemy it was, though it seems tame to us: making fun of the notion that not a sparrow falls, etc., having a character defy the Universe —why, in *Maggie* they even removed a line saying 'as God says' when it meant 'as it says in the Bible.' I think it is a pretty good bet that Hitchcock said the ironic ending had to go, that there had to be an inspiring ending. So Crane took out philosophical sections where Henry had alternately praised and condemned the Universe and put in a sentence of specious upbeat religiosity which was obviously at war with the meaning of the manuscript. ('Over the river a golden ray of sun came through the hosts of leaden rain clouds.') Crane was a kid and he wanted the book published. He really messed it up, because the excisions left numerous large and small loose ends. My feeling is pretty strong, in short, that after Garland criticized the MS Crane probably yielded halfheartedly to one or another advisor, gradually losing his sense of the work as an aesthetic unity and relinquishing his practical control of it in order to get it into print, however maimed.

"If this is so, we must acknowledge that no literary critic will ever hold in his hand the 'ideal' text Crane created, for during the post-Garland revisions the original chapter 12 was discarded (and part of it lost, then or later) and other pages were discarded from the ends of certain chapters. One can pretty much reconstruct all of this, all but a couple of pages, total . . . This is as near as we can get, and it is a powerful work of art, even slightly maimed, an entirely unified work of art, much superior to what everyone has been reading and writing criticism on.

"I think Norton could score a great coup by printing the text in the form I have described. If not, I have a student named Henry Binder whom I've put onto the 'loose-ends' problem; he's going to be publishing on the novel, and might edit it this way for his dissertation if you choose not to take my suggestion here. The great thing is the way the really authorial text affects basic prob-lems such as the shape of Crane's Naturalism. And having read the text that Crane wrote rather than the one that he later botched up puts you in a position to throw out a great deal of the criticism or to see that it goes at good things in muddled fashion.

"I asked Binder to go through Don's new 'Criticism' section spotting any places where problems which the critics deal with inconclusively or avoid altogether would be solved if they had been reading the excised passages. Binder picked out several passages which reflect mistaken concepts of *Red Badge* that have grown out of the Appleton printing and others which demonstrate the sound intuition of scholars and critics that something is amiss in the book as they read it, even though they fail to see that the confusion arises from an imperfect text. Let's look at some.

"216: On the reflections toward the end of the Appleton text ('He had rid himself of the red sickness of battle,' and so on), Charles C. Walcutt says 'It is not obvious whether the young man who thinks these thoughts is deluding himself or not.' True, but only because of the excisions. The ending of the MS is definitely ironic.

"230: Stanley B. Greenfield argues from the excised portions that there '*is* irony in the end of the novel' but he never quite focuses on the fact that after the excisions you can't really be *sure* there is irony. What the Appleton edition cuts out is Crane's continuing ironic judgments on Henry. You can't argue from the MS that the irony is *still* present in the first edition, as Greenfield does; but you can argue that it was in the MS and that it was so violently removed that every cautious reader will be bewildered by the published ending.

"239: Mordecai Marcus rightly says that 'the general affirmation of Crane's conclusion still jars' (slightly, he says) with 'the ironic treatment of Henry,' but he does not go on to say that the jarring is the result of those violently performed excisions and the addition of the final upbeat paragraph.

"239: Marcus gets hopelessly confused. He's right that the 'suddenness of Henry's insight,' the remaining 'traces of irony in the last chapter,' and 'Crane's departure from naturalism' are 'the causes of scepticism about the effectiveness and straightforwardness of the denouement'—at least he's right in the sense that critics are skeptical about the unity of the book because Henry's final insight comes too suddenly, too unprepared-for, because the irony is either removed or rendered dubious, and because Crane suddenly begins treating Nature in a non-Naturalistic way. But the *real* cause of the uneasiness of critics is that the text was truncated so carelessly that it was rendered unintelligible. Then (p. 240) Marcus wrongly goes on to say the excisions *keep* the final chapter from being ambiguous: on the contrary, it is ambiguous only *because* the cuts were made. Crane's ironic attitude toward Henry's self-delusions are altogether unambiguous at the end of the MS version.

"280-81: John Berryman is wonderful, though he goes at it as a brilliant reader, not through the textual evidence. He's right: the 'rhetoric' is just rhetoric. After quoting the 'red sickness of battle' passage, Berryman says, 'But *then* comes a sentence in which I simply do not believe. . .!' Beautiful: Berryman is so good that he gets it just right though he misses the textual reasons; he couldn't have known back then about the way the manuscript reads.

"299: Pizer gets it right too, saying that Fleming's own sanguine view of himself at the close 'cannot be taken at face value.' As Don says, 'Fleming's self-evaluations contrast ironically with his motives and actions throughout the novel.' But the implication of this is that Pizer expects a pattern to be followed throughout a unified novel. The pattern is *not* followed in the last chapter, so Pizer has to appeal to the rest of the book. What this amounts to is admitting that the ending doesn't make sufficient sense by itself. You can strain and make it have a kind of sense if you resort to the pattern set up elsewhere in the book, but you are walking on air since the last chapter keeps pulling the supports from under you.

"301: James B. Colvert says 'the problems raised in the story are not clearly defined or resolved.' True of the published book, *not* true of the MS. 'As a consequence the ending is confused and unconvincing.' Well, the ending *is* confused and unconvincing, but *not* as a consequence of Crane's failure to resolve or define the problems: it's that way because of the carelessness and illogicality of the late excisions and the inappropriateness of the late addition. There's a textual explanation.

"301: Colvert rightly notes 'the deterioration in the quality of the writing' in the last chapter, 'the appearance of a tendency toward incoherence.' But these faults are not in the MS version and they result from the loose ends left when excisions were clumsily made. There are various sentences in the last chapter which are literally incoherent because of the excisions. Colvert is quite wrong in blaming Crane for being unable to convince us of something: he had done it right in the MS.

"324: John W. Rathbun says that 'Wilson and Fleming become virtually inseparable and take on essentially the same qualities of courage.' Not true in the MS, which is carefully designed to show Wilson's superiority to Henry in basic generosity of spirit. Binder points out that the excision of the report of Jimmie Rogers's death drastically alters the reader's sense of a *contrast* between Henry and Wilson. If Henry is to be heroic, after all, this passage had to be excised (it shows Wilson much concerned at Jimmie's death while Henry is totally self-absorbed and indeed gleeful). Deleting the last mention of Jimmie makes the retention of the earlier references meaningless.

"334: Marston LaFrance rightly says that a 'sense of uncertainty' plagues Fleming 'until the last two or three pages,' but the point is that the ill-planned excisions have left Henry's new certainty uncontrolled by Crane's irony.

"349: Robert M. Rechnitz rightly says that studies of the novel 'continue to question whether the intention of the novel's final paragraphs is literal or ironic.' In fact, one just can't tell: the published book is just not clear enough. The clues—those which survive in the text—go all one way till the last chapter, then they begin to go the other way but not wholly so. The novel as published is incapable of providing a clear meaning, though Don and Berryman can get one by disregarding the last chapter. Critics have all had to work round the ending somehow, unless they ignored it altogether. Whatever they do is unsatisfactory because they have not done so in terms of the textual evidence. The point is that no unifying concept is discernible after the revisions: it is maimed text, much worse maimed than the reconstructed pre-Garland text would be.

"So, if I were editing *Red Badge* I would print as close as possible to what Crane wrote before he began getting pressure from outside. I think such a text over the next years would revolutionize Crane scholarship. I have no idea whether Don will be at all persuaded by my arguments, though I hope to at least be able to clarify anything that needs clarifying when I see him here before Christmas. I do think that once my review comes out in *NCF* the best Crane scholars will have to begin talking about the challenge I throw out there, the possibility that the pre-Garland text is what everyone should be reading.

"I don't know exactly what to urge on you, except awareness that the new knowledge will be appearing and it would be nice to have Norton ahead of the pack. If Don wanted, I could help Binder write some sort of textual overview which could be included in the NCE.

"So, I offer this in good spirits and won't feel bad if Don decides to disregard it all, though I think it would be great for Norton to capitalize on the new publicity being generated by the Bowers editions and new writings by me, Binder, and surely others."

Pizer's response to Phelps on 13 December 1975 was temperate enough but quite final. He had, he told Phelps, given considerable thought to the problem of what text to use and in fact had been thinking about Crane textual problems for some years, unlike (he tactfully did not say) the author of the reader's report. My choice of text, he said, arose from my reading of the novel: I liked the book best as coherent philosophical natural-ism and with Crane adopting a consistent ironic attitude toward Henry. Pizer saw the whole thing as a problem in criticism, not in editing. Mine was a critical effort in that I would be seeking to convince Crane scholars of the rightness of my interpretation of the novel. If I and my student succeeded, perhaps in ten or twenty years Norton might wish to publish the text as Crane wrote it, but our argument was only an argument and Pizer was not convinced by it. I was wanting to solve all controversy about the conclusion of the novel by printing a specific text. This was going about the problem from the wrong end. First I and my student should convince others in critical essays that all diffi-culties can be resolved by a choice of the right text, and then the world would beat a path to our doorsteps and plead with us to edit such a text. In other words, as Pizer was to say in print later on, Parker was not a Crane scholar and did not know what he was talking about.

Of course I did not *have* to be a Crane scholar to be inter-ested in reading and having others read what Crane actually wrote. And of course I had not, as Pizer assumed, started with an interpretation and looked about for a variant text which would support it. I had known for years that particular passages did not make sense because of cuts in the last chapter, or at least did not make the sense they had originally made, but I had not thought through the implications of that knowledge until I at last focused on the similarity between what had happened at Apple-ton's both to *The Red Badge of Courage* and to *Maggie*. I also started with a conviction about the creative process—that writ-ers write the way they write for good reasons, though they may lose sight of these reasons later on. Work on *Tender is the Night* had taught me, as Higgins and I had said, that art may not be magical or mystical but good art is subtle and coherent, is the way it is for good reasons, even if the artist himself under later compulsions loses part of his faith in—or recollection of—his original design and the validity of his first 'final' intentions. And of course I knew that critics had been known to argue about the interpretation of literary texts which had no problems in their textual histories. There is a great difference between a complex,

162

ambiguous text which invites competing critical interpretations and a text which is radically flawed because the author died before reconciling anomalies, or because the author pieced it together hastily in order to have something to sell, never mind if it were incoherent, or let an editor censor it in order to have something in print, however mangled.

Pizer's rejection of my offer left me, once more, to decide how to handle the discovery. There was hardly a conscious decision, since Henry Binder was on the scene, ready to "study textual editing with Hershel Parker," as he said, and resourceful and competent. I gave Binder his title, in wry parody of a title that went back beyond Joseph Katz's article on *Maggie* and an article on Howells by Katz's teacher Edwin H. Cady to the 1920s and Henry Wadsworth Longfellow: "*The Red Badge of Courage* Nobody Knows."[9] Binder later dropped the italics on the first word, but he had his assignment and was off and running.

What you do with an idea like this is market it, over the objections of a great many people, over, I remember, a public bray of ridicule from one of my colleagues: "If Crane didn't like it he could have said so later on!" In this particular case, I had the support of my chairman Max F. Schulz, and the dean of humanities, David H. Malone, once it came time to fund Henry Binder's trip to look at the bound manuscript and the scattered leaves.[10] We had, like everyone else, the resources of the MLA convention, where Elaine Reed approved Binder's Forum for the December 1977 meeting in Chicago. (Pizer rebutted us from the floor.) I had the cooperation of Ronald Gottesman, the editor of the realistic period of the *Norton Anthology of American Literature*, who in 1976 got John Benedict's blessing to print there the reconstructed text of the novel. I still had to make a decision about how to market the unwritten "The *Red*

9. Joseph Katz, "The *Maggie* Nobody Knows," *Modern Fiction Studies* 12 (Summer 1966): 203-12; Edwin H. Cady, "The Howells Nobody Knows," *Mad River Review* 1 (1965): 3-25; Howard Mumford Jones, "The Longfellow Nobody Knows," *Outlook* 149 (8 August 1928): 577-79, 586.

10. A good chairman is hard to find. If Schulz had not let me teach graduate courses in what I was working on ("Interpretive Implications of Textual Evidence," "Aesthetic Implications of Textual Evidence," were some early course titles), I could never have written this book. Dean Malone always backed me and my graduate students.

Badge of Courage Nobody Knows." *Proof* was already in trouble. I gave no thought to having Binder submit it to *American Literature* or another specialist journal: it would be too long, and it would be considered textual and, worse, bibliographical. (*American Literature* was, in fact, to turn down Binder's demonstration of what really happened to four pages which were anomalously missing from the manuscript in Chapter 4; the piece was declared too bibliographical, even though it proved that the four pages were given to the editor of *Current Literature* as setting copy for a pre-publication excerpt [one which Bowers had overlooked] which was the nearest text to the manuscript. *PBSA* accepted the piece promptly enough.)[11]

So I resorted to the academic network. Through a friend at Austin, James T. Cox, a graduate student who was book review editor of *Studies in the Novel* (not the Crane critic James Trammell Cox, and not the Mark Twain critic James M. Cox who appears in the previous chapter of this book), I arranged to edit a special issue of *Studies in the Novel* on Stephen Crane. We could follow Binder's article with one I had assigned Steven Mailloux ("Your job is to use what you have learned from Stanley Fish and Ross Winterowd and explain how the book became a classic if I am right in saying it has been known only in a maimed form"). I could salvage a little of the work Brian Higgins and I had already done on *Maggie*, and I had what I considered a shrewd plan for co-opting Don Pizer: bring him on board to update his old essay on scholarship and criticism on Crane, the one published in *Fifteen American Authors Before 1900* (1971). I asked the temperate David Nordloh to review the entire Virginia Edition, and he was, in the end, more scathingly critical than I had known enough to be.[12] All this took many months—the lead essay was not finished until the fall of 1977.

11. Henry Binder, "Unwinding the Riddle of Four Pages Missing from the *Red Badge of Courage* Manuscript," *PBSA* 72 (First Quarter 1978): 100-06.
12. Steven Mailloux, "*The Red Badge of Courage* and Interpretive Conventions: Critical Response to a Maimed Text," *Studies in the Novel* 10 (Spring 1978): 48-63; see also Mailloux, *Interpretive Conventions* (Ithaca: Cornell University Press, 1982), pp. 160-65. In the Crane issue of *Studies in the Novel* see also Donald Pizer, "Stephen Crane: A Review of Scholarship and Criticism Since 1969," pp. 120-45, and David J. Nordloh, "On Crane Now Edited: The University of Virginia Edition of *The Works of Stephen Crane*," pp. 103-19.

In the meantime, I had heard from Fredson Bowers about the *Nineteenth-Century Fiction* review. He did not want to see any more of my fantasies about the editing of American literature and was thinking, in fact, of suing me and the editor of *Nineteenth-Century Fiction* for that particular review. It was easy to reassure the editor of the journal, for I had the kind of evidence we assumed any court would understand—evidence, for instance, of failure to make the Hinman collations stipulated by the CEAA as a condition of funding.

During the prolonged wait for the special issue (dated Spring 1978, the first copies came in December 1978) and for the publication of the *Norton Anthology of American Literature* (April 1979), I taught *Red Badge* in successive semesters (often bringing back Binder and Mailloux for star turns) and worked repeatedly through Pizer's assemblage of criticism. Here I want to make only a few points about that body of work.[13] First, all these modern critics were basically New Critics, even Edwin H. Cady (who had studied the bound manuscript of *Red Badge* in Virginia) and Pizer himself. They all focused on the received text, in one or another reprint of the Appleton edition, and looked backwards from it to the manuscript (if they mentioned the manuscript) rather than behaving as the best 1930s biographical scholars might have behaved—that is, rather than starting at the beginning, with accounts of the process of composition, with the evidence of the draft manuscript, with the evidence of the direction of Crane's revisions and expansions from draft to manuscript, and finally with the direction of the Appleton alterations. When these critics mentioned a manuscript passage it was usually to elucidate something that was not clear in the Appleton text. Thus Cady could say (p. 251) that although a passage of "bathetic anti-climaxes" had been cut (with the rest of Chapter 12), "its irony remains operative in the pivotal next chapter." He mentions (252) Henry's egotism in "two suppressed pages" at the end of Chapter 15 (Chapter 14 in the Appleton text) then says that "It will take all the rest of the

---

13. I cite Donald Pizer's revised Norton Critical Edition of *The Red Badge of Courage* (New York: W. W. Norton, 1976), not only for the convenience of me and my readers but also because I want to avail myself of Pizer's selection of "the best that has been written about *The Red Badge of Courage*" (p. viii).

last part of the book to try that egotism [that is, the egotism which was in the manuscript] in the fire of a real, if minor, heroism and reduce it to the human modesty achieved by Wilson on the first day." Throughout, Cady rejects the manuscript variants as heavy-handed, overly explicit, yet he repeatedly recurs to the full manuscript version in order to make sense of the published text. (At least, he does so until he reaches the last chapter, where he inexplicably quotes the "With this conviction" passage in the Appleton form but does not quote the manuscript version which contains the deleted referent of "conviction.") The dominant formula Cady relied on was a favorite of the New Critics, of course, who exalted showing over telling, the implicit over the explicit. At no point did Cady acknowledge how problematical, theoretically and practically, was the terrain he had moved into once he resorted to the manuscript to elucidate the book. The other critics who referred to manuscript variants did so with even less clear a rationale than Cady had articulated for himself.

Second, not one of these critics attempted to tell afresh the story of the composition and publication of *Red Badge* as a chapter in Crane's biography, one with intricate relationships to works he had already written (and had or had not already published) and with intricate relationships to works he was to write and, especially, with the novel he was soon to expurgate in order to have it republished. This is not to say that none of the critics made biographical judgments. They *all* did, for despite their New Critical allegiances critics inevitably fall into biographicizing—though often without a grounding in the ascertainable data of biography. In fact, critics biographicize in the particular way they now tend to do *because* of their New Critical orientation. Sometimes, as with Mark Twain and *Pudd'nhead Wilson*, they are amazingly lenient toward a slapdash author. In the case of *Red Badge*, when they find flaws in the Appleton text they often make harsh judgments on Crane's failures as a thinker, as an artist, and as a human being. James B. Colvert condemns "Crane's inability to control" the central metaphor of his entire oeuvre, the figure "of the little man in conflict with the hostile mountain." In *Red Badge* Crane reveals "imperfect mastery" of that figure (301). The "problems raised in the story are not clearly defined or resolved," Colvert says, in the passage I quoted to Peter Phelps, and as a consequence "the ending is confused and unconvincing." The "deterioration in the quality of the writing" in the last chapter shows that the task Crane had set himself was "too much for him": "The tone shifts inappropriately, the irony is erratic and often misdirected, and the hero is permitted certain assumptions inconsistent with his previous characterization and Crane's established attitudes toward him" (301). Having set up a situation in which Henry's sentimental delusions about himself as a conquering hero are to be corrected, "Crane disappoints us" (302). Taking Crane's irony as so "erratic," Colvert proceeds to denounce the "insecurity" of his "control over his point of view" (302). The failure of the book, Colvert decides, "is a failure in tone and theme" (304), and must be explained in different ways. It is "relatively easy" to explain the "failure of tone" on the basis of "Crane's biography," for the young writer was merely "an imperfectly suppressed sentimentalist laboring under the spell of a naive heroic ideal." To explain the failure in theme Colvert looks not only at this one "flawed novel" but at all Crane's "important fiction and poetry" (304). It turns out that Crane was unable to work the story out in a way compatible with his "master symbol —the metaphor of the little man before the mountain" (310).

This denunciation of the "failed" novel in terms of the intellectual, aesthetic, and moral failures of Stephen Crane illustrates again how critics fixate on the published text as the achieved literary work. When they do not impute to it a nonexistent unity, they frequently batter the poor writer for having failed to achieve precisely what he had brilliantly achieved in the manuscript. Colvert's analysis of the flaws of the Appleton text is excellent—irrefutable; but those flaws have nothing at all to do with Crane's intellect and his artistry, and relate to his morality only by showing he could be beaten down from his principled determination to get his works into print the way he wrote them. Colvert biographicizes perfunctorily on the basis of his accurate perception of flaws in the received text: "Crane's biography" exposes him as "an imperfectly suppressed sentimentalist" (304); Crane's "biography reminds us of his characteristic ways of turning his irony against his own egotism and pride" (309), something he tried unsuccessfully to do with Henry's egotism and pride because he could not always do it successfully with his own. Colvert might have been spared this hypothesis about Crane's personal weaknesses if he had known to take cognizance of textual evidence.

I do not at all intend to imply that Crane critics have not said wise and witty things about *The Red Badge of Courage*. Colvert, I emphasize, is right about the weaknesses of the Appleton text, though wrong about how to account for them. Sensible and even brilliant passages are strewn through the pages of the criticism Pizer assembled. I think of Charles C. Walcutt's passionate argument about Crane's meticulous picture of Henry's "self-delusion and vainglory" (220) and about the concluding paragraphs as representing "a climax of self-delusion" (221). I think of Mordecai Marcus's saying that "Crane must have intended irony about Henry's cowardice as well as about his delusions regarding his fate," since Chapter 15 (in the Appleton numbering) "emphasizes Henry's luck in being spared public shame for his flight." Therefore Crane had "planned a terminal irony both about Henry's early cowardice and later delusions of his importance to the universe" (238). I think of Cady's way of reading most of the book pretty much as Crane wrote it, using omitted passages to explain cryptic passages in the Appleton text, as when he emphasizes "Crane's association of philosophic naturalism with Henry Fleming's panic syndrome" (248). I think of Marston LaFrance's productive strategy of progressing through the Appleton text in terms of the series of problems Crane had to solve in order to go on.

All these good essays are guilty of what Colvert wrongly accuses Crane of—that is, of throwing everything away at the end. Marcus compromises his essay at the end by deciding that, revisions having to be improvements, Crane had "vastly improved his conclusion by his excisions," for without the excisions "the final chapter would be quite ambiguous" (240); in fact, of course, the manuscript reading was quite unambiguous, as Marcus himself had recognized when he attributed the critical debate about the ending to the revisions (239). As I have shown, Cady, who had consistently used manuscript variants throughout his analysis, suddenly stops doing so when he discusses Henry's glee and his store of assurance. Having been patiently persuasive throughout his analysis, LaFrance at the end abruptly resorts to intimidation: "The endless critical squabbles which have arisen over this final chapter hinge upon a single question: does Fleming achieve any moral growth or development of character? Yet any Crane student should be able to answer this question almost without consulting this chapter at all" (346).

Sorting resolutely among the essays by the critics given prominent place in Pizer's collection, I could in fact have achieved a close approximation of perhaps half of the interpretive parts of Binder's essay by the simple device of snipping sentences from Cady and the others apart and joining them with small connectives: good critics say good things, even when they are working with imperfect evidence and faulty rationales. I could even have included in such a pieced-together essay a superb reading of the function of the original Chapter 12, mainly lifted from Cady's essay. Yet however brilliant their local insights are, none of the critics deals with everything which was left out of the Appleton text and still retrievable. In this no man's land where biographical evidence is avoided and mistrusted but where biographical conclusions are leapt to, where textual evidence is avoided, at times, or adduced when it supports a point the critic wants to make, yet never fully analyzed under some rationale about the limits of the creative process or the authority of the author, even fine critics falter and flounder. No pastiche of even the best essays on the novel could have provided what was wholly new in Binder's essay, such as his sections on the function of certain characters (primarily Jimmie Rogers and Wilson), on the interrelationship of certain chapters (especially Chapters 16 and 26), or on the meaning of the concluding chapter. None of the critics could have approximated the reading that Binder ultimately arrived at, since none of them had read and reread the text reconstructed as close as it can be to the way Crane wrote it.

In the concluding section of his essay Binder offered a comprehensive reading of the reconstructed text. Here I quote two passages. The first is an explanation for the critical impasse:[14]

14. Henry Binder, "The *Red Badge of Courage* Nobody Knows," *Studies in the Novel* 10 (Spring 1978): 9-47; the quotation is from pp. 32-33.

The great divergence of opinion about the Appleton text exists not because of critical subjectivity, but owing to the incomplete nature of the text critics have read. In *Red Badge*, as he wrote it in manuscript, Crane tied together Henry's ambivalent conclusions about his place in the universe, his desertion of the tattered soldier, his continuing egotism, his failure to change in battle, and the very different matters of Conklin's blindly fated death, the cherry-voiced stranger's courageous optimism and kindness, and Wilson's step toward manhood and understanding. In Crane's original conception, all of these matters worked in close concert. But with the rebellious passages deleted, Henry's extreme rationalizing was no longer the focus of his characterization in the novel. And with the final mention of Jimmie Rogers cut, Wilson's function as Henry's foil was blurred. Also the importance of Henry's promise to remain with the dying Conklin and the significance of his immediately subsequent desertion of the tattered man was obscured when Henry's justification for the desertion was deleted from the final chapter. Which is all to say that, after the cuts were made, the most marked clues to Crane's intentions in the story were gone.

Binder concluded with this tough, eloquent paragraph:[15]

> *The Red Badge of Courage* as Stephen Crane wrote it is the story of an episode in the life of Henry Fleming. The final mystery of heroism in this episode is that Henry finds no real identity or selfhood in battle; and his notions of "fate" remain justifications for his own errors, reinforcements for his youthful vanity. The intricacies of each character's thoughts and feelings in the continuum of the war press along their own paths, perhaps breaching final walls, perhaps not. Conklin is a man before he goes to battle; Wilson becomes one; Henry does not change. From the first, we sense the advancing edge of Henry's expectations for himself; but as the story proceeds, in the no-man's land between his wavering self-image and his intermittent scorn and eagerness concerning bravery, there is no footing for a real change to prevail, never an awakening in him to what manhood is, only the confusion of his delusive explanations.

15. "The *Red Badge of Courage* Nobody Knows," p. 41.

170

As it had turned out, Binder had earned the right to make such sweeping judgments by doing the dogged work of scholarly research (he found several documents which Bowers had missed, including an important letter from Hitchcock to Crane in January 1896 accepting *The Third Violet* but making it clear that some changes would be required) and by an equally dogged struggle to understand Crane's own character and his aesthetic intentions.[16]

After the *Norton Anthology of American Literature* appeared in the spring of 1979,[17] the users' reports which trickled in seldom mentioned the text of *Red Badge*, though there was occasional praise and some complaints about the novelty of the expanded text, and especially about the ellipsis dots Binder had placed at points where the source of the text changed. The main objections came from Donald Pizer, as we expected. In keeping with his longstanding notion that we are stuck with whatever the author agreed to have published, Pizer complained:[18]

> If an author himself has seen a book through the press, as Crane did for the *Red Badge* (he made the cuts in the manuscript, he— there is no evidence to the contrary—made the cuts in the typescript, and he corrected proof), then we should demand hard and incontrovertible proof that specific revisions were forced upon him before we reject those revisions. It is significant in this regard, I think, that though there has been much discussion of Crane's revision of the *Red Badge*, and that though all the evidence used by Binder except the *Third Violet* letter has been available to scholars engaged in this discussion for almost twenty years, no one has hitherto [that is, before my 1976 review] suggested that the basic reading text of the novel be returned to its manuscript form.

16. "The *Red Badge of Courage* Nobody Knows," p. 46. The importance of the letter is hard to describe in the absence of a full account of Hitchcock's edgy dance around Crane. Hitchcock was correct, polite, and resolute; he habitually got what he wanted from writers.

17. *The Norton Anthology of American Literature* (New York: W. W. Norton, 1979), II, 802-906.

18. "*The Red Badge of Courage* Nobody Knows: A Brief Rejoinder," Donald Pizer, *Studies in the Novel* 11 (Spring 1979): 77-81; the quotation is from pp. 79-80.

Pizer continued with an extended claim that my original preference for the manuscript, and Binder's preference, was based not
on editorial principles but literary taste:[19]

> Present throughout the preference by Parker, Binder, and Mail-
> loux for the manuscript version of the *Red Badge* is the assump-
> tion that a clear and consistent novel is better than an ambivalent
> and ambiguous one. The manuscript version is a good novel
> because we can readily understand Crane's contempt for Henry's
> egotism and delusions, the Appleton text is a bad novel because it
> is extremely difficult to fathom Crane's attitude toward Henry. The
> good and authentic Crane may be cynically subversive but he is
> clear; ambiguity, critical disagreement, and more than a hint of
> mixed authorial feelings about Henry are the result of a "maimed
> text" and also constitute bad fiction. But how valid is this assump-
> tion, one wonders, in the context of Crane's major work besides
> the *Red Badge*?... Crane's mature narrative voice, most close
> readers have sensed and Frank Bergon has recently brilliantly
> shown, made for complexity and fuzziness because he sought to
> render the impact of immediate experience on character rather
> than an authorial reading of experience. The best students of
> Crane, those attuned to the maturing of this voice and of Crane's
> responsiveness to the human condition—among them Green-
> field, Chase, Crews, Cady, and most recently and fully Levenson—
> have never doubted that the cutting of the heavy-handed and
> contemptuous irony of chapter 12 and the conclusion represents
> Crane's recognition, in the act of revision, of the falseness of this
> material to his fully conceived intent and strategy in the novel....
> We have, in other words, in the position taken by Parker, Binder,
> and Mailloux an expression of a preference for clarity through
> ironic heavy-handedness by three scholars whose work on Crane
> has largely been confined to Crane's writing before 1896, while
> two generations of critics who have tuned their responsiveness to
> Crane's vision and art on his work as a whole have found that the
> cut portions of the *Red Badge* are well cut indeed.

19. "A Brief Rejoinder," pp. 80-81. Pizer continued his campaign indirectly in
the attack on the Pennsylvania *Sister Carrie, American Literature* 53 (January
1982): 731-37, in commentary on those who are guilty of "a superficial editorial
romanticism which posits that an author's initial and 'instinctive' expression is of
greater worth than his later critical reflection" (p. 733); he also attacked the
restored *Red Badge* and the restored *Sister Carrie* at a 1982 textual conference at the
California Institute of Technology.

Some of this Pizer had said in 1975 to Peter Phelps. Of his new objections perhaps the most curious was the claim that Crane's mature narrative voice "made for complexity and fuzziness," made for, in Pizer's honorific word, ambiguity. I was as much a devotee of ambiguity as Pizer, or William Empson, I would have thought; in the late 1970s Brian Higgins and I were, after all, struggling to find the right praise for *Pierre; or, The Ambiguities.* But authorially planned and aesthetically functioning ambiguity was the desired quality, not fuzziness, or, still worse, indeterminateness. In 1979 Albert Rothenberg provided a powerful statement of the position I was taking against Pizer:[20]

> Among modern critics, ambiguity has been heavily emphasized as a factor in aesthetic appeal. While production of such ambiguity could surely be considered to be one of the functions of janusian thinking, a particular caution about the term "ambiguity" must be stressed in connection with literature and with art. Aesthetic ambiguity could not consist merely of indefinite or indeterminate meaning. Such ambiguity would be merely confusing and incomprehensible, and consequently of little value. Structured and defined ambiguity suggesting and yielding multiple meanings is the valuable, or the aesthetic, factor. Such definition and structure is not overt but implied, and consequently there is a quality both of indeterminacy and of control.

Quite contrary to Pizer's charge, I was prepared to assume that "a clear and consistent novel" could also be "an ambivalent and ambiguous" novel. It just happened that Crane had written a clear and consistent novel but that Appleton had published one which, at the end, was hopelessly confusing.

Aside from Pizer's, there were few comments in the next years. In *American Literary Scholarship, 1978* (published in mid-1980), Thomas Wortham accepted the superiority of the reconstructed text and declared that "the coherence of Crane's

---

20. Rothenberg, *The Emerging Goddess* (Chicago: University of Chicago Press, 1979), p. 364. Janusian thinking, in Rothenberg's definition (p. 55) "consists of *actively conceiving two or more opposite or antithetical ideas, images, or concepts simultaneously.*" In his remarkable but much earlier essay, "The Iceman Changeth: Toward an Empirical Approach to Creativity," *Journal of the American Psychoanalytic Association* 17 (April 1969): 549-607, Rothenberg had a slacker notion of ambiguity, just as he held a simpler Freudian view of revisions.

ironic vision is solidly established."[21] However, Wortham added these two sentences: "But the manuscript does not represent Crane's 'final' intention, any more than does the Appleton text. *The Red Badge of Courage* nobody knows is *The Red Badge of Courage* nobody will ever read because it was never completed in full accordance to Crane's artistic vision." I would disagree with the first of these sentences to the extent of saying that in this case the manuscript does represent, in all important respects, Crane's original intentions, which are the only intentions to possess artistic finality. I think the second sentence confuses the issues. Nothing of documentary nature suggests that Crane ever thought he had not completed the book in full accordance with his artistic vision. To the contrary, he knew he had written a wonderful book.[22] For the revised edition of his Twayne series book on Crane, Edwin H. Cady (one of Wortham's teachers) wrote a new introductory essay on "The Elusive Stephen Crane" in which he spoke out against the Virginia *Maggie*: "Like Donald Pizer, Joseph Katz, and Hershel Parker (and almost everybody else), I thought Bowers was wrong. As an original member of the CEAA Board and the quondam general editor of a major edition, I felt betrayed."[23] In Cady's view, the jury was not even out yet on *Red Badge*, although the "adversary process" was "in full swing." Turning from comments on Levenson's introduction, Cady appraised the state of the controversy over the text.[24]

Meanwhile, back on the stricken bibliographical field, Bowers and his hard-worked staff have two opponents—each of whom would seem to have something to fear from the other. The one seems to be a platoon led by Professor Hershel Parker, also textual editor of the Melville Edition, who, in a sense being more orthodox than the Pope, more royalist than the king, have found Bow-

21. "19th-Century Literature," *American Literary Scholarship: An Annual, 1978* (Durham: Duke University Press, 1980), p. 221.

22. See for instance his letter to Ripley Hitchcock, 30 January 1895, reporting the way the staff of the Philadelphia *Press* had spoken of the newspaper serialization; *Stephen Crane: Letters*, eds. R. W. Stallman and Lillian Gilkes (New York: New York University Press, 1960), p. 49.

23. Edwin H. Cady, *Stephen Crane*, rev. ed. (Boston: Twayne, 1980), p. 24.

24. Cady, pp. 24-25; the "chthonic" quotation below is from p. 25.

ers's text replete with error according to Bowers and have returned, perhaps puritanically, to the one true "conservative" copy-text, the Barrett manuscript. The third party [sic] is Professor Donald Pizer, who says of his new "Norton Critical Edition" that, in the light of Crane's long, hard effort to revise and revise and get it right, "we should permit Crane the last word—that of the Appleton text. . .the 1895 edition, conservatively emended" for "obvious errors."

Some of Cady's phrasings require commentary. I am associate general editor of the Melville edition—Hayford, Tanselle, and I are all "textual editors." Second, I advocated return not only to the Barrett manuscript but to the other surviving manuscript pages, and now, having learned from my student, would use *Current Literature* for copy-text where it supplies text of Chapter 4 missing from the manuscript. Third, although the quotation from Pizer is accurate, except that "obvious errors" should be "obvious typographical errors," Pizer does not say anything in this context about Crane's "long, hard effort to revise." Most interestingly, perhaps, Cady saw Binder's new text as "a very chthonic *Red Badge* indeed"; most disappointing, beyond doubt, was Cady's failure to revise his discussion of the novel to reflect the issues raised in the *Studies in the Novel* special issue and in the restored text of the novel.

As Pizer foresaw, critics were very slow to begin to come to terms with the new text and the claims made for it—or even to recognize that there is any need to come to terms with them.[25] The tendency among the very few who have mentioned the new evidence and new text has been, so far, to take quick evasive action.

Then on Friday, 2 April 1982, the front page of the New York *Times* appeared with a handsome photograph of Crane as a war

25. See Chester L. Wolford, *The Anger of Stephen Crane: Fiction and the Epic Tradition* (Lincoln: University of Nebraska Press, 1983), pp. xiii and 67. Wolford explains that he has "used the Virginia edition rather than Binder's edition in the *Norton Anthology of American Literature* (1979) not because the former is better but rather because all of Crane is conveniently available in that edition." Wolford focuses momentarily on the original Chapter 12 but says, rather cryptically, that since the restored "passages do little more than reaffirm the greatness of *The Red Badge*, the classical dicta of economy and symplicity ought to apply, and one giving a supposedly classical reading of a work ought to side with his sources."

correspondent and the opening paragraphs of Herbert Mitgang's story, " 'Red Badge' Is Due Out as Crane Wrote It." The
article began:

> A classic work of American literature that millions of readers have
> long regarded as the great Civil War novel—Stephen Crane's "The
> Red Badge of Courage"—is about to be brought out in full, just as
> the author wrote it.
>
> The novel was cut and changed for publication in 1895 to
> popularize it and to play down some of its gloominess. The new
> edition is 55,000 words—5,000 longer than the edition that stu-
> dents have considered the last word.
>
> The new version of the handwritten novel restores phrases,
> sentences, paragraphs and even an entire chapter...

All hell broke loose. Phones were ringing when the Norton
offices opened: people wanted to place orders. Binder was
interviewed by several radio stations, including National Public
Radio. A question about the text of *The Red Badge of Courage*
showed up in the New York *Times* Saturday Quiz on 3 April.
Time Magazine soon referred to the new text as a fact of literary
life. The Book of the Month Club bought the volume as an
Alternate (*"A classic restored to its original form*, Publisher's
price $14.95, Your price $10.95. One Book-Dividend Credit.").
Publisher's Weekly ran an article on the extraordinary sale of the
paperback rights to Avon for $60,000—this for a book that had
been long out of copyright.[26] All that remained, it seemed, was
the choice of the reconstructed text by the Library of America.

The furor quickly faded, and I began looking at indications
of the staying power of the restored text. The January 1983
Choice hailed the volume:[27]

26. Paul S. Nathan, "Rights & Permissions," *Publishers Weekly* 221 (18 June
1982): 53: "*Out of Public Domain.* Avon has paid $60,000 for a book frequently
reprinted without any money changing hands, and editorial director Bob Wyatt
exults in a note to this department: 'I can't tell you how happy this purchase makes
us.'... On the chance that other houses might be planning to compete at auction
for softcover rights to the reconstituted novel, Avon had registered a floor bid with
Norton. Encountering no such competition, it got the book for the floor."
27. *Choice* 20 (January 1983): 704.

. . . there has not been, heretofore, a good, readable text of Crane's "final intention"; now there is—a compact, handy little volume, scholarly, "definitive," yet not formidably for scholars only. Binder restores Crane's final intentions, unobtrusively appends supporting editorial apparatus, and nicely establishes the superior claim of author Crane over his editors. Ambiguities resulting from editorial intrusion are one thing; ironies carefully orchestrated by the author are another. Binder's text clarifies the former, and, in so doing, reveals more of the latter. Crane wins. Binder's accompanying 50-page essay is a masterful account of the tangled tale of the revision of *Badge* en route to publication and persuasively argues for the aesthetic and thematic superiority of Crane's final manuscript intention. Highly recommended for all libraries, all levels—secondary school through graduate school.

Choice later listed the book in *Outstanding Academic Books*,[28] one of 561 titles out of the 6849 books reviewed in the last time period. The importance of being on this list, of course, is that many libraries on restricted budgets use the *OAB* listing as a guide in their book buying. Libraries, decades hence, will have the volume.

But whether teachers of American literature will teach the book as Crane wrote it is another matter. High school teachers may well find it hard to justify teaching a book which cannot be used as a maturation story but instead is an ironic story in which an egotistical kid gets away with desertion and at the end is so gleeful that no one caught him that he has no time for compassion for a fallen comrade. As for the possible fate of the text in college courses, professors of American literature tend to be more shortsighted in such matters than their nonacademic contemporaries. Journalists, themselves inured to editorial slashings of their prose, understand how a writer can let something be published in some imperfect form if the alternative is not to have it published in any form. Furthermore, journalists know that ordinary people are interested in restored texts of classic works, whether of literature or film; they even know that an alert minority of the purchasers of the Sunday New York *Times* will want to know about restorations of text and music in Verdi and

28. *Outstanding Academic Books and Nonprint Materials* (Middletown, Conn.: Choice, 1983), p. 14.

177

Berg. The Mitgang article, in fact, was picked up all over the country, and Noel Polk sent me a clipping from the Paris *Herald-Tribune*. Obviously the best judges of newsworthiness, the journalists, are sure that the restoration of a classic is news. Professors, however, are inhibited by their marked-up texts of the old *Red Badge*, beautifully scored for two fifty-minute sessions, and they also have, if they have published on the book, vested interest in what they used as text, a matter of some importance if they counted animal images or religious symbols. Matters are still worse for the professor who has heard of literary theory from James Thorpe and knows that the published text is the only one which can possibly have integrity. Ironically, it may not matter what the professors think. There may not be, after all, ready access to the book as Crane wrote it. In the fall of 1984 the *Norton Anthology of American Literature* is being revised, and the preliminary contents sheet shows other Crane selections, not *Red Badge*. Worse, the price of the Avon paperback, available in September 1983, is $6.95.[29] The University of Delaware Bookstore kicked back my order form with the suggestion that I choose a cheaper text. No, I said, I had a reason for specifying the Avon edition. How many professors will choose it, especially for an undergraduate class? If Norton does drop the restored *Red Badge* from the anthology, will a competing anthology rush to purchase rights to it?

If I had foreseen all that has happened, I would have copyrighted the text myself so I could have made it available, free, to any publisher who wanted it. My purpose always was to disseminate the text, not to profit from it. Even now, I suppose, I could break the Norton copyright, since I laid out the method for reconstructing the text in 1976, risking, I knew very well, the possibility that someone would rush into print with it. But could I get a publisher to agree to keep it available at a dollar or

29. In August 1983 Avon mailed out an extraordinary sixteen-page promotional brochure, *A Guide to the Only Complete Edition of the Famous American Classic, "The Red Badge of Courage"*—including, on page two, a facsimile (pasted up in three columns) of part of Mitgang's review, slashed diagonally across the page by two larger-type paragraphs from Binder's celebration of the restored text; then on pp. 3-4 followed the opening three paragraphs of Binder's essay and on pp. 5-16, the final section of the essay (as printed in the Norton hardback). The only failing was that the orange envelope contained no clue to the contents.

two a copy, or even better, in a 50¢ paperback? As it stands, I may have defeated my idealistic purpose by not keeping control of the text. Here we go into an area ambivalent and ambiguous enough to delight Donald Pizer. It's a tough situation, one with unforeseen and undesired ironies. A $6.95 paperback is not what I had in mind. You see, now, why I could not call this chapter "The Private History of a Campaign that Succeeded."

Chapter 7

Norman Mailer's Revision of the *Esquire* Version of *An American Dream*:

The Authority of "Built-in" Intentionality

As I have suggested in previous chapters, a number of classic American novels until recently have been known only (or most commonly) in forms which resulted from perfunctory alterations, often performed by a publisher, after the works had been completed. Among such works are *Huckleberry Finn*, *Maggie: A Girl of the Streets*, *The Red Badge of Courage*, *Sister Carrie*, and *Flags in the Dust*. The posthumous *Billy Budd, Sailor* is still commonly printed with a "Preface" which was merely a section discarded from a late chapter, and another posthumous work, Mark Twain's *The Mysterious Stranger*, until recently was known only in a form which combined the body of one version with the conclusion of another. Norman Mailer's Dial Press version of *An American Dream* belongs among these books as a text which the author himself damaged by a handful of small excisions and slight verbal substitutions during his careful polishing of the version which he had serialized in *Esquire*.[1]

Whatever status critics ultimately accord the work (either in the *Esquire* text, still available in libraries or purchasable from

1. This chapter grew out of a collation of the *Esquire* text against the Dial Press text which Bruce Bebb and I made in 1976. It originally appeared in the *Bulletin of Research in the Humanities* 84 (Winter 1981): 405-30 (actually published in January 1983).

dealers in old magazines, though not readily available for class-room use, or in an eclectic text Mailer could construct to retain the passages misguidedly omitted while incorporating the improvements), certain of the revisions for the Dial version deserve attention not only from students of the American novel but from anyone interested in theoretical problems of literary revision, in particular those that arise out of a writer's retrenching a small part of a complex, coherent pattern. The history of *An American Dream* illustrates the fact that passages left untouched by the revising author may nevertheless be drastically affected—may be drained of authorial intentionality or may seem to acquire intentionality which is only adventitious, not authorial at all, though the words are still the author's. It also sheds light on the problem of when intentionality is built into a passage or a work as a whole (and what kind of revision is required if an author is to alter it). The evidence may be seen as continuing the argument of some previous chapters against Michael Hancher's theory that intention is something a writer pours into his text at the mystical moment he completes it, and against James Thorpe's opinion that intention is somehow infused by the act of publication. The evidence of Mailer's revisions of *An American Dream* supports the concept powerfully argued by John Dewey in the 1930s (and reaffirmed by Murray Krieger and Albert Rothenberg in the 1970s) that intentionality is built into a passage at the moment of composition, if at all; and I would add that aspects of it may persist, despite the author's attempts to remove it.

This chapter, you should know, does not purport to offer a complete textual history of *An American Dream*. In a vault of Mailer's are two large boxes of material on this novel, including manuscript and typescript pages antedating the magazine publication (most intriguing, perhaps, are the several versions of the opening) and two sturdy $1.19 F. W. Woolworth ledgers with covers stamped "RECORD" and "CASH" which contain paste-ups of the *Esquire* text on the rectos and some authorial notes and revisions.[2] The boxes do not contain the setting copy for the Dial edition (presumably another set of paste-ups from

2. These ledgers and other unpublished material are used through the courtesy of Robert Lucid and with the permission of Norman Mailer.

Esquire, more heavily revised) and do not include any Dial proofs. All Mailer's revisions of the *Esquire* text would interest students of his style—both those revisions which can be seen in his own handwriting and those which must be inferred from study of the variants in the book. (Some of the Dial variants, as you would expect, are editorial or compositorial.) Mailer had prided himself on learning to write while revising *The Deer Park*, and he refined his art as he prepared copy for the Dial *Dream*.[3] There is no reason to doubt his claim to have sounded every sentence ten times for timbre as he revised (indeed, sounding out sentences one at a time may have contributed to his missing a few places where his excisions leave passages dangling some lines or pages away, as when the narrator, Stephen Richards Rojack, still speaks out of "that calm" although the earlier reference to the calm has been deleted).[4] Certainly his claim to have revised forty percent of the pages (even thinking in terms of book pages) is a very low estimate. Most of the revisions are local—within a sentence, or involving only two or three contiguous sentences. Among the few extended passages which Mailer reworked thoroughly are (in the first chapter) the sexual adventure Rojack (former Congressman, professor of existential psychology, and television talk-show host) has with the maid, Ruta, in her room just after he has strangled his wife, Deborah, and his confrontation the next night with Deborah's father, the trucking tycoon Barney Oswald Kelly (in the eighth

3. See *Advertisements for Myself* (New York: G. P. Putnam's Sons, 1959), quoted from the reprint with a new preface by the author (New York: Berkley, 1976), pp. 204-14.

4. I will cite two editions of *An American Dream*: *Esquire* (abbreviated *Esq*) for January-August 1964, and the first book edition (New York: Dial Press, 1965). My discussion will make it clear which *Esquire* passages appear in the Dial version in revised form or not at all and (in a few cases) which passages appear in the Dial for the first time. I will not be telling you the precise point in the Dial text where an excision from *Esquire* was made or the precise point in the *Esquire* text where an addition was made in the Dial, but the revisions will be easy to locate. Anyone would still need to have the *Esquire* in hand in order to work seriously with my evidence. This system of citation is, I think, less cumbersome than it sounds.

For the deleted "calm" the citations are *Esq* (July), p. 44 and Dial, p. 184. Rojack's reference to "that calm" is at *Esq* (July), p. 42 and Dial, p. 184. The deletion weakens the pattern in which moments of profound calm occur during crises.

Here and in the next sentence Mailer's comments on the revision are from the paraphrase in Conrad Knickerbocker, "A Man Desperate for a New Life," *New York Times Book Review* (14 March 1965), p. 39.

chapter). In this last, and most revised chapter, Mailer added about three pages to Kelly's provocative hints of his incestuous relationship with Deborah (and his paternity of her daughter Deirdre) and a half-page coda in which Detective Roberts confesses wifebeating to Rojack. Mailer also introduced (or reintroduced—I've not been able to check the typescripts yet) more explicit sexual language throughout. Mailer also made a series of tiny changes which enhance the portrait of Cherry, the nightclub singer with whom Rojack falls in love several hours after murdering his wife, revisions which slightly alter (but do not damage) the hierarchy of characters by making her more nearly Rojack's equal, a fitter partner in talking metaphysics as well as in risking love. From most of this evidence someone could write a convincing analysis of Mailer's remarkable skill and thoroughness as a reviser. My concern, however, is with the small number of alterations which sabotaged characterization, structure, and even meaning in ways which Mailer could not have foreseen, much less intended. Mailer was simply wrong in thinking he could remove a few little pieces of the novel and still have the remainder mean what he had written it to mean, and be as good as it had been.[5]

A strange additional category of revisions was forced upon Mailer. He began writing *An American Dream* in September 1963, in answer to a self-imposed public challenge to write an important novel against a monthly deadline, just as Dickens and Dostoevsky had done.[6] Serialization began in the January 1964 *Esquire* and continued each month through the August issue, where book publication by Dial Press was promised for the fall of 1964, although in fact it was delayed into March 1965. Mailer began writing the book to take place in a month and a year that had not yet occurred, March 1965, so that the action would take place early in the year after the serialization and, he expected, the book publication. In the first installment an offstage character, minor but exerting powerful influence, is John F. Kennedy;

5. I should emphasize the craftsman's concentration displayed in most of Mailer's revisions and also in his notes to himself about checking for previous uses of a word or a close synonym, but that kind of careful aesthetic control frequently, as in this case, is accompanied by small lapses.
6. Mailer's promise to write a serial is in his "The Big Bite," *Esquire* (December 1963), p. 26.

and in all likelihood Mailer had already determined upon the similar offstage use he would make of Kennedy later in the novel, in passages yet unwritten. The January 1964 issue of *Esquire* was set up in November 1963, before President Kennedy was assassinated. Apparently the presses were stopped in order to put blue rectangles in place of Kennedy's and Lyndon Johnson's faces on the annual Dubious Achievement pages, but the cover was allowed to go out with photos of both men among the block of thirty-six faces of dubious achievers, and the opening of *An American Dream* was not reset. (In a cagy note for the March 1964 issue, the publisher, Arnold Gingrich, without mentioning Mailer's novel, indicated that some copies were distributed with the former President and the new President still on the Dubious Achievement pages.)[7] Quite aside from its effects on him personally, the assassination left Mailer with literary messes that had to be dealt with.

One problem was minor—that of liberties allowable with a living President but in bad taste with a slain one. In the first installment Rojack portrays himself as Kennedy's rival—and sometimes superior—in two ways. On a double date in Washington in November 1946 (or a few months later?) he stole—and seduced—his fellow congressman Jack Kennedy's girl, Deborah Caughlin Mangaravidi Kelly, the trucking heiress. Furthermore, during the war he had looked upon "the abyss" in consequence of killing men at close range: "Jack, I suspect, never saw that abyss. I don't think he ever executed anyone close enough to see their face." For the book version Mailer kept the double date but dropped the assertion that Deborah had been Kennedy's girl, and he reduced Rojack's now flippant-sounding speculation about Kennedy's military experience to "Jack, for all I know, never saw the abyss," a comment that carried fewer unintended resonances.

The other problem was more serious: Kennedy's death wrecked the original time scheme of *An American Dream*,

7. "Editor's Note" (March 1964), p. 16: "We felt that it would be in the interests of good taste to delete some of the pictures from our January issue, although we did not have enough time to make the changes in all editions" (a response to a reader who had asked if one of the "ominous blank blue spaces" had been meant to carry a picture of LBJ).

compounding the minor problems that were already there, such as the confusion of election month with month of taking office. Someone tried to salvage the situation for readers of *Esquire* by naming 1962 as the year of the action in the synopses which accompanied the February and March installments, but that year was plainly impossible.[8] As he revised for the book version Mailer took the only alternative to dropping Kennedy as a character and tried to move the action back to March of a year when Kennedy was living and was President. Since the death of Marilyn Monroe (August 1962) and the Cuban Missile Crisis (October 1962) were also built into the novel, March 1963 became the only possible date for the action. Mailer changed the year Rojack remet Deborah in Paris and married her from 1956 (I assume, a little uneasily, that the double date was in 1947 and not in 1946, the year reasonably accepted by the synopsis writer) to 1954, keeping the duration of the marriage as nine years (eight together and one separated). Mailer did a fairly thorough job, at the cost of cutting out a reference to Rojack's age (forty-four) and Deirdre's (twelve) while retaining a now impossible reference to women working for Rojack's election eighteen years ago (meaning eighteen and a half or almost nineteen), and in one overzealous stroke pushing back the time it took Rojack to acquire a doctorate in the Midwest and a full professorship in New York from a breathtaking nine years in the *Esquire* (around 1958, counting from 1949) to a near-miraculous seven years in the Dial (around 1956). (Neither the Esquire nine nor the Dial seven squares with the accompanying information that Rojack married Deborah in the year he became a full professor.)[9] As far as I know, no one has mentioned any connection between the assassination and the time scheme of *An American Dream*, but that tragedy accounts in large measure for the serial version's seeming eerily out of time and the

---

8. Mailer would not have made some of the errors in the synopses, such as giving the Sutton Place address to Deborah instead of the friend Rojack first visits and giving the year of the action as 1962 (a date accepted in at least one book on Mailer).

9. Rojack's age: *Esq* (April), p. 98 and Dial, p. 100; Deirdre's: *Esq* (August), p. 42 and Dial, p. 211; election workers: *Esq* (May), p. 127 and Dial, p. 136; academic wizardry: *Esq* (June), p. 115 and Dial, p. 167; first year at the New York university as the first year of marriage: *Esq* (May), p. 151 and Dial, p. 158.

book's containing not only anomalies but the overriding strangeness of having the story told retrospectively yet at a time when the narrator does not know Kennedy is dead. In literal terms, it is possible (Rojack could write the book between April and November 1963), but literalism is at war with the indefiniteness with which he departs at the end, bound for Guatemala and the Yucatán.

The damaging revisions I am concerned with, those made without such historical constraints, fall into a few overlapping categories. Some cuts were made, I suspect, because Mailer decided they were too obviously autobiographical or might seem so. Three of Rojack's memories of Harvard (enough to have filled a page or so in the book) make up, in number of words, roughly half of these deletions. Numerically, the largest set deals with Rojack's fears of various kinds, including fear of women and fear of failing in sex with women as well as fear of being raped homosexually or (if imprisoned) of longing for a young man.[10] Other deleted passages deal with Rojack's thoughts which are explicitly about the topic of homosexuality or which have some homosexual component. Two short but crucial deletions deal with his response to other male characters as having psychological complexities equal to his own—a response which violates the venerable American taboo against portraying men as being sensitive to each other in ways which cannot exclude awareness of their sexuality. In the novel as he wrote it, Mailer explored the psychology of masculinity more courageously than any major American writer had done since Melville (*Pierre, Clarel*) and Whitman (*Leaves of Grass*). It was in the men's magazine, at that time a periodical more welcome in barber shops than on coffee tables, rather than in the later hardback, that Mailer's hero possessed a sexual consciousness

10. *Esq* (March), p. 144 and Dial, p. 72 (the serial reads "I was game to them at this moment, but in about the way a naked whore would be game if she were dragged into their hut on the dawn and they took her one by one rather than ripping overpowered charges of Magnum into ducks sitting on the water fifteen yards away"); *Esq* (March), p. 148 and Dial, p. 87 (the serial reads "I would lie in a cell at night with nothing to do but walk a stone square floor and dream through heats of desire for one of the girls in the men's wing of the prison, one of those girls with all but a woman's body (and a man's organs) and I would die through endless stupors and expired plans").

liberated beyond the banalities to which masculine conscious-
nesses were soon to be raised en masse. During the next decade
representatives of Women's Liberation routinely denounced
Mailer for his regressive and repressive sexual attitudes, and a
representative male critic (having completed his manuscript
with the support of "men's groups" in two states) could loftily
observe that "Rojack, in accord with Mailer's own biases, is
caught up in the savage world of *machismo.*" Not in *Esquire*, he
wasn't, although he may seem to be in the Dial version.[11]

As that last quotation reminds us, we cannot talk for long
about the excisions of passages dealing with male sexuality
without running dead against Mailer's celebrity. By having his
hero murder his wife Mailer guaranteed that reviewers would
recall, and gloat over in print, the notorious fact that he had
stabbed his wife (his second wife) in 1960, and he provided an
abundance of other parallels between himself and his character.
The equation of writer and hero was made immediately and still
persists; just as we used to encounter "Ishmael-Melville" in
critical discussions, we encounter the term "Norman Rojack"
or, coyly varied, "Stephen Mailer." And in fact the book did
draw on Mailer's own experiences, sometimes in ways which he
was aware of but reviewers could not be, as when he adapted his
own account of witnessing an autopsy in the Ozarks for Rojack's
narrative.[12] Having put so much of his public and private life
into his hero during the extraordinarily pressured composition,
having pushed his ambitious novel-on-demand onward even as
hostile comments were accumulating about the monthly installments, Mailer had ample cause to become hypersensitive to
aspects of the book that could be seized upon by critics dis-
posed not to like it. Even excluding members of the anti-Mailer
cliques, would not many reviewers leap at the chance to point
out passages referring to homosexuality and make arch comments about what Mailer might be revealing? An uneasy state of
concern for how passages were being or might be taken may
account for Mailer's otherwise peculiar deletion of Rojack's

11. Stanley T. Gutman, *Mankind in Barbary* (Hanover: University Press of
New England for the University of Vermont, 1975), pp. viii, 110.
12. Robert F. Lucid's introduction to Laura Adams, *Norman Mailer: A Comprehensive Bibliography* (Metuchen: Scarecrow, 1974), pp. xiv-xv.

explanation to Cherry of how he had always felt about being a breech baby—a passage which was part of a pattern in the novel of miscarriage, deliberate abortion, and unnatural birth. Did Mailer cut it because he didn't want readers to assume he had been a breech baby himself? Now that the question comes up, had he been? With another writer, one less compulsive in his self-exposure, such questions could constitute inappropriate intrusion into his privacy, to say the least, but the erosion of ordinary decencies is one of the prices Mailer has paid for his intermittent exhibitionism. He has also paid for remaining intensely alive, in his life and in his work, to the realities of latent homosexuality—paid by giving others the opportunity to bait him with homosexual innuendo (as when a reporter dubbed him and Jimmy Breslin "The Odd Couple" during his mayoralty campaign) and paid by displaying, on occasion, an excessive dread of being associated with homosexuality (as when he at first rejected a poster as "faggy green").[13] We know too much about him and guess at more. My guess, in the case of *An American Dream*, is that he became concerned, at some late point during the revisions, that some passages were conspicuously liable to be used against him. As clinical psychiatrists are telling us, literary revision may involve disguise and defensiveness;[14] having been open as he composed, a writer may well seek to make himself less vulnerable as he revises. Maybe Mailer's retrenchments for the Dial version prove that growing

13. Joe Flaherty, *Managing Mailer* (New York: Berkley, 1971), pp. 47, 71.

14. Albert Rothenberg, *The Emerging Goddess* (Chicago: University of Chicago Press, 1979), p. 353. Rothenberg goes on to declare that in his experiments creative writers demonstrate greater anxiety when faced "with their substituted or later used words and phrases from successive revisions than with all other types of stimuli," but he does not speculate specifically on why this is so. Are they more anxious because they remember the earlier anxiety which compelled them to substitute new words for those they had written? In his earlier essay on O'Neill, "The Iceman Changeth: Toward an Empirical Approach to Creativity," *Journal of the American Psychoanalytic Association* 17 (April 1969): 549-607, Rothenberg cited with less qualification the argument "that deletions in the writing of patients in treatment can represent attempts to conceal unacceptable thoughts" (p. 563; see I. Roxon-Ropschitz, "The Act of Deleting and Other Findings in Writings of Neurotics," *Psychiatry* 9 [1946]: 117-21). The whole of Rothenberg's long essay on O'Neill is of great significance for literary critics, although it has been generally ignored, never, for instance, having been mentioned in *American Literary Scholarship*.

up in macho U.S.A. is a burden to the best male literary mind around as much as it is to every little boy who dreads being called a sissy.

Whatever his motives, Mailer paid for the retrenchments—paid in ways and degrees that cannot be precisely measured, both in the reputation of *An American Dream* itself and in the consequent darkening of his general reputation. But he also paid in ways that *can* be measured, for we can readily enough see how the excisions led critics to misunderstand the book. I do not mean the reviewers; it would take a separate study to chart their motives in misunderstanding it, for no major American novel of the century, indeed none since *Pierre*, has evoked such vehement and even perverse abuse of both author and book. I mean later, calmer critics, especially those who have cared enough about Mailer to write books on his works. These critics of *An American Dream* display a remarkable inconclusiveness about who the main characters are. Knowing the whole of Mailer's writings, they see perfectly well what most (not all) of the themes are and recognize most of the structural patterns, but although they all agree that Kelly is Rojack's most formidable opponent, they don't know how to rank all the other characters Rojack confronts. Robert Solotaroff plays up Rojack's "silent contest with the Mafioso nightclub manager," Tony, while mentioning Detective Roberts's name only once until three pages before the end of a fifty-five page chapter, where he frankly admits that he doesn't know what to make of him and so improvises, since "*some* explanation can always be worked out" for the importance of a character. Gutman does not even mention Roberts by name, and Robert J. Begiebing barely mentions him, while declaring that "Rojack tests his courage and new psychic powers against the ex-prize fighter Romeo and the mafioso Tony." Begiebing says that Rojack confronts "four principal figures," Deborah, Ruta, Cherry and Kelly.[15] In any list of major

---

15. Robert Solotaroff, *Down Mailer's Way* (Urbana: University of Illinois Press, 1974), p. 165 (on Tony) and p. 176 (on Roberts). Robert J. Begiebing, *Acts of Regeneration* (Columbia: University of Missouri Press, 1980), pp. 71 and 62. Andrew Gordon in *An American Dreamer* (Rutherford: Fairleigh Dickinson Press, 1980) comes closest to seeing Roberts's significance but (as I will show later) cannot make up his mind as to Roberts's function. Begiebing rightly calls attention (p. 60, n. 5) to Solotaroff's "tone of tongue-in-cheek" throughout the chapter, but

opponents, Ruta, Romeo and Tony don't belong, but Roberts and the black singer Shago Martin do belong—and most critics all but ignore Roberts and argue about Shago's function. These recent critics are not flounderers or wafflers but earnest readers of a text which is radically flawed. The failure of such good critics to agree on something so simple as who the main characters are strikes me as the best possible sort of empirical evidence that Mailer had indeed damaged his novel—and by the smallest of excisions.

The Harvard memories were not all deleted. Mailer retained the implied initial contrast of athletic careers at Harvard, "Prince Jack" taking honors over "Raw-Jock," and he left in other mentions—Rojack's memory of House Football that comes as he runs toward East River Drive and Deborah's body, the memory of the cold in Sever Hall as he gets into Cherry's chilly bed before she joins him, and the memory of once acting the role of young Harvard banker while on an excursion with Deborah to hear Shago Martin.[16] From the description of Rojack's journey to his apartment on the second day of the story, Mailer cut a Harvard-connected passage (in which Rojack looks into an imaginary mirror):

> So I attempted to see my face. Literally. As if I were looking into a mirror. And I conceived that face. I looked at myself, my face with its large head, a victim's face at its worst, weak and puffy, and at best—I was a Doctor of Mirrors—strong good rugged features always seemed more impressive than myself, yes that well-groomed rugged head came near to satisfy the features of a war

---

the exasperating tone (as well as the refusal to settle down to reading the novel) may owe something to frustration at trying to make sense of the Dial text. Like others who first read the novel in the serial version, Solotaroff seems to have forgotten its special qualities and thinks almost exclusively of the Dial text. I am in all seriousness when I say that in James J. Gibson's terms, Solotaroff's peculiar behavior (peculiar to this chapter) is understandable as a consequence of an absence of stimulation. In extreme cases, such as sensory deprivation experiments, the "perceptual systems seem to go on trying to function even without input, racing like a motor without a load." See *The Senses Considered as Perceptual Systems* (Boston: Houghton Mifflin, 1966), p. 303.

I reviewed the very different and very good books by Gordon and Begiebing in *Studies in American Fiction* 10 (Spring 1982): 121-24.

16. House Football: *Esq* (March), p. 90 and Dial, p. 58; Sever Hall: *Esq* (May), p. 125 and Dial, p. 126; banker: *Esq* (July), p. 41 and Dial, p. 180.

hero, quite a head to have grown from the thin self-doubting face of a young lieutenant fresh out of Harvard. I never felt as if I belonged to that older face, the interior was poorer than the surface, the interior was still related to some dark thin frigid college boy locked in a crush on big brother's virile head, yes a weak part of me put on that face each morning like a young squire lifting his helmet.

Mailer also cut a Harvard recollection from Rojack's trip from his apartment to meet Roberts at the precinct house:

There was a hint of a good sunset on the river which promised the next day would be clear. And for a minute I stopped on a side street and watched some boys playing stickball in the near-dark, getting some ten seconds of play between the passing of the cars. On a premature spring night twenty-five years ago I had come back to New York from Harvard and walked the streets, pulling out of the damp mild air some intoxication for the future. I had been full of Thomas Wolfe and swore a vow I would conquer the city someday, and later spent the evening alone in a burlesque house, the powdered breasts of the back line and the noise of the traffic horns outside riding a velvet roller coaster of apprehension and desire.

Finally, from the aftermath of Rojack's brutal beating of Shago Martin, the black singer who was Cherry's previous lover, Mailer cut Rojack's memory "of trips up to Harlem" and his "old Harvard pride for having a Negro as a close friend":

That was gone a little now, along with the rest. Twenty plus years ago one had Negroes for close friends and was fiercely snobbish of it; now one signed petitions, initiated interracial programs on campus, contributed money, attended mass meetings. . . .

These excisions involved no rewriting: Mailer took the hunks out and slapped the loose ends together.[17]

---

17. Mirror: *Esq* (May), p. 127 and Dial, p. 133; Wolfe: *Esq* (May), pp. 148-49 and Dial, p. 152; Negro friends: *Esq* (July), p. 107 and Dial, p. 201. Perhaps Mailer decided that the literary ambition implied in the memory of Thomas Wolfe would seem too autobiographical (despite his own majoring in aeronautical engineering); Rojack, a government major, makes no other references to an ambition to emulate a fiction writer.

All three of these Harvard memories are powerful passages. The first is part of one of the best aspects of the novel as it appeared in *Esquire*, an attempt to explore the gap between Rojack's inner doubts and exterior strengths, a gap defined in the first chapter of the novel as the distance between Rojack's "public appearance" and his "secret frightened romance with the faces of the moon" ("phases" in the Dial text). In particular, the first Harvard memory is an attempt to deal honestly with the persistence of his idealized adolescent emotions into middle age in the form of suppressed doubts about his maturity and distrustful envy of his own rugged outer self. The passage is part of the *Esquire* version's acute sensitivity to male psychology, in particular the consequences of growing up male (or being male but not quite growing up) in an America where suppressing dangerous emotions is a mark of maturity. It is, to look at it in formal terms, the third mirror scene; the earlier two survive in the Dial version, the one in Deborah's apartment after Rojack has killed her and the one in the men's room of Tony's night-club, after Rojack has vomited there. One would expect the first two scenes to prepare for the third: buildup, buildup, payoff. If that was the case, then the Dial text has two buildup scenes but no payoff.[18]

The second deleted Harvard memory also deals with the discrepancy between aspiration and achievement. Rojack "had been full of Thomas Wolfe" and had sworn to conquer the city —a vow ironically commented upon by the way the young Rojack concluded the evening and by his present condition as a murderer, in danger of life imprisonment, his six-to-twenty-volume work on existential psychology unwritten, his seed going out on separate voyages to extinction and to life.[19] The third passage, dealing also with the contrast between youthful

18. My point is that the first two scenes are left in some sense dangling, uncontrolled. One of the crucial excisions from the original version of *The Red Badge of Courage* left the Appleton text with two buildup scenes involving Jimmie Rogers but without the payoff scene toward which the earlier two were building. This may not be mere irrelevant coincidence; such emotionally charged payoff scenes are more apt to attract the attention of a revising editor like Ripley Hitchcock or a revising author like Mailer.

19. Unwritten volumes: *Esq* (January) p. 80 and Dial, p. 17; voyaging seed: *Esq* (May), p. 127 and Dial, p. 133.

idealism and adult compromises, sheds light backwards on Rojack's protesting the beating of the Negro at the precinct the night before and also complicates the motives behind the way he had first responded to Shago and the way he had lost control and brutalized him. In the *Esquire* text killing Deborah has given Rojack grace with which he can confront what Begiebing calls his stifled obsessions, according to Mailer's theory of "the close relationship of one's being to one's deepest cellular functions":[20]

> Mailer incorporates his theory in *An American Dream* that by airing one's obsessions, by confronting the messages of disease and waste, and by engaging death, perversion, and fear, one may help a disproportionate or stifled self to become a balanced self growing toward Life.

Rojack's new struggle to grow toward Life has loosed a flood of memories of twenty or more years before—bittersweet memories which challenge him with their ironic interplay of youthful ambition against imperfect success, present actuality against future possibility. He remembers so vividly because after killing Deborah he has been freed to feel the same ardent emotions which had suffused his experiences during his college years and which had been suppressed throughout the long manipulative tyranny of his marriage. In the Dial, without such an outpouring of memories, less was at stake for Rojack in the past, less is at stake in the present, and less is at stake for the future.

Under what looks like a similar impulse to reduce Rojack's emotionality, Mailer systematically removed from throughout the *Esquire* text some three dozen references to his being fearful. Sometimes the changes almost reverse the meaning, as when "I was not even unduly scared" becomes "I was not even scared." At particular points in the Dial version, Rojack does not have a "hint of fear" or a "mincing" fear, is not "as close to hysterics" as he has ever been, does not have a "tremor" in his handwriting, does not need to avoid being photographed for the tabloids with his head humped "in fear" behind a hat, does not have a "familiar dread," does not feel a fear as "acute as

20. Begiebing, p. 68.

stage fright," is "always afraid" but not "always afraid of a woman," does not feel "anxiety," "apprehension," and "quick fear" about being on his way to see Kelly, does not admit to being afraid (but only to being "a little" afraid), does not say that he is a coward but only that he thinks he is, does not admit that fear was "all" of him, and does not have a hand "fluttering" (femininely?) out of control but merely "shivering."[21] These tiny changes make a difference, partly by sheer number but more because of the kinds of fears which are reduced or denied in particular situations, especially confessions of sexual fear and, perhaps even more important, intellectual fear—the fear like that of a savage at the moment of conceiving the wheel, the fear of following out all the implications of a thought.[22] Fear and trembling remain built into the Dial version (Mailer even added Kelly's reference to Kierkegaard).[23] But Rojack's "not inconsiderable thesis" as a professor of existential psychology, after all, is that "magic, dread and the perception of death" are the "roots of motivation."[24] In Kelly's sarcastic summary (cut from the book) Rojack's "little idea" is that "God is not love but courage." In both versions, Kelly recapitulates Deborah's account of Rojack's ambition—how he "would like to blow up poor old Freud by demonstrating that the root of neurosis is cowardice rather than brave old Oedipus." Such a hero might well, in Kelly's taunting word, do "fieldwork" on the parapet of

21. Unduly: *Esq* (January), p. 77 and Dial, p. 3; hint: *Esq* (January) p. 80 and Dial, p. 17; mincing: *Esq* (February), p. 112 and Dial, p. 48; hysterics: *Esq* (March), p. 91 and Dial, p. 63; tremor: *Esq* (March), p. 92 and Dial, p. 70; tabloids: *Esq* (March), p. 144 and Dial, p. 73; familiar dread: *Esq* (March) p. 148 and Dial, p. 86; acute: *Esq* (April), p. 99 and Dial, p. 104; anxiety: *Esq* (June), p. 114 and Dial, p. 165; little: *Esq* (June), p. 148 and Dial, p. 175; think: *Esq* (August), p. 43 and Dial, p. 213; all: *Esq* (August), p. 104 and Dial, p. 255; fluttering: *Esq* (August), p. 104 and Dial, p. 257.
22. *Esq* (March), p. 149 and Dial, p. 87 ("I wanted to get away from this trap I had created for myself out of the sensual lazy incapacity to start on the dangers of following my thought from the beginning to the end"); *Esq* (May), p. 151 and Dial, p. 159 (in *Esquire* the considerably longer quotation from the lecture included the sentence: "This fear has been expressed best perhaps by Robert Oppenheimer, who said, "I know I am on the track of something huge when I realize the idea and am filled immediately with terror and awe."); *Esq* (June), p. 114 and Dial p. 165 ("This thought came to me with the fear equal to the fright of the savage who first conceived of the wheel").
23. *Esq* (August), p. 103 and Dial. p. 250.
24. *Esq* (January), p. 78 and Dial, p. 8.

the terrace of a Waldorf penthouse;[25] at least he should live with acute sensitivity to fear in his own actions and motivations, as Rojack does in the *Esquire* version. The changes make Rojack less a tough thinking-man, a little more the mere stolid tough guy. Once he had made his hero a professor of psychology with such a thesis about human motivation, Mailer had denied himself any chance of settling for a tough-guy hero for his book version, but he still could, and did, somewhat reduce Rojack's emotional complexity, whether or not that was his purpose.

Even Mailer's crucial reduction of psychological complexity in two other male characters, Roberts and Shago Martin, involves a reduction of Rojack: if they are not complicated, neither is his reponse to them. The first of these deletions occurs when Rojack meets Roberts on East River Drive beneath Deborah's apartment. Having thrown her body out of the window (and paused for a second fast stand-up sexual encounter with Ruta), Rojack has reached the street and begun playing the bereaved husband, making sure to get blood on his hands and cheeks. His detachment reminds him of having to say "Oh, darling; oh, baby" while having sex with some woman who was not attractive to him. Mailer deleted the detachment along with the description of what Rojack sees when he finally meets Roberts's eyes after having avoided them:[26]

> to my considerable surprise (although half of me after all seemed sufficiently far removed from all of this to be living like a gentleman at liberty) I liked him. There was a glint in his eye. I'd met an equal. This man had detachment to equal mine.

Just below, Mailer also deleted mention of "the controlled murder which rested in the eyes of this detective"—a contrast with Rojack's own uncontrolled murder. The next deletion of this kind occurs when Shago Martin lets himself into Cherry's apartment and orders Rojack out. Mailer cut a passage in which Rojack feels a fine little joy in knowing that Shago, like Roberts, is capable of killing him. In the Dial, Shago is "capable of murder," still, but Rojack does not, when he looks at him, have a

25. *Esq* (August), p. 103 and Dial, p. 251.
26. *Esq* (March), p. 90 and Dial, p. 60.

"poor tortured beast" of a soul which was, in Kiplingesque rhythm and language, "ready to sing out, 'Your last best chance is one good war with an equal face to face.'" In the *Esquire* version, Shago, like Roberts, is an equal to Rojack, and their confrontation is memorable: "Our eyes met and stayed together for a long time. There was an even raw gaze in his, which stung like salt on the surface of my eyes, and something back of that, a sense of a man so locked in complication that I almost looked away." In the Dial version their eyes stay together, but not for long, and Rojack does not mention Shago's psychological complexity, does not say there was "something back" of the raw gaze, "a sense of a man so locked in complication" that he almost looked away.[27] Like the Harvard memories and like the admissions of failure and fearfulness in the *Esquire* version, these passages about Roberts and Shago complicate Rojack's characterization: tormented as he is, as Andrew Gordon says, by fears "of failure, homosexuality, castration, and death,"[28] he retains or has somehow achieved (but only in the *Esquire* text) the ability to acknowledge similar complications in other men.

Mailer had built *An American Dream* upon a series of confrontations, always stern business for a man who sees a confrontation as "a meeting whose outcome is unknown."[29] The confrontations in the *Esquire* version are mainly with worthy opponents, with "equals," to use Mailer's recurrent word, although some of the stronger effects derive from his deliberate debasement of the pattern, as when Rojack brings a cheap version of his psychic artillery to bear upon someone conspicuously his inferior. Almost always the confrontation involves eye-to-eye contact, as the derivation of the word suggests—often a stare-down. (Obvious—and novelistically clever—variations are Rojack's encounters by telephone with Arthur, his television producer; with his department chairman, Tharchman; and with Deborah's friend Gigot.) Kennedy is the first of these worthy

27. *Esq* (July), p. 42 and Dial, p. 183.
28. Gordon, p. 147. A critic determined to celebrate Mailer's genius as a reviser could argue that by deleting Rojack's explicit equality with Roberts and Shago he was creating subtler effects, showing instead of telling. I would say that *An American Dream*, in serial and in book version, is a novel in which Mailer tells and shows, tells and shows.
29. *Cannibals and Christians* (New York: Dial Press, 1966), p. 175.

opponents. No eye-contact is mentioned, but Rojack prides himself (in *Esquire*) on stealing Kennedy's girl, and measures his capacities and achievements against Kennedy's, never having "any illusion" that his heroism "was the equal" of Kennedy's. The first stare-down is with the fourth German, whom Rojack has mortally wounded but who nevertheless advances upon him with a bayonet. Rojack "could not face his eyes," then when he did look into them he "faltered before that stare." It is memory of the fourth German that makes Rojack quit his career in politics because he "was lost in a private kaleidoscope of death." Rojack's host at a Sutton Place party is not a rival to stare down, but there is a possibility that in his sexual adventures he is "precisely like" Rojack. The question of a worthy adversary comes up again in the memory of Rojack's boxing with another guest at a party, only to have Deborah accuse him of "bullying that poor man"—a man older than himself; then when Rojack refused a later challenge Deborah treacherously accused him of being afraid to fight a younger man. With heels on, Deborah is a least an inch taller than Rojack, and his struggle with her in the first chapter is presented as a battle between equals, or even against a foe more formidable than he: she almost has the strength to lift him off the ground, something few male wrestlers can do. Having killed her, Rojack gains so much grace that as he looks in the mirror he has "eyes to equal at last the eyes of that German." Soon afterwards he has a staring contest with Ruta: "there was a look in my face—I suppose I was ready to kill her easy as not; my look cracked the glitter of fury in her eye." Then Rojack meets Roberts, who both in the serial and the book has "the sort of cold blue eyes which live for a contest." But in the book there is not the same contest, for there is no meeting of equals, and there is no longer any "controlled murder" in Roberts's eyes. (This deletion leaves Roberts's behavior the next day inexplicable, when after learning that he must free Rojack he looks as if he will attack him with the telephone receiver then seizes his own jaw "in a grip which must have been equal to pressing a button in the machinery of himself for it served to return his control.") Later Rojack does his best to "stare back" at Leznicki, the other detective, and Roberts and Rojack stare at each other until the policeman looks away. Then in Tony's club Rojack and Romeo engage in a stare-down ("We locked one stare into the other") which Rojack wins—an easy contest, since Romeo has "no ideas in his eyes, only pressure." Of sex with Cherry, Rojack says: "our wills now met, locked in a contest like an exchange of stares which goes on and on."[30]

Then the rest of the book begins to take shape around two major confrontations. Rojack must get ready to meet Roberts the second day and afterwards must prepare himself to meet Deborah's father. During the dreaded interview at the precinct house Rojack and Roberts compliment each other as worthy adversaries (the Dial reduces Roberts by omitting Rojack's compliment), then when the threat of arrest has passed, thanks to Kelly's intervention, Rojack sees himself and Roberts as equal antagonists, but equal in shame, like sold-out wrestlers relaxing in the dressing room after one of their fixed bouts. Cherry tells of a confrontation in Las Vegas when she "finally stood up to somebody, even to even"—the king of narcotics in Los Angeles —and she recalls how Rojack had faced up to Romeo. Rojack goes from having met Roberts to getting ready to meet Kelly, but Mailer introduces a major surprise—Shago enters Cherry's apartment and an unexpected confrontation follows, although not fully a contest of equals in the Dial, since the explicit reference to their equality is deleted. Shago draws a knife but does not use it (and would not have used it, according to Cherry). Rojack grabs him from behind and batters him against the floor then shoves him down the stairs. Later in the *Esquire* version (but less so in the Dial) Rojack and Cherry honestly face their ambivalent feelings about his unfair victory over Shago, in a scene that recalls by contrast Deborah's malevolent taunting of Rojack for taking advantage of a weaker opponent and evading a superior one. And we learn from Cherry that Shago had come in on her and Tony and that Tony, unlike Rojack, had

30. Kennedy: *Esq* (January), p. 77 and Dial, p. 2; faltered: *Esq* (January), p. 78 and Dial, p. 5; kaleidoscope: *Esq* (January), p. 78 and Dial, p. 7; precisely like: *Esq* (January), p. 79 and Dial, p. 10; bullying: *Esq* (January), p. 80 and Dial, p. 16; German: *Esq* (February), p. 109 and Dial, p. 38; glitter: *Esq* (February), p. 111 and Dial, p. 42; blue eyes: *Esq* (March), p. 90 and Dial, p. 60; controlled murder: *Esq* (March), p. 90 and Dial, p. 60; telephone: *Esq* (May), p. 150 and Dial, p. 158 (I quote the Dial version because that is the text where the passage is inexplicable; it differs in minor ways from the serial text); stare back: *Esq* (March), p. 144 and Dial, p. 74; Romeo: *Esq* (April), p. 100 and Dial, p. 107; Cherry: *Esq* (May), p. 125 and Dial, p. 127.

"cracked up before him."[31] Then the climactic contest with Kelly goes off in the book much as in the serial, despite the numerous revisions, except that, as I will show, the contest lacks some of its power because Rojack's characterization in the first seven chapters has been pervasively weakened. The pattern of confrontation remains built into the Dial version, but the deletion of Roberts's and Shago's explicit equality with Rojack sabotages the structure of the novel as effectively as the assassination had wrecked its time scheme.

When Rojack no longer perceives Roberts as an equal, the stakes in the ensuing contest are changed, for if Roberts is not a dangerous adversary, one with "controlled murder" in his eyes, then Rojack has less to dread through the two interrogations and less reason to identify with Roberts as he does. In the magazine version it was fitting for Rojack to rely on an equal, to feel as if Roberts were his "first ally and last best friend," his protection from the vicious other detective, Leznicki, and the brutal subordinate, O'Brien, but in the Dial version Rojack seems dependent on Roberts in an almost whiny, childish way, and his sense of a special "physical communion" coming from Roberts is bereft of the information which had made it acceptable. The most basic damage is to the hierarchy of the characters. Merely by the brief deletions, Roberts seems reduced toward (not all the way down to) the level of Leznicki and O'Brien. There is an awkwardness even in the *Esquire* version, where Leznicki sometimes takes charge and where on the second day Rojack, while mustering his courage to see Roberts again, thinks once with more dread of seeing Leznicki. But this problem is much worse in the book, where Roberts's higher status is not established at the outset. In the *Esquire*, it is a shocking comedown when Roberts begins to absorb some of the odor of the fat, farting O'Brien; not so much so in the Dial. And when the early comment about Roberts, "I liked him," is cut while "I liked Leznicki enormously—it was part of the fever" is retained, Rojack's hectic state of mind is less easy to understand, and the

31. Compliment: *Esq* (May), p. 178 and Dial, p. 155; sold-out wrestlers: *Esq* (May), p. 151 and Dial, p. 160; narcotics: *Esq* (June), p. 116 and Dial, p. 172; Tony: *Esq* (July), p. 106 and Dial, p. 198.

set of relationships shifts further.[32] The reader of the book will
have picked up the pattern of worthy adversary before Roberts
and Leznicki are introduced, so he may well feel that Leznicki is
the tougher opponent, but more likely he might just experience
some subliminal uneasiness at the disruption of a barely set up
pattern. The deletions cannot actively make Leznicki take on a
new role, but they do confuse his old role in relation to Roberts.

The trickiest alteration of Roberts's characterization is the
half-page paragraph Mailer added to the last chapter just after
Roberts and Rojack have watched Cherry die, beaten to death
(in grim mistake) by a friend of Shago's, and just after Roberts
has told Rojack that Shago is also dead, beaten to death in
Harlem. In this paragraph, the new ending to the chapter, Roberts takes Rojack to an after-hours joint where he first lies about
the night before, claiming to have drunk with an old mistress
till dawn and beaten her up, then, after a perfunctory query as to
Rojack's involvement in Shago's death admitting instead it was
his wife he had beaten up, then asking (with shocking lewd-
ness) if Cherry had been "a good piece of ass" and suggesting
ambiguously that she had worked for the police, then (rather
than fighting Rojack in the street) dissolving into a blubbery
lament for the way policemen lose their standards, shedding
tears for "the dirty polluted blood of all the world."[33] Did Mailer
write this sordid coda before he had deleted the initial equality
beteen the two men? If you imagine it added onto the *Esquire*
text, you'd say not likely, for although it produces a dramatic
revelation of character, the new view of Roberts is unbelievable.
Did Mailer add it as part of the attempt to blur Rojack's equality
with Roberts and Shago in the book version? If so, it seems a
gratuitous debasement, foul but not astonishing, of a character
who was not very important anyhow, who no longer had a high
position to fall from. Did Mailer add it forgetting that he had cut

32. Friend: *Esq* (March), p. 144 and Dial, p. 72; physical communion: *Esq*
(March), p. 90 and Dial, p. 62 (*Esquire* has "the sort of communion"); Leznicki: *Esq*
(March), p. 147 and Dial, p. 82.
33. *Esq* (August), p. 107 and Dial, p. 264.

the equality, in the hope of achieving some sort of grisly cathartic transition while enhancing his depiction of Rojack's superiority?[34] The critics can't tell, since they have read the coda only in the context of the Dial version, or haven't thought about the *Esquire* version carefully, even if that's what they first read. Not knowing what to make of the character of Roberts, at the end and throughout the book, some critics barely mention him. Solotaroff's diffidence is striking—he doesn't know what to say about him, except that Mailer likes that "type" (whatever type that is) and played the lead role, Police Lieutenant Francis X. Pope, in his second movie, *Beyond the Law*. Others try harder but also don't know what to say: Gordon can't decide whether Roberts is "the kindly father" or "the threatening authority figure" or the "feminized father" or maybe not a father figure at all but "another double for Rojack."[35] Again, these are not new-fangled connoisseurs of imprecision but very sensible critics not knowing what to do with something which does not make sense. A self-conscious practitioner of novelistic techniques, Mailer of course knows how easy it is to shift the relative ranks of characters, as he shows in the comment he gives to Rojack: "I have given an undue portrait of Deborah, and so reduce myself."[36] But during his revisions Mailer did not focus on the ways such effects could be created inadvertently.

In revision shock waves travel far, and the deletion of Roberts's equality with Rojack upsets the hierarchy of characters even in later scenes where Roberts is not present. Notably, in the absence of a previous contest with Roberts as an equal

34. Perhaps the documents in Mailer's vault will answer these questions. Meanwhile, we should remember that Mailer revised over a period of months, under different influences and impulses. In the *Esquire* version the section in Chapter 5 about the Clark Reed Powell Prize Lecture contained Rojack's parenthetical comment that he "could not even remember now whether it was *Harper's* or *The Atlantic*" which had reprinted it from the "professional journal" where it first appeared. In the ledger stamped "RECORD" Mailer in pencil elaborated Rojack's admission: "the fact that I could not remember that sort of fact thrust me into a passing panic. how could I ever stand up to Roberts if I could not even remember this." Here Mailer was building up to the confrontation between Rojack and Roberts, but by the time the revisions were finished he had not only *not* elaborated this particular scene, he had *diminished* it (by deleting the entire parenthetical comment). It would be a mistake to think of Mailer's revisions as if they were of a piece.

35. Solotaroff, p. 177; Gordon, p. 157.

36. *Esq* (January), p. 81 and Dial, p. 18.

adversary, the psychic battling in Tony's after-hours club lacks the clue that would tell the reader how to measure it. Readers of *Esquire* know that Rojack is hurling his psychic bullets not at worthy adversaries but at a tawdry assortment of after-hours boozers, and the fact that he engages them in conflict shows how near to collapse he is after his harrowing evening and night. For readers of the *Esquire* version, the scene comes as a kind of comic relief. Having survived the confrontation with Roberts and been allowed to go free, at least for the night, Rojack now in drunkenness and near-hysteria engages inferiors in trivial battles, from which the only gain is time to prepare himself for the risk of loving Cherry. The ludicrous, frantic quality of the original version was akin to the feverish mood which led Rojack to like Leznicki "enormously" and to the "exhilaration" which Mailer commented upon in the ledger marked "RECORD" as he added a passage in Chapter 5 for the Dial edition.[37] In the Dial, with the larger contest between Rojack and Roberts reduced, the psychic dueling seems to take

---

37. The *Esquire* version of Rojack's telephone conversation with Gigot did not contain the passage about the "kind of exhilaration" Rojack felt in talking with person after person on the telephone. The Dial addition is short but oddly redundant: "I was in a kind of exhilaration by now. There was a curious exhilaration as if we were all the subjects of a nation which had just declared war." The "RECORD" ledger contains a longer and clearer version of the passage than the one which appeared in the book: "It was idiotic to have said this, but I was in a kind of exhilaration by now, a fever which I could feel rise up in me, and pass over the line of the telephone. Separately they might all be sitting in shock, but talking to me, there was a curious exhilaration in Deborah's death, as if we were the subjects of a nation which has just declared war, and so tomorrow will be different." Mailer commented on his addition: "a reaction to the flipness of the conversations," and wrote a further comment on Rojack's state of mind as revealed in his addition: "He is in a kind of exhilaration of fever and feels as if he passes it to others. That all of them separately might be shocked, but talking to him, the exhilaration of a death (like the exaggeration of the secret glee with which we sometimes—to the unhappiness of our idea of ourselves—laugh internally as the misfortune of a friend." The illustration in the version of this paper in the *Bulletin of Research in the Humanities*, p. 428, lets you see at a glance what Mailer did. (In my quotations I have spelled "exhilaration" in the regular way.)

Since in this revision Mailer was adding a passage which explicitly characterized the feverish quality of Rojack's mood at the time of his conversation with Gigot, it seems highly unlikely that he would consciously have sabotaged the similar, though more nearly hysterical, mood Rojack had experienced at Tony's bar. Yet his deletion of Roberts's equality with the hero has had the effect of making even the best critics miss the ludicrous, parodic quality of Rojack's confrontation with Romeo.

on undue proportions. In particular, the stare-down with Romeo seems to gain significance, Romeo being elevated, by default, merely because Roberts has been diminished. Romeo is physically strong and possesses genuine wit, the mental equivalent of his tricky left hook, but in psychological terms he is not a worthy opponent. Yet he looks like one in the book, since he fits into the stare-down pattern with the fourth German and cannot be perceived in contrast to Roberts, who, unlike Romeo, had ideas in his eyes, in the *Esquire* text, as well as "controlled murder." A little later even the Mafia hood Tony is magnified by Rojack's cheap psychic battle with him, magnified again by default, since a trivial contest does not look so trivial when the previous contest with a worthy opponent has been blurred. Critics, of course, have given undue prominence to both Romeo and Tony, sometimes treating them more seriously even than Roberts, if not Shago.

The consequences of Mailer's removing Rojack's sense of Shago Martin as his psychological equal are also disastrous. *Esquire* offers a superbly dramatic confrontation. After Rojack has survived his dreaded second meeting with Roberts and is getting up his courage to see Kelly, there comes this wholly unprepared for confrontation with a man whose "sense of control" (coupled with a capacity to kill) reminds the *Esquire* reader of Roberts, but who is even more complicated, even more dangerous, than the detective, and whose voice (singing or speaking) is a weapon at least as powerful as Rojack's own, whether in his published writings (briefly quoted) or his spoken words, or in the narrative as a whole. Almost all the words about Shago or said by Shago remain in the Dial version, but without the initial tribute from Rojack that had informed them. The result is that Shago's characterization is pervasively weakened. His musicianship is a little more like a stereotype, what whites expect from a Negro, his love for Cherry is slightly shallower, and the pain he suffers at losing her is a little less tormenting, merely because he is not introduced as being locked in complication, as the kind of man who will always respond to experience profoundly and ambivalently. Rojack's fight with Shago becomes quite different. Rather than unfairly battering an equal, Rojack almost seems to be fighting bravely back against the stereotyped knife-wielding black intruder. The

204

effects are difficult to analyze, since the later respect for Shago remains in the Dial, but the initial deletions cheapen all of Cherry's and Rojack's subsequent talk about their feelings, especially her admission that at moments she wanted him to "throw that nigger down the stairs."[38] Cherry and Rojack have been portrayed as good early 1960s liberals during the beating of the Negro at the precinct house, a scene which in the *Esquire* version (more clearly than in the Dial) prepares for the Shago scene. But since Shago is reduced in the Dial (as Rojack is, by default), there is no chance for Rojack and Cherry to show their full acceptance of him as an equal. What in the *Esquire* version was a complicated, lacerating picture of white liberal attitudes towards blacks (a picture filled out by the ironic Harvard memory of pride in having a Negro for a close friend) is confused and at moments turned inadvertently into something nearer ordinary middle-class white racism. As with Roberts, critics simply do not know what to say about Shago. Begiebing insists that Shago "is not the heroic figure" that Stanley T. Gutman says he is (Gutman says he is a man "bearing his defeat with honor and pride") but rather a "defeated Soul and a double for Rojack who shows the hero the possibilities of defeat."[39] Critics have been known to disagree on texts which have no problems of composition, revision, and transmission, but these Mailer critics, I insist again, are doing the best they can with the evidence in the Dial text, and they come closer to Mailer's intentions only as they go by what he *should* be saying, in the light of what he says in other writings, instead of going by what the Dial edition actually says.

The nature of the alterations in the last chapter shows that Mailer had no intention of altering the complexity of Rojack's last and most formidable male rival, Barney Oswald Kelly, yet he did so, indirectly, by reducing Rojack. That process, largely inadvertent, continues into the last pages of the seventh chapter, where Mailer deleted the passage in the cab near Harlem when Rojack, delaying on his way to see Kelly, realizes that his state of mind, having taken advantage of Shago physically, is

---

38. Shago's control: *Esq* (July), p. 41 and Dial, p. 181; stairs: *Esq* (July), p. 106 and Dial, p. 198.
39. Gutman, p. 117; Begiebing, p. 75.

somehow akin to his state of mind earlier in the day after having, in effect, taken advantage of Roberts when he benefited from Kelly's intervention. The unintended consequence is that in the Dial version the stakes of the contest with Kelly, like the stakes of the contests with Roberts and Shago, are reduced, since to make Rojack even a little simpler (by sacrificing his chances to acknowledge the complexity of these two men and his chances to engage in battles of wit and courage with them as worthy opponents) is to alter, however slightly, his capacity for battle on intellectual, moral, and erotic grounds with Kelly. In the *Esquire* version, Kelly is the third and climactic antagonist Rojack has faced since he murdered Deborah, and he faces Kelly only after he has proved himself by the previous confrontations, not only besting Roberts and Shago, but realizing the consequences of taking advantage of both of them. At last Rojack is in the seductive presence of the master of evil, whom he must conquer if he is to escape Deborah and earn a chance for a new life. Kelly's story of his marriage to Leonora, paralleling as it does Rojack's earlier account of his own marriage to Deborah, enlarges his stature as demonic rival, in both versions, and his calculated storytelling forces the numbed Rojack to let the messenger enter his brain at last with the realization that Kelly had taken Deborah incestuously when she was fifteen and had continued the liaison to the present. The climax of the confrontation occurs as Rojack admits to murdering Deborah, accuses Kelly of incest, and is powerfully swayed by the urge he feels in Kelly to have the three of them, Kelly, Rojack, and Ruta, in frenzied orgy on the same bed where Kelly and Deborah had gone off "to the tar-pits of the moon." Rojack's triumph is in resisting, in choosing "to be free of magic, a man again, rational, promiscuous, blind to the reach of the seas," and his means of escape is the decision to walk the parapet. (In the Dial version Kelly's invitation is more explicit, a murmured "'Come on, shall we get shitty?'" and Rojack's saving counter urge is "to be some sort of rational man again, nailed tight to details, promiscuous, reasonable, blind to the reach of the seas.")[40] At last, partly as a result of the two earlier contests which are reduced in the Dial

40. *Esq* (August), p. 104 and Dial, p. 255.

text, Rojack is in control of himself and does not give way to the temptations, including the grotesque possibility of attacking Kelly with an incongruous weapon, Shago's telepathic umbrella. In the *Esquire* version, as in the Dial, Rojack learns much in the final chapter—not only of Kelly's incest with Deborah and the paternity of Deirdre, but something about being a man again, sane, in control, something that makes full sense only in the *Esquire* version, where he has grown through his previous encounters with formidable equals.

An American Dream is a classic case of an author's damaging his text by trying to alter a few patterns or parts of patterns. The importance of psychological equality of male characters— and the hierarchy of characters, male and female—is built into the Dial version as well. Almost everything else in Rojack's scenes with Roberts and with Shago is the way it is because at impressive moments in the *Esquire* version he saw each of them as his equal. These are crucial motivating passages, crucial structural passages. When Mailer closed up the wounds after the excisions, sometimes the words that remain do not make any good sense, as I have shown. More often, the words which remain make sense, but not precisely true authorial sense, not the sense that the author put there when the passages were being composed, and not any new sense that he later built into them. In the *Esquire* version, everything about the initial scene with Roberts led up to the meeting of eyes and to Rojack's perception of him as an equal, and then everything else followed from that passage. The Shago encounter worked the same way. Now the words leading up to the crucial lines are joined to the words that followed from them, but the vitalizing passages are missing. The words that remain in the Dial version are still Mailer's words (and an overwhelming percentage of them are still words from the *Esquire* version), and they have his authorial blessing as the words in the authorized book edition of his novel, but no amount of authorial blessing can endow the ravaged passages with full intentionality. They are as they are because they meant something else at the time they were being composed. Even if nothing anomalous sticks out like a broken bone through skin, passages are drained, and in subtle ways the whole book is drained, of intentionality.

When I wrote the first version of the preceding paragraph for a talk in 1979 at the South Atlantic Modern Language Association and when I revised it early in 1981 for the Autumn 1981 issue of *Studies in American Fiction* (published in December 1981), I was not interested in Mailer the man and Mailer the writer nearly so much as in the lessons which I could learn, and then teach, from a particular textual situation. Up to that point, I had learned enough from collating the two texts without doing archival research. When David V. Erdman accepted the essay late in 1981, he wanted illustrations, so I called Robert Lucid, Mailer's official biographer, who very generously arranged to meet me in the vault in Manhattan where Mailer's papers are kept. None of the items on my wishlist of the eight or ten most desirable illustrations was in the boxes of *An American Dream* material, but I got some quite acceptable substitutes, and in due course the *Bulletin of Research in the Humanities* reproduced four of the glossies sharply and provided them with succinct captions. In the meantime I had profited from Lucid's criticism of the current draft of the essay, and had profited even more from the impressive example of his sense of responsibility toward Mailer and toward himself. With a fresh sense of the opportunities, not just the pitfalls, that might await anyone working on a living writer, I reworked the entire essay and wrote a new concluding paragraph designed to woo Mailer into undoing the damage I was sure he had done unwittingly. In the form of its appearance in the *Bulletin* the paragraph, like the rest of the essay, was freighted with my own memories of the 1960s and subsequent years, not lightest of which was my sympathetic association of the reviews of *An American Dream* with the reviews of *Pierre*: like Melville, Mailer had been cruelly and perversely abused. It had become a purposefully rhetorical paragraph meant for Mailer's eyes:

"Since Mailer survives, unlike the authors of the other novels I cited at the outset, and indeed flourishes, he could repair the damage to *An American Dream*. In a day or two, if he restrained himself from revising yet again, he could make the restorations from *Esquire*, though at the small cost of losing some local stylistic revisions which he made at or around the deleted passages. It would be a remarkable literary curiosity,

the chance to see how a new edition of the old text would be received. Now it is plain that the original reviewers were not only vindictive but simply wrong in castigating Mailer for violating aesthetic probabilities by a plot which linked American institutions everyone knew were distinct—academia, the entertainment industry (television, night clubs, recordings), transportation (in the person of a trucking tycoon), the Mafia, the CIA, the Presidency, and (crowning impossibility) expensive women who moved back and forth among representative members of these institutions. Now the sociologists are telling us that incest is no mere gothic plot contrivance and no fit subject for jests about family romances but a common occurrence at all levels of American life, household fact if not household word; like Fitzgerald, Mailer knew a horrific literal truth about America and projected from it a powerful symbolic malaise, a witch's brew into which he stirred not only national institutions and violation of primal taboos but such tamer bits of Americana as the prevailing manifestations of alcoholism, cancer (literal, psychically induced, and metaphorical), electronic eavesdropping, and extremes of poverty and wealth. Now, also, many of the feminists of the 1960's and 1970's who denounced Mailer as their most conspicuous, if most resilient, target, have decided that they cut too many losses too soon; one small loss, worth retrieving, is Mailer's complex scrutiny of American masculinity in the *Esquire* version. There is not a person reading this chapter who has not felt superior to Norman Mailer—feeling superior to him is an occasional pastime of all literate Americans. Yet there may not be another man or woman of our time who has written so profound and prescient a meditation on manhood, marriage, and the American Dream. I have come round to thinking that *An American Dream* is very possibly a great novel, or that it used to be, back in 1963 and 1964, before Dial published it."

I learned fast enough that writing on Mailer was more controversial than writing on Melville. On 10 February 1983 Herbert Mitgang, the textualists' friend at the New York *Times*, author of front-page stories in 1981 on the Pennsylvania *Sister Carrie* and in 1982 on the Norton reconstruction of *The Red Badge of Courage*, gave space to the *Bulletin* essay under the

209

heading "On the Scholarly Trail of the New Revisionists."[40] Mitgang's comments were descriptive, not judgmental, and the only thing I winced at was his saying I had "coined the phrase 'authorial intentionality,'" I who had lobbied hard for the aesthetics of editorial apparatus and who in an immensely long psychological exploration with Brian Higgins of "The Flawed Grandeur of Melville's *Pierre*" had used only one word of jargon, one time ("individuation"). Doing his job right, Mitgang had asked the author of *An American Dream* what he thought of the essay:

> Mr. Mailer said that he had glanced at the professor's article and found it interesting as a literary matter. But, he said: "I'm not sure he's right. I think the Dial book is better. The publisher preferred to print the Esquire serial, but I devoted four months to revising it for the book. I probably made some errors in some sentences, but there is nothing wrong with making changes. Henry James rewrote all of his novels. It gives you a chance to cut out some of your darlings."
>
> Mr. Mailer doesn't intend to change "An American Dream" a second time. At the moment, he said, his mind is on his 800-page novel "Ancient Evenings," which is coming out in April.

Fair enough: maybe sometime Lucid or Begiebing or someone would encourage Mailer to glance back at the article; meanwhile I had done the best I could do, and it was merely tough luck that Dial was announcing a forthcoming paperback of *An American Dream* just at this time.

Then a graduate student called me with the news, haltingly delivered, that a reporter named Jonathan Yardley had savaged me in the Washington *Post*, in an article which was being reprinted all around the country, in everything from the Chicago *Sun-Times* to the student's source, the Easton, Pennsylvania *Express*, where the headline read "MAILER BATTLES ACADEMIC CHUTZPAH" and an inset explained, in extremely legible type, that "An obscure college professor has decided that the published version of Norman Mailer's *An American Dream* is not the one he meant to write nor as good as his first

40. *Esq* (August), p. 104 and Dial, p. 255.

draft."[41] Well, not exactly, but there was no point quibbling. The article began as an extravaganza on a partially hypothetical Dryasdust: "Furrowing his brow and scratching his rapidly thinning hair, our hero reaches as deeply as he can into his lexicon of academic gobbledegook and postulates this stunner: 'What was the authorial intentionality?'" (I have, in fact, a full head of rapidly graying hair.) Then Yardley got down to personal insults and vigorous posturing designed, apparently, to reassure Mailer that with Yardley on his side he had nothing to fear from me. Calming himself a little, he asked: "Are we seriously to believe that an obscure professor is more reliable than the person who actually wrote the book? The question may seem preposterous on its face—but to those who specialize in tracking down real or imagined 'authorial intentionality' it most certainly is not. The revising of important and not-so-important works of literature has become an industry at many English departments, and not a small one."

For several reasons I did not lose any sleep over the Yardley attack. First of all, as soon as my student had given me the gist of the piece I asked him to go over Yardley's quotations from my article again, slow. As I had suspected, all the quotations in the *Post* were from the *Times*: Yardley had excited himself so immoderately after reading Mitgang and had not bothered to look at my article for himself. Well, a man with such fervent convictions about literature wouldn't want to risk looking at the evidence. Besides, I had learned to take the long view of such criticism: if you keep getting your ideas into print, sooner or later they may make some difference. More particularly, Yardley did not upset me because what he was saying, after all, was merely a more demagogic version of the sincere if irrational conviction that many scholars hold: anything an author had allowed to go into print must have been what he wanted and he must have known best and even if he hadn't known best it was no one else's business to second-guess him. As it happened, Mailer took any lingering sting off the Yardley article. The day

41. See "After 80 Years, Publisher Plans Uncut 'Sister Carrie,'" New York *Times* (17 April 1981): A1, A16; "'Red Badge' Is Due Out as Crane Wrote It" (2 April 1982): A1, C30; and "On the Scholarly Trail Of the New Revisionists" (10 February 1983): C22.

after I picked up the clipping from my student, I showed it to Mailer in Philadelphia, where he was giving the Pappas lectures, and he autographed it, directly above the "MAILER BATTLES ACADEMIC CHUTZPAH" headline: "To Hershel—may his ideas prevail to the sticking point, Norman."

Not one to underestimate the laborious collating that lay behind the article, and not one to underestimate the possible long-term financial benefits to his children from scholarly monographs on his manuscripts and typescripts, Mailer welcomed my working more thoroughly with the papers so I could write a little book on the making of *An American Dream* (a friend of mine having been promoting a series of such books). Mailer may yet read the article more carefully and be persuaded by it, but he says, with finality, that he would never be content with merely restoring a few passages: if he were to turn back to the book, he would want to revise it again, seriously. So the winsome rhetoric of the last paragraph in the *Bulletin* may have failed in its covert purpose, but the story may not be over.[42]

42. I assume the headline was the same in the Washington *Post*. There are limits to the research one should be expected to do. I am pleased to report that Stanley Fish takes on Yardley (among others) in "Profession Despise Thyself: Fear and Self-Loathing in Literary Studies," *Critical Inquiry* 10 (December 1983): 349-64. Mailer can take care of himself, without the help of a journalist who has, like Romeo, more pressure in his eyes than ideas, but I'll take any help I can get.

Conclusion

Textual Evidence and the Current Practice of Theory

In the course of defining and demonstrating a textual-aesthetic approach to literary study I have offered a critique of academic writing on American literature in the last several decades, one with broad application to literary criticism as practiced by American professors of English, whatever their fields. I want now to focus my evidence on literary theory as currently practiced. The young theorists Steven Knapp and Walter Benn Michaels now deny the value and power of theory, decrying it as a game that they and others play without strong chance of scoring, much less winning.[1] An incorrigible empiricist, I bow to the power of theory. It was, after all, theory, however simplified, which led to the habit of ignoring of biographical-textual evidence and its implications, the condition which has warranted my writing this book. Just as diluted New

1. Steven Knapp and Walter Benn Michaels, "Against Theory," *Critical Inquiry* 8 (Summer, 1982): 723-42; and their "A Reply to Our Critics," *Critical Inquiry* 9 (June 1983): 790-800. Lawrence I. Lipking's "The Practice of Theory," *Profession 83* (New York: Modern Language Association of America, 1983), pp. 21-28, a refreshing overview, takes note of "one growing school of theorists devoted to the proposition that theory is useless and ought to be discontinued" (p. 28). The title of my Conclusion had reached its present form before I saw Lipking's title, but I would have stolen his in a minute if I had heard about it when he gave the paper at the 1983 ADE Summer Seminar at Southwest Texas State University.

Criticism winked out from the scores of essays on Henry James's fiction I surveyed in Chapter 4, so has diluted, do-it-by-the-dots deconstructionism already been perfected by the newer critics.[2] Curiously enough, some of the most influential recent theory rests on weak tenets of older theory, as I will show.

It is customary and correct to attribute to the triumph of the New Criticism the severing of American academic criticism and theory from almost all (not just stupid and maudlin) biographical scholarship, and from almost all (not just incompetent and pedantic) bibliographical and textual scholarship. Other factors were at work. If university enrollment had remained stable throughout the 1950s, if there had been no proliferation of new junior colleges, colleges, and universities which possessed libraries unequal to those at Harvard and Yale, perhaps the triumph of the New Criticism would have been delayed or even prevented: it thrived when the professor could make a career from writing about a few paperback novels or collections of short stories which he (and increasingly she) carried to the beach at summer. But the more I try to understand the neglect of biographical, bibliographical, and textual evidence in modern criticism and theory, the more W. K. Wimsatt, Jr.'s and Monroe C. Beardsley's "The Intentional Fallacy" looms up as the most influential piece of theory in the century, more influential even than the standard classroom text, René Wellek and Austin Warren's *Theory of Literature*, which labeled as "quite mistaken" the "whole idea that the 'intention' of the author is the proper subject of literary history."[3] As one expects with such a seminal document as "The Intentional Fallacy," its influence goes far beyond its actual readers and indeed beyond its actual arguments, which, while tendentiously phrased, were not as

2. A clear recent example of such mechanical imposition of post-structuralist strategies on Melville is Brook Thomas, "The Writer's Procreative Urge in *Pierre*: Fictional Freedom or Convoluted Incest?" *Studies in the Novel* 11 (Winter 1979): 416-30. As early as 1978 Henry Sussman was pointing out the fact that the academy had begun to assimilate and tame deconstructionism: see his "The Deconstructor as Politician: Melville's *Confidence-Man*," *Glyph* 4:32-56.

3. "The Intentional Fallacy," first printed in the *Sewanee Review* 54 (July-September 1946): 468-88, reprinted in W. K. Wimsatt, Jr., *The Verbal Icon* (Lexington: University of Kentucky Press, 1954) and in paperback (New York: The Noonday Press, 1958), pp. 3-18; *Theory of Literature* (New York: Harcourt, Brace, 1949), p. 34; and second edition, in paperback (New York: Harcourt, Brace, 1956), p. 31.

extreme as they were often taken to be. Reacting against crude biographical criticism in which an author's sincerity might be adduced as evidence that a given poem was important, Wimsatt and Beardsley did not deny that biographical evidence might be somehow relevant—just that it was "neither available nor desirable as a standard for judging the success of a work of literary art."[4] Wimsatt's later "Genesis: A Fallacy Revisited" was more disdainfully couched, especially in its contempt for biographical critics who, "wishing to throb in unison with the mind of the artist, will wish to know all about that individual artist and as much as possible about his historic context."[5] His disdain seems to have affected the nature of the work graduate students undertook at Yale during the 1950s and 1960s to the point that to interest oneself in the creative process became a confession of impossible gaucherie if not grossness, and, then as now, what was in vogue at Yale rapidly was adopted elsewhere.

In retrospect, we can see just how rapidly the triumphant new ideology installed its biases not only in graduate programs but also the newly-multiplying undergraduate courses. Less quantifiably, it soon effected the shift in departmental hierarchies which exalted literary critics (and later exalted theorists) over their literary historian and biographer colleagues (with a few exceptions) and which relegated bibliographers and textual scholars to the most inferior status of all, where Bruce Harkness by the late 1950s could speak out as a classroom teacher turned textualist-prophet in an academic community overrun by critics, and call, without many results, for critics and textual scholars to join forces. By around 1960 the tenured

4. "The Intentional Fallacy," p. 3. See *The Disciplines of Criticism*, eds. Peter Demetz, Thomas Greene, and Lowry Nelson, Jr. (New Haven: Yale University Press, 1968), for Wimsatt's "Genesis: A Fallacy Revisited," pp. 193-225, where (on p. 222) he revises the sentence: "The design or intention of the author is neither available nor desirable as a standard for judging either the meaning or the value of a work of literary art."

Cleanth Brooks cautions me not to forget Wimsatt's own biographical studies and assures me that he does not believe Wimsatt would have found anything to disagree with in my description of the author at work in Chapter 2. While accepting Brooks's judgment, I think the history of criticism shows that the language of Wimsatt and Beardsley lent itself to extreme interpretations.

5. "Genesis," p. 194.

students of the original New Critics were publishing their inter-changeable one-page "explications" and their interchangeable ten-page "readings," and the hierarchies were set.[6] Almost nobody talked to anybody outside his (and gradually her) own group. Do you think young theorist Graff and young textualist Parker chatted on the stairs in University Hall at Northwestern on the intricate interrelationships between authorial second thoughts and determinate meaning? About as much as Fredson Bowers and E. D. Hirsch, Jr. chatted on the Lawn at Charlottes-ville about validity in interpretations of Maggie's last night, I suspect. If you were a critic, "scholarship" soon became some-thing that other people did, so you could toss off a comment on what "scholarship has shown" (ignorant of the strong possibil-ity that scholarship probably had not yet done a very good job of showing it, whatever it was).

As New Critics were joined (and succeeded) by phenome-nologists, structuralists, reader-response critics, deconstruc-tionists, feminist critics and theorists, post-structuralist Freudians, and the rest, the influence of Wimsatt and Beardsley (and even of Wellek and Warren) remained manifest in a perva-sive distrust of biographical, textual, and bibliographical evi-dence.[7] ("The Intentional Fallacy" has of course cast a longer

6. I borrow from E. D. Hirsch, Jr.'s comments on the emergence of "readings" (see below). See also Gerald Graff, "Who Killed Criticism?" *American Scholar* 49 (Summer 1980): 337-55, especially p. 340, on the relationship between such readings and explications and "the democratization of the university." I do not share Graff's sense that today "the words 'scholarship' and 'criticism' are used interchangeably" (p. 337), except in the most general way, as in the title *American Literary Scholarship*. There's still a gap to be recognized and bridged.
7. In a simplified version, the intimidating weight of the "genetic fallacy" is joined to the oppressive weight of Wellek and Warren in Robert Milder's strictures in *American Literary Scholarship, An Annual, 1981* (Durham: Duke University Press, 1983), pp. 60-61: "Reliable criticism requires reliable texts, but when Parker presses critics to learn the "textual history" of a work, he sometimes means two different things, the history of revision and publication, which helps scholars estab-lish an authoritative text (and critics choose between the rival texts available), and the history of composition, which may be important only to critics concerned with the work as it unfolded in the author's mind. At issue here is what Wellek and Warren long ago called the "ontological situs" of a work of art, or the question of where meaning resides; and once a text has been established, there is no compelling reason why a formalist or a reader-response critic, neither of whom shares Higgins and Parker's disposition toward authorial meaning, should need to know its genesis." ("Long ago" is of course relative. As far as I can see Wellek and Warren's discussion of the "ontological situs" of a work of art, as distinguished from

pall than its companion essay, "The Affective Fallacy," which the reader-response critics had to repudiate before setting up their shop.)[8] I have already commented on the irony that by minimizing biographical and textual evidence (including evidence about the creative process) the New Critics and their followers cut themselves off from their best allies in celebrating the unity of literary texts, since the working assumption of any textual critic or editor and the working assumption of any student of the creative process is that the direction of any developing aesthetic object is toward unity.

There were curious consequences as critics (drawn to biographical commentary despite themselves) fumbled for ways to justify their dodging into and out of the realm of biography without doing the rigorous labors of biographers, refusing as they did to treat a textual problem as one requiring conscientious study of the creative process and the possibly built-in authorial purposes for particular scenes and sections of a novel. The creation of a disembodied Henry James was one such strategy, whether or not it was ever perceived as a strategy. In Chapter 6 we saw examples of unearned and uncharitable biographicizing on the basis of a flawed text as one critical substitute for traditional biography. An alternate way of playing at the biographical game without investing any capital derived from personal research was to abstract a problem from the realm of textual criticism (or "textual bibliography") and biography of the writer during the creative process in order to treat it as if it

---

the less epistemological "ontological status," first appeared in the 1956 edition, at the beginning of the revised and newly titled Chapter 12.) Milder is saying that textual information is all very nice if you are interested in that sort of thing but there is no reason anyone who is not already interested should have to bother with it. That is, critics don't necessarily need to pay any attention to scholarship; if they want to criticize a text, they don't need to let facts deter them. This kind of thinking where diluted Wimsatt and Beardsley or diluted Wellek and Warren are still cited as champions of the verbal icon is the same sort of thinking which propelled the profession, four decades ago, toward an impasse in criticism and theory. We have hardly budged from the chic 1940s distrust of biographical evidence, and we have not, as a profession, paid enough attention to textual evidence even to begin to formulate a rationale for excluding it.

8. Wimsatt and Beardsley's "The Affective Fallacy," *Sewanee Review* 57 (October-December 1949): 31-55; reprinted in Wimsatt's *The Verbal Icon*, pp. 21-39. See p. 31 of the original text or p. 21 in *The Verbal Icon*: "The Affective Fallacy is a confusion between the poem and its *results* (what it *is* and what it *does*)."

had only to do with the author's philosophy. Thus Milton R. Stern says that the choice of the 1934 text of *Tender is the Night* or the Cowley text must be made on the basis "of the book's thematic purpose and of Fitzgerald's own relationship to it"; similarly, John F. Callahan says the problem of form (or text) in the same novel "comes down to Fitzgerald's own doubts about the nature of time and personality."[9] Somehow these critics feel safer when they can convert a textual issue into an issue involving the writer's philosophy or psychology, two areas that others might find as treacherous as any textual terrain.

Having abstracted the subject of variant texts from biography, critics who still were moved, against the power of the New Criticism, to acknowledge the authority of the author found themselves free to envision him as possessed of mysterious powers, not only displayed during the impenetrable obscurities of the compositional process but also capable of being exercised as he confers meaning on a completed text with the wave of a hand or by ripping a book apart and reordering a hunk of it. Writers possess, according to these critics, the power to bestow new intentionality at will; writers can take an old work and wish it, oh, *wish* it, into meaning something it had not meant when it was composed. During the few hours Mark Twain spent pulling out part of the typescript of *Pudd'nhead Wilson* to publish separately, he created a "tragic masterpiece" which surpassed *Huckleberry Finn* "in unity of theme and general organization."[10] Evan Carton says that after capitulating "to the pressure of his upstart characters" as he wrote, Mark Twain reestablished "his own control by severing the double story and disposing of one half"; he reestablished not the original control but a new control, apparently, and infused it, poof poof poof, into every

9. Milton R. Stern, *The Golden Moment* (Urbana: University of Illinois Press, 1970), p. 385. Stern assures us (p. 391) that "Fitzgerald's own instincts about the relationship between the structure and what the book is all about remain most trustworthy, and he was right in wanting to tear the book apart and reassemble it." See John F. Callahan, *The Illusions of a Nation* (Urbana: University of Illinois Press, 1972), p. 65.
10. See Philip C. Kolin, "Mark Twain, Aristotle, and Pudd'nhead Wilson," *Mark Twain Journal* 15 (Summer 1970): 4 ("tragic masterpiece"); and John Freimarck, "*Pudd'nhead Wilson*: A Tale of Blood and Brotherhood," *University Review* 34 (June 1968): 303 ("it surpasses that great novel in its unity of theme and general organization").

word of the parts he salvaged and the new little passages he wrote to tie some of the parts together.[11] Wayne C. Booth said that the achievement of Fitzgerald's revision of *Tender is the Night* (a revision which required even less rewriting than *Pudd'nhead*), is "to correct a fault of over-distancing, a fault that springs from a method appropriate to other works at other times but not to the tragedy Fitzgerald wanted to write."[12] Thus poor, inept Fitzgerald had wanted to write a tragedy, all during the years he worked on what became *Tender is the Night*, and failed, only to succeed, a few years later, in those triumphant moments when he tore apart a copy of the book and masterfully thrust a section of it into a different place: instant, though long-belated, tragedy. It is as if the right order were latent in what Fitzgerald wrote, awaiting only a magic touch to restore it to a platonic ideal which had had no reality during the years of composition. In all of these comments the failure to think of the writer as a human being who worked meaning into the text line by line and page by page—the failure to engage in detailed analysis of the aesthetic implications of the growth and variation of texts—has freed the critics to imagine the author as possessed with superhuman powers, though powers which do not stand up to much close scrutiny.

The reality is less magical, but authorial powers are, at best, very great—authorial power is the only literary power there is. The evidence in this book suggests that textual meaning is not something living in a text which has (in Susan R. Suleiman's ironic summary) an "existence as an autonomous, identifiable, and unique entity: *the text itself*"; not something that a reader actively participates with the text in producing (see Jane P. Tompkins on Wolfgang Iser); not something which "takes place in the text itself and in the reader's encounter with the text" (Jonathan Culler); not an experience that takes place in "the reader's mind rather than the printed page" (Stanley Fish); and not something which is the "property" of "interpretive

11. Evan Carton, "*Pudd'nhead Wilson* and the Fiction of Law and Custom," in *American Realism: New Essays*, ed. Eric J. Sundquist (Baltimore: Johns Hopkins University Press, 1982), pp. 82-94; the quotation is from p. 88.
12. *The Rhetoric of Fiction* (Chicago: University of Chicago Press, 1961), p. 195.

communities that are responsible both for the shape of a reader's activities and for the texts those activities produce" (Fish).[13] E. D. Hirsch, Jr., who argues that "textual meaning" is "the verbal intention of the author," insists that the New Critical doctrine of textual autonomy (the "metaphorical doctrine that a text leads a life of its own") "undercuts *all* criticism, even the sort which emphasizes present relevance.... The 'life' theory really masks the idea that the reader construes his own, new meaning instead of that represented by the text."[14] The evidence of this book shows further that while a text may have existence as an "identifiable" and "unique" entity, it never is an autonomous entity. During composition a text is contingent on the author, if not on others as well, and before or after publication it is vulnerable to the author and others such as family members, editors, publishers, and compositors.[15] Textual

13. Suleiman, in her "Introduction: Varieties of Audience-Oriented Criticism," *The Reader in the Text*, eds. Susan R. Suleiman and Inge Crosman (Princeton: Princeton University Press, 1980), p. 40; Jane P. Tompkins, *Reader-Response Criticism* (Baltimore: Johns Hopkins Press, 1980), in her "An Introduction to Reader-Response Criticism," pp. ix-xxvi (see p. xv); Culler, *Structuralist Poetics*, p. 264; Stanley Fish, *Is There a Text in This Class?* (Cambridge: Harvard University Press, 1980), pp. 22-67 (the quotation is from p. 36 and is quoted and discussed by Tompkins in her introduction, p. xvii); Fish, *Text?*, p. 322. Steven Mailloux writes to me that he does not think I do justice to Fish's theory of interpretation here: "Both you and he would say that it is the assumption of New Critics (about texts, authors, etc.) that determines what they see. And both of you would also say that if other assumptions were accepted and acted upon, the discipline would see very different things and write very different essays. Fish's 'interpretive community' is just the name he gives to the critical beliefs and interpretative assumptions that enable literary study to proceed in a particular way. If your approach were to prove persuasive, then what would have happened, according to Fish, is that one interpretive community (bio-textual-aesthetic) had replaced another (neo-New Critics) in affecting the discipline." If Mailloux is right, Fish's doctrine is not outrageous so much as platitudinous: i.e., we see whatever we're equipped to see.
14. *Validity in Interpretation* (New Haven: Yale University Press, 1967), pp. 224, 212, 213.
15. Other people frequently interfere with the words of the author and therefore prevent the textual meaning from being precisely "the verbal intention of the author." This fact is of course deplorable, for often such tampering cannot be identified and corrected. Some theorists, rather than regretting such tampering, accept it on the same terms as anything the author wrote, particularly if he tacitly or explicitly "accepted" the changes, or "expected" that such changes would be made. Donald Pizer propounds the not uncommon view that if an author "accepts an editorial change or suggestion, his acceptance is the equivalent of a creative act, even though the act is the initial responsibility of an editor." See "On the Editing of

meaning is the verbal intention of the author, as long as we acknowledge that the text may be so imperfect or so maimed as to distort or remove that intention, assuming that it was ever fully embodied in written words.

Beginning in 1960 with the publication of part of what became, seven years later, *Validity in Interpretation*, Hirsch was for years almost the solitary defender of validity in interpretation based on authorial intentions, almost alone in insisting that a theory of reading which aims at achieving "the practical goal of every genuine discipline," consensus ("the winning of firmly grounded agreement that one set of conclusions is more probable than others") must be based on the intention of the author. Taking an ironic look at the process by which in the 1950s it "became fashionable to talk about a critic's 'reading' of a text," Hirsch observed that the word "seemed to imply that if the author had been banished, the critic still remained, and his new, original, urbane, ingenious, or relevant 'reading' carried its own interest."[16] The nearest thing to a classic argument against such solitary or group subjectivity is the section on "Determinateness of Textual Meaning" where he argues "that hermeneutics must stress a reconstruction of the author's aims and attitudes in order to evolve guides and norms for construing

---

Modern American Texts," *Bulletin of the New York Public Library* 75 (March 1971): 147-53; the quotation is from p. 148. Similarly, James Thorpe in *Principles of Textual Criticism* (San Marino: Huntington Library, 1972), p. 31, says "the integrity of the work of art depends very much on the work being limited to those intentions which are the author's together with those others of which he approves or in which he acquiesces." Echoing both Pizer and Thorpe, and carrying their ideas to a further extreme, Jerome J. McGann in *A Critique of Modern Textual Criticism* (Chicago: University of Chicago Press, 1983), pp. 62-63 (and *passim*) celebrates not the creative process but the "social" process "where intentions are plainly shifting and changing under the pressure of various people and circumstances." It is "social relationships" which give literary works their lives, says McGann (p. 81), not authors. To do as Pizer, Thorpe, and McGann do is to insist on integrity in something after integrity has been lost and to confuse two separate phases, the creative phase and the publishing, marketing phase. While it is possible that a writer could think through all the textual implications of someone else's suggested change, in practice writers rarely think through even the most important effects such a revision can have locally, much less how shock waves can affect remoter parts of a long work. Until the time comes that we are more interested in John Murray and his staff than Byron, more interested in Ripley Hitchcock than Stephen Crane, the "social" process has to be differentiated from our search for what the writer wrote.

16. *Validity in Interpretation*, pp. ix, 3.

the meaning of his text."[17] I would qualify Hirsch only by the reminder that textual evidence (evidence of composition and revision) should not be neglected in the reconstruction of the author's aims and attitudes. Hirsch's position is similar to the "interpretive assumptions" which M. H. Abrams describes himself as sharing "with all historians who rely on texts for their basic data":[18]

> the authors . . . wrote, not in order to present a verbal stimulus (in Roland Barthes' term, *un vide*) to the play of the reader's interpretive ingenuity, but in order to be understood. To do so, they had to obey the communal norms of their language so as to turn them to their own innovative uses. The sequence of sentences these authors wrote were designed to have a core of determinate meanings; and though the sentences allow a certain degree of interpretive freedom, and though they evoke vibrations of significance which differ according to the distinctive temperament and experience of each reader, the central core of what they undertook to communicate can usually be understood by a competent reader who knows how to apply the norms of the language and literary form employed by the writer. The reader has various ways to test whether his understanding is an "objective" one; but the chief way is to make his interpretation public, and so permit it to be confirmed or falsified by the interpretations of other competent readers who subscribe to the same assumptions about the possibility of determinable communication.

I would qualify Abrams only by recalling that writers who do not try hard enough to be understood can fail to achieve a precisely determinate meaning, while very often after a writer has achieved his determinate meaning in a text something happens which distorts, conceals, or removes some of that meaning.

Since a mystery widely remarked upon is Hirsch's failure to have swept the field with his arguments, I am going to make some intrusive speculations under cover of the theory of aca-

17. *Validity in Interpretation*, pp. 224-35; the quotation is from p. 224.
18. "Rationality and Imagination in Cultural History: A Reply to Wayne Booth," *Critical Inquiry* 2 (Spring 1976): 447-64; the quotation is from p. 457.

demic genealogy, according to which it matters who your father or uncle was (and is already mattering who your mother or aunt was). I wonder, on the evidence of Hirsch's rather odd failures to make the best use of the biographical and textual arguments available to him, if as a graduate student at Yale he felt profound reluctance to perform biographical-critical acts that Wimsatt regarded with contempt. Whatever the cause, Hirsch (in the passages cited in Chapter 2, paragraph 4) weakened his position with the gratuitous rhetorical concession that "the immediate effect" of the banishing of the author by the New Critics "was wholly beneficial and invigorating," however much academic disarray followed from that banishment; later, even while appealing to biographical evidence about Wordsworth's attitudes, he declared in much the spirit of "The Intentional Fallacy" that "we shall never be certain what any writer means,"[19] and he never sufficiently engaged himself with the likelihood that when we talk about what a writer means we are talking about, at times, provable inferences.

My hunch about how Hirsch failed to make the most of his evidence is somewhat corroborated by Suresh Raval's recent analysis. Saying that "Hirsch's logico-experimental approach consists in subjecting one's interpretive hypotheses to the control of observation which is provided by the invariant verbal construct" (Hirsch does in fact regularly regard the form of a literary work as fixed, an "unalterable sequence of words"), Raval explains that although Hirsch links the work to the mind which produced it he "does not go by simple notions of examining what the poet said in his notes, essays, or memoirs,

---

19. *Validity in Interpretation*, pp. 3 and 240. I am less the nosy Parker than I seem here. My personal speculations grow out of years of trying to see why Hirsch has not had the impact he ought to have had with those trying to think their way beyond the New Criticism. While I would now ascribe the cause mainly to his failure to sever his own ties with the New Criticism, I would also suggest some other causes, such as his tendency to want other people to accept his special meanings for commonly used words, his self-inhibiting decision to make his study theoretical rather than half practical, half theoretical, and the seeming arbitrariness of some of his readings of texts, as of Blake's "London." Hirsch is one of the heroes of my study, all the more to be defended because of the grotesqueness of some of the recent attacks upon him.

though he would not altogether reject them."[20] Raval sees a curious affinity between the author of *Validity in Interpretation* and the authors of "The Intentional Fallacy":[21]

> Interestingly enough, then, Hirsch, like Wimsatt and Beardsley, seeks to avoid psychologism and the search for the author's private meanings, though, contrary to them, he also seeks to reinstate intentionality as central to interpretation. Hirsch's argument thus does not really confront the antiintentionalist position, since in order to deny that position he would have to recognize the importance of private meanings. The question, then, becomes whether Hirsch's reinterpretation of the concept of intention succeeds in countering the antiintentionalist position. The answer, it seems to me, has to be No, because Hirsch's authorial intention does not entail a biographical person but rather a "speaking subject," not really distinguishable from the New Critical persona.

Raval's analysis goes far to explain the odd way Hirsch has of standing at arm's length from some aspects of what he ought to be seizing as the stuff of his arguments, a stance which has contributed to his failure to have had the effect he ought to have had.

More than a decade after *Validity in Interpretation* such a historian of structuralist and deconstructionist theory as Jonathan Culler shows no visceral dread of being caught trying to explore the creative process. Like many others of his academic generation, he has so internalized the Intentional Fallacy that he never seriously pauses to think about what he might learn if he decided to find out for himself whether or not evidence about authorial intention might be, in fact, available, and perhaps even a desirable literary tool. Culler ingenuously excuses himself from seeking information about the author on the grounds that it is "easier" to gain information about how readers read (we can read their interpretive essays) than about how writers write: "for the assumptions of writers are of difficult access and their statements about their own works are

20. Suresh Raval, *Metacriticism* (Athens: University of Georgia Press, 1981), p. 63; for "unalterable sequence of words" see *Validity in Interpretation*, pp. 224 and 236.
21. *Metacriticism*, pp. 63-64.

motivated by such varied factors that one is continually led astray if one tries to infer from them the conventions assumed."[22] Thus, instead of doing the scholarly work on the way literary texts are created and altered, we can spend our time reading other critics. One must indeed be skeptical about authorial statements of purpose, but Culler, a good post-Wimsattian, assumes too quickly that evidence of authorial intention could come only from authorial statements such as, to supply an example, those in James's *Notebooks* before or during composition of a work or those in his letters or Prefaces after the completion of it, where it may well be that what James did in a given instance was different from what he said he was going to do before he did it, from what he said he was doing while he was doing it, and what he said he had done after he did it. Ironically, even as he identifies himself as an adherent of "facts," facts of how critics read, Culler would presumably rule out textual evidence of considerable evidentiary heft—evidence of the direction Stephen Crane was taking as he revised and expanded the rough draft of *Red Badge* into final manuscript, or evidence of the shifting plans Mark Twain pursued during the composition of the large manuscript called *Pudd'nhead Wilson*. He would also rule out other biographical information such as the Harper contract for *Pierre* and a draft passage of that contract in the hand of Melville's brother.[23] Elusive in his distrust of information about authorial intention, Culler seems to want to pay all necessary deference to the importance of the author, but he radically distorts the variety, complexity, and significance of available evidence about authorial assumptions, thereby depriving himself of evidence (textual and other documentary evidence) of great potential value for creating and for testing his notions about literary competence.[24] Looking at Culler's rejection of such evidence, I would say, in defiance of the "genetic fallacy" and its later

22. Jonathan Culler, "Prolegomena to a Theory of Reading," in *The Reader in the Text*, pp. 46-66; the quotation is from p. 51. For a similar statement see Culler's *Structuralist Poetics* (Ithaca: Cornell University Press, 1975), p. 117.
23. These examples are perforce mine since Culler does not explore any possible means of gaining information about the author's intentions.
24. "Prolegomena," p. 51: "As a reader oneself, one can perform all the experiments one needs, and one has access to what numerous other readers have

permutations, that one's sense of a text is inseparable from inferences about how the author's intentions developed, changed, and perhaps came into conflict with themselves over the temporal process of the creation and subsequent adventures of the work. When such inferences are derived from, for instance, demonstrable patterns of revision, they are of an order of provability entirely different from casual authorial statements often cited by those eager to abandon the search for validity in interpretation.

Oddly, the New Critical assumption that the unified, perfect verbal icon, "the text itself," is always a sufficiently reliable source of information about the author's intentions for a work has haunted even editorial theory up through G. Thomas Tanselle (the editor, like the critic, "will be turning to the text itself as his primary evidence") just as much as it has haunted critical theory up through Tzvetan Todorov ("What exists first and foremost is the text itself, and nothing but the text").[25] In many cases, however, "the text itself" does not even contain all the text that is necessary for understanding the author's intention in it. I would challenge Tanselle for not adequately qualifying his claim that "the work itself is the controlling factor in statements made about its meaning, whether or not those statements aim at elucidating the author's intended meaning,"[26] for not specifically anticipating situations where what is thought of as the text itself—the 1895 *Red Badge*, the 1896 *Maggie*—does not contain the parts of the original text itself which would allow confident statements to be made about the meaning of the text.

---

said about a given text, while the statements of its one author are few and problematical." All but a handful of the essays ever written on *Pudd'nhead Wilson* are useless in the light of the surviving authorial manuscript. Crane's revisions of *Red Badge* from draft to final manuscript provide irrefutable evidence of a consistently clarifying and persisting authorial intention. You do not need authorial "statements" when such textual documents survive.

25. G. Thomas Tanselle, "The Editorial Problem of Final Authorial Intention," *Studies in Bibliography* 29 (1976): 180; Tzvetan Todorov, "Reading as Construction," in *The Reader in the Text*, pp. 67-82 (the quotation is from p. 67).
26. "Final Authorial Intention," p. 181.

I am closer to a formulation by Hirsch, especially when I read into his words a meaning which I feel sure he did not intend:[27]

> Of course, the text at hand is the safest source of clues to the author's outlook, since men do adopt different attitudes on different occasions. However, even though the text itself should be the primary source of clues and must always be the final authority, the interpreter should make an effort to go beyond his text wherever possible, since this is the only way he can avoid a vicious circularity. The harder one looks at a text from an incorrect stance, the more convincing the incorrect construction becomes.

Concerned with the difficulties of distinguishing "the author's subjective stance," which the text can never in any sense "represent,"[28] Hirsch once again reveals (as at other crucial points in his arguments) that he has not wholly escaped the anti-scholarly influence of the New Critics: he is willing, as I have pointed out, to adjudicate an impasse in criticism on the basis of biographical evidence, a reconstruction of Wordsworth's "probable attitudes so far as these are relevant in specifying the poem's meaning," but he too readily concedes (in the passage I have already quoted) that "we shall never be certain what any writer means." Furthermore, he does not sufficiently identify the variety of such extrinsic evidence and does not sufficiently emphasize its possible importance. Saying Hirsch's words in my own voice, imposing a new intentionality on them, I would make "beyond his text" mean rough drafts, manuscripts, contracts, and the like—materials which are usually thought of as quite beyond the text itself. Hirsch does not deny the relevance of such documents (indeed, he tosses off those brilliant textual questions I quoted in Chapter 1) so much as fail, because of his theoretical text-centered stance, to think habitually in terms of aesthetic anomalies which may originate in the creative process or later, during the process of publication or republication.

Focusing as they do on "text" as a disparate entity, textual theorists and literary theorists talk about revised texts in

27. *Validity in Interpretation*, p. 241.
28. *Validity in Interpretation*, p. 241; the following quotations are from p. 240.

unrealistic terms as routinely as the critics of Henry James have done. Hirsch defines the problem of revised and interpolated texts by saying that the question is not how we are to interpret the text but *"Which* text are we to interpret?" Our "only problem is to choose" a text, either the original one or a later text made up of heterogeneous elements, then, "having chosen, rigorously to refrain from confusing or any way identifying the two quite different and separate 'texts' with one another." Hirsch too quickly assumes that the critic will be justified in regarding a "heterogeneous compilation" as carrying a new unified intentionality.[29] John M. Ellis pretty much echoes Hirsch's notions:[30]

> Before we can see what it is that has occurred when a text has been changed from one version to another, we must look at the effect of the parts of the text concerned on the whole text; that is, we must interpret their function within both complete texts. And only after that can we form any judgment about the nature of the changes, which must be viewed not merely as the change of a few words that can be compared directly to each other, but as a change from a whole text meaning one thing to a whole text meaning another thing.

Similar formulations come from textualists. According to the revised CEAA *Statement,* "Two or more texts of certain works may vary so frequently and so widely as to constitute, in effect, two different works, each with its own copy-text"; and Tanselle has argued that in a particular case Henry James's revisions created two "discrete works."[31]

The problem with such very appealing formulations has already been suggested: routinely, when novels are revised, hunks are re-used, unaltered or only slightly altered, and even in extensive revisions it often happens that whole paragraphs or pages or chapters go unrevised. In these cases, what goes

29. *Validity in Interpretation*, p. 233.
30. *The Theory of Literary Criticism: A Logical Analysis* (Berkeley: University of California Press, 1974), p. 118.
31. *Statement of Editorial Principles and Procedures*, Revised Edition (New York: Modern Language Association of America, 1972), p. 6; "Final Authorial Intention," p. 196.

unrevised to a greater or lesser extent goes unrethought, unrestructured, carrying its original intentionality in a new context where that intentionality is more or less at war with the different intentionality in the altered or newly written passages. If many sentences or paragraphs or even pages are unrevised, we cannot assume that the author has belatedly rejected his original intentions for such passages and has reconceived each unrevised passage so as to restructure it for the new and discrete work. If unaltered or scarcely altered hunks of the original text remain in the later text, that later text is not truly a "separate" one, and our focus should not be on keeping texts separate but on seeing ways they are still the same. Versions are harder to create than we acknowledge and revisions produce discrete works much more seldom than we say. The failure of textual theorists and literary theorists to provide a good definition of "version" may be laid directly at the foot of "The Intentional Fallacy," for the failure springs from a reluctance to focus on the imposition of authorial meaning during the process of composition (or recomposition) and only then.

The long dominance of the notion of the text as a stable embodiment of organic unity is such that there is very little difference between the proliferation of "interesting" private "readings" which Hirsch deplored and the attitudes, at times, of the theorist of structuralism and deconstructionism, Jonathan Culler. As a structuralist Culler assumes that the text is stable and that that stability somehow derives from the author, but, following Roland Barthes, he sees pleasure as a main value "that a structuralist study of literature might serve" and he is powerfully swayed toward an individualistic aesthetics "based on the pleasure of the reader." Such an aesthetics would reject the "myth" of organic unity as "a standard of value," but might retain the myth "to function simply as a hypothesis of reading."[32] We could escape any slavish bestowing of equal attention upon each part of a text and could bestow our attention on points where we could derive most enjoyment, finding pleasure not in unity but in "the fragment, the incongruous detail, the charming excess of certain descriptions

32. *Structuralist Poetics*, p. 264 (the first quotation) and p. 263 (the following ones).

and elaborations, the well-constructed sentence whose elegance exceeds its function, or the flaws in a grand design." Culler's pleasure principle is tempting in what it promises along the way toward the end of the text—small pleasures which can be enjoyed for themselves rather than being seized on and fitted or refitted for their places in a grimly sought overarching organic unity. Yet when Culler embraces the pleasure principle without discarding his New Critical faith that the text he is reading so sensuously is authoritative, he sets up a situation in which he may be thrilling to adventitious pleasures never intended by the author.

I regard with tolerance Culler's notion that "the major task of criticism" ought to be "that of making the text interesting,"[33] for he goes on to approve of responsible reading, but it is hard not to regard as frivolous other theories which justify the reader's bending any text to his or her personal fantasies, whether the theory is that of the reader-response and subjectivist theorist Robert Crosman ("In order to serve the various needs and desires of various readers, texts *ought* to have plural meanings") or the theory of the subjectivist Norman N. Holland ("With a transactive theory of response, you can relate the rich variety of literary experience to the rich variety of human beings themselves"). Stanley Fish now holds that "meanings are the property neither of fixed and stable texts nor of free and independent readers but of interpretive communities that are responsible both for the shape of a reader's activities and for the texts those activities produce."[34] Politically, these notions may be categorized as bleeding-heart liberal (the conviction that the lowliest of God's critters deserves to have his or her own special meaning of a text, just for him or her). Crosman, without quite calling Hirsch a fascist for believing there can be a correct reading, nevertheless calls him "coercive" and concludes that his "theory of meaning" is quite "unsuited to a modern democ-

33. *Structuralist Poetics*, p. 262.
34. Robert Crosman, "Do Readers Make Meaning?" in *The Reader in the Text*, pp. 149-64; the quotation is from p. 162; Norman N. Holland, "Re-Covering 'The Purloined Letter,'" in *The Reader in the Text*, pp. 350-70 (the quotation is from p. 367); Fish, *Text?*, p. 322.

racy.''[35] Alternatively, these notions may be in their way authoritarian (consider Fish's subtitle, "The Authority of Interpretive Communities"—announced before publication as "The Authority of Hermeneutic Communities"). As a former Californian, like Fish, I spook easily around authority-wielding hermeneutic communities, whether political, sexual, or textual; spooked enough, I recite Shakespeare on "brief authority" and get on with study of the author and literary authority.

To a textualist perhaps the most beguiling fact about literary theory from structuralism to deconstructionism is the persistence of innocent trust in the text itself as a New Critical given. According to Jonathan Culler, structuralist poetics took "the intelligibility of the work as its point of departure."[36] For Roland Barthes, "Structural analysis. . . bypasses the problems associated with the figure of the author as well as other criteria exterior to the text and instead focusses its attention on the text, understood as a construct whose mode of functioning must be described."[37] A text was *lisible*, readable, even though Barthes denied the author as the source of textual unity and located that unity in the reader who would focus, in Culler's words, "on the codes and conventions responsible for the work's *lisibilité* or intelligibility."[38] Structuralists and reader-response critics alike, in Culler's survey, have "come to rely on the text as a source of insight, suggesting that one must grant some authority to the text so as to try to learn from it, even when what one learns about texts and readings puts in question the claim that anything in particular is definitively in the text."[39] In deconstructionist criticism, according to Culler, the text itself still remains a given: "Any reading involves presuppositions, and the text itself, Derrida suggests, will provide images and arguments to subvert those presuppositions. The text will carry signs of that difference from itself which makes explication

35. "Do Readers Make Meaning?" n. 9, p. 160.
36. *On Deconstruction* (Ithaca: Cornell University Presss, 1982), p. 32.
37. *Textual Strategies*, ed. Josué V. Harari (Ithaca: Cornell University Press, 1979), Harari's "Critical Factions / Critical Fictions," pp. 17-72 (the quotation is from p. 23).
38. *On Deconstruction*, p. 33.
39. *On Deconstruction*, pp. 82-83.

231

interminable."[40] "What is deconstructed in deconstructive analyses," Culler continues, "is not the text itself but the text as it is read, the combination of text and the readings that articulate it." Paul de Man without being an intentionalist can put the case that the author's texts "in themselves provide the only starting-point for deconstructive treatment."[41] And in de Man's view deconstruction "is not a matter of mere critical gamesmanship precisely because it uses—*can* only use—the figural leads and devices advanced by the text itself."[42] Even when he rejects Barthes, saying that "the possibility of reading can never be taken for granted," de Man still relies on the text as a given.[43] Bemusing as such formulations are, when Jacques Derrida sees deconstruction as "a technique of de-sedimenting the text in order to allow what was *always already* inscribed in its texture to resurface,"[44] I resort to *Pudd'nhead Wilson* as proof that what the critic thinks was always already inscribed there wasn't, in some cases, inscribed there at all but is imputed by the reader to be inscribed there.

Where structuralists attempted to direct research in the humanities toward "broad, systematic projects," deconstruction "is now urged to return to close reading," to (in what Culler admires as a "happy phrase" of Barbara Johnson's) "'careful teasing out of warring forces of signification within the text.'" There is, Culler recognizes, "some measure of continuity between the goals of the New Criticism and those of the newer criticism," but he makes the distinction that "the 'closeness' of deconstructive readings lies not in word-by-word or line-by-line commentary but in attention to what resists other modes of understanding."[45] The text remains a given; excluding the author as the source of unifying elements, denying value in a

40. *On Deconstruction*, p. 214; the quotation in the next sentence is from p. 215.

41. Christopher Norris, *Deconstruction: Theory and Practice* (London and New York: Methuen, 1982), p. 106.

42. Norris, *Deconstruction*, p. 108.

43. Paul de Man, *Blindness and Insight* (New York: Oxford University Press, 1971), p. 107.

44. Harari, *Textual Strategies*, p. 37.

45. *On Deconstruction*, p. 220 (the words "happy phrase" are on p. 213, where Culler first quotes Johnson's words); the following quotations are from p. 220 and 256.

reader's imposing any unifying "closure," deconstructionists still begin uncritically with "a particular text" and explore how, within that text, "elements that a unifying understanding has repressed work to undo the structures to which they seem marginal"; the goal of the deconstructive reading "is not to reveal the meaning of a particular work but to explore forces and structures that recur in reading and writing." The achievements of deconstructive criticism, Culler says, "lie in the delineation of the logic of texts rather than in the postures with which or in which critical essays conclude."[46] Barbara Johnson, in the essay on *Billy Budd, Sailor* which Culler so admires, assumes the logic in a text which, as the editors Hayford and Sealts showed, contains internal illogic simply because Melville's latest revisions altered the direction the work was taking and in effect called Captain Vere's behavior into question.[47] No more than any New Critic does Johnson avail herself of the evidence of the Genetic Text of *Billy Budd, Sailor* as a source of those crucial but apparently "marginal" elements which unity-seeking readers have repressed.

Thus for all their cosmic recklessness, the deconstructionists hold to the bland New Critical assurance that any text is complete and ready for their manipulations. Just like ordinary critics they assume that they start with an unproblematic "text," which only then do they proceed to "problematize." J. Hillis Miller cannot begin his game of unraveling unless he starts with what he calls the "poem in itself." More than this, the deconstructionists essentially mystify the process of contradiction and conflict whereby the text's unity is "disrupted." For them, the disruptive effects are attributed seemingly to some mysterious perversity of discourse, writing itself, which is always undoing itself from within. By definition, for Miller, all

---

46. *On Deconstruction*, p. 260.
47. *The Critical Difference* (Baltimore: Johns Hopkins University Press, 1980), Chapter 6, "Melville's Fist: The Execution of *Billy Budd*," pp. 79-109, 151-52. Johnson's disregard for scholarship is plain in n. 7, pp. 151-52, where she cites "commentators" as if Hayford and Sealts had not discredited their claims that the story had "its origin" in the *Somers* mutiny case. In *Billy Budd, Sailor*, eds. Harrison Hayford and Merton M. Sealts, Jr. (Chicago: University of Chicago Press, 1962), see pp. 221-425 for the Genetic Text; and see "Perspectives for Criticism," pp. 34-39, for an analysis of the effects of the late revisions.

texts are "'unreadable,' if by 'readable' one means open to a single, definitive, univocal interpretation."[48] With his conditional construction Miller has safely ensconced himself at the cozy traditional hearth, since no one would seriously insist on such an extreme definition of "readable."

Miller plays at being outrageous, but he is more right than he guesses, for many familiar texts are literally unreadable, if by "readable" one means open to a coherent interpretation growing out of a sequential perusal of a text. Many familiar texts do not, in large ways or small, make sense, however driven critics may be to find sense in them. By tracing textual anomalies and conflicts to the processes that authors work through in creating their texts and to the adventures of texts subsequent to their composition, I advance a more plausible, rationally explicable account of what deconstructionists have in an intriguing but dim way discerned and then have proceeded to mystify. I hold up for contemplation by deconstructionists what Harrison Hayford has written on "unnecessarily duplicates" in *Moby-Dick*, a conjectural essay (necessarily so, given the paucity of documentary evidence) which dares to take scenes and even paragraphs and sentences apart in an attempt to find compositional patterns which will explain anomalies in the published text.[49] As I have suggested, deconstructionists do not live up to their own claims of risk-taking: they don't start far enough back and don't go far enough ahead. In relying on the text as a constructed given rather than venturing into more perilous textual terrain, taking the risks that only biographers and textualists know enough to take (those intuitive leaps across fragments of texts, across the gaps created by authorial or editorial mayhem; the dizzying integrity of the spaces between those editorial ellipsis dots in the restored *Red Badge*), deconstructionists are camping, as it were, in their own

48. J. Hillis Miller, "The Critic as Host," *Critical Inquiry* 3 (Spring 1977): 439-47; the quotations are from p. 445 and 447.

49. "Unnecessary Duplicates: A Key to the Writing of *Moby-Dick*," in *New Perspectives on Melville*, ed. Faith Pullin (Edinburgh: Edinburgh University Press, 1978), pp. 128-61.

backyards. Such timid deconstructionists have bypassed the deconstructive and reconstructive opportunities I have identified in this book.

Nor has there been much to learn about texts, so far, from two movements which ought to be still closer to the textual-aesthetic one I have been defining. The first, the search for a feminist canon, was begun by critics who broke away from the New Criticism in the late 1960s, about the time some of us textual-biographical scholars did, and in some of its phases pursued biographical investigation and sought to understand writers in cultural contexts. The appealing goal, in these years, was, in Annette Kolodny's words, "rigorous biographical research and critical judgment," and Elaine Showalter from the first stressed the need to resurrect works with genuine literary value.[50] There was from the start a nonsexual handicap for the new feminists: their academic generation was ill-trained in American literary history, having been brought up to explicate a limited number of "standard" texts. As a graduate student of an earlier period, I had combed American literary histories for a list of some two hundred "neglected" novels and read those I could find—all of Stowe's, for instance. I knew the merit of books by women which the feminists were "discovering," but I was uneasy when they discovered the wonderful Caroline Kirkland without discovering her wonderful son Joseph Kirkland. We needed not a new sexist canon but a new nonsexist canon. Yet there seemed every reason to hope that the feminists' research would inevitably involve forms of textual scholarship, at least as a by-product of the new study of literary history.

In the crossfighting of the ensuing decade (the demand for a black feminist aesthetic as well as a white feminist aesthetic,

50. See Kolodny's review essay "Literary Criticism," *Signs* 2 (Winter 1976): 404-21; the quotation is from p. 416. In the "Literary Criticism" review essay in *Signs* 1 (Winter 1975): 435-60, Elaine Showalter had no illusions about "the need to focus, to clarify, to investigate"; it takes time "to retrain ourselves, let alone our departments, to do the basic research, to locate the documents, and to develop the framework for future investigations" (p. 436). Showalter added: "It is not enough to discover new writers or new materials; one must demonstrate their worth, a task which has been assumed to require authority and maturity" (p. 438).

the demand for a lesbian aesthetic),[51] the chief theorists of the movement ceased calling for rigorous study of literary history and biography. Ignoring Showalter's plea in 1975 for historical investigation into the milieux of women writers, Kolodny (whom Showalter had called "the most sophisticated theorist of feminist interpretation") adopted some of the weakest of the fashionable, male-instigated theories.[52] Kolodny began to speak impatiently of research, especially as it relates to finding out what authors meant: "Short of time machines or miraculous resurrections, there is simply no way to know, precisely or surely, what 'really was,' what Homer intended when he sang, or Milton when he dictated," and she paid homage to Wimsatt and Beardsley: "Critics more acute than I have already pointed up the impossibility of grounding a reading in the imputation of authorial intention because the further removed the author is from us, so too must be her or his systems of knowledge and belief, points of view, and structures of vision (artistic and otherwise)."[53] She also accepted the subjectivism being promoted by David Bleich, Norman N. Holland, and Robert

51. The plea that there be, or that there could be, a feminist aesthetic is of course recurrent in this literature. Showalter (1975), p. 437, was clear that "feminist criticism is still more coherent as an ideology than as a methodology"; Kolodny (1976), p. 414, faced up to the "thorny problem of generating 'a feminist aesthetic'"; Cheri Register in her review essay on "Literary Criticism," Signs 6 (Winter 1980): 268-82, even more resolutely asks, in a subheading, "Is There a Female Aesthetics?" (p. 271). Earlier Sydney Janet Kaplan in the review essay on "Literary Criticism," Signs 4 (Spring 1979): 514-27, had referred (p. 525) to a "hard-hitting, well-supported attack on the neglect of black literature by feminist critics," a "sorely needed statement about the absence of black women writers from the 'canon' and the need for a black feminist aesthetic." (This was Barbara Smith's "Toward a Black Feminist Criticism," Conditions 1 : 25-44.) Register (p. 277) addresses the possibility of whether "a distinctly lesbian aesthetics exists," and in "Zero Degree Deviancy: The Lesbian Novel in English," Critical Inquiry 8 (Winter 1981): 363-79, Catharine R. Stimpson sets out to ground lesbian writing "in the domain of feminist criticism" (p. 363).
52. Showalter, "Feminist Criticism in the Wilderness," Critical Inquiry 8 (Winter 1981): 179-205; her praise of Kolodny is on p. 182. See Kolodny's "Dancing Through the Minefield: Some Observations on the Theory, Practice, and Politics of a Feminist Literary Criticism," Feminist Studies 6 (Spring 1980): 1-25.
53. Kolodny (1980), p. 10; the following quotation is from p. 11. For Crosman see the citation in n. 34. See also Norman N. Holland, 5 Readers Reading (New Haven: Yale University Press, 1975), and David Bleich, Subjective Criticism (Baltimore: Johns Hopkins Press, 1978). For a salutary argument against subjectivism see Israel Scheffler, Science and Subjectivity (Indianapolis: Bobbs-Merrill, 1967).

Crosman: "we appropriate meaning from a text according to what we need (or desire) or, in other words, according to the critical assumptions or predispositions (conscious or not) that we bring to it. And we appropriate different meanings, or report different gleanings, at different times—even from the same text —according to our changed assumptions, circumstances, and requirements." This was to abandon the research into literary history which might have led to the establishment of a feminist canon, and indeed was to renounce the very idea of establishing a canon based upon aesthetic values. Thus abandoning its earliest goals, the movement set new ones—"to acknowledge the aesthetic potential of the female body," and to be willing to "speculate that anatomy is part of epiphany";[54] to pursue "the tantalizing riddle of the differentiation of male and female language," a search which has degenerated into sexist questioning of the relation of women's writing to women's conversation;[55] and to show that the literary creative process is different in women than in men, a claim that opens the door again to treating women not only as different but also as inferior.[56]

The evidence of Rothenberg and others suggests that the creative process is not gender-related but simply human, just as linguistic evidence (as Showalter says) does not support the notion that "the sexes are pre-programmed to develop structurally different linguistic systems."[57] From my vantage point, there is obvious merit in any movement which began with a renewed interest in literary history and recognized, at the outset, that laborious archival work would have to be performed, and which may return to such goals after a decade of buying cheap goods and pursuing delusory aesthetic goals. One

54. Cheri Register (1980), p. 275; the speculation that anatomy is part of epiphany is quoted by Register from Catherine F. Smith, "Jane Lead," in *Shakespeare's Sisters* (Bloomington: Indiana University Press, 1979), p. 18.

55. The "tantalizing riddle" is from an uncharacteristically incautious passage in Showalter (1975), p. 449; see Register (1980), pp. 272-73, for a survey of dismayingly impressionistic attempts to define a specifically feminine and feminist language.

56. See various essays in *Critical Inquiry* 8 (Winter 1981), the special issue on *Writing and Sexual Difference* edited by Elizabeth Abel; the issue, considerably enlarged, was reprinted by the University of Chicago Press as a Phoenix paperback (1982).

57. Showalter (1981), pp. 192-93.

encouraging sign is that the special issue of *Critical Inquiry* devoted to the idea of canons contains an essay in which Barbara Herrnstein Smith (writing as a critic and a theorist, not calling attention to her gender) reexamines basic questions which Kolodny and others had repudiated;[58] ultimately, of course, reconsideration of canons will require biographical, bibliographical, and textual research. Another extremely encouraging sign is the appearance of Paul Lauter's compilation of sixty-seven syllabi which "reflect the efforts of instructors to incorporate in their teaching the fruits of two decades of scholarship in minority and women's art, literature, and culture." The syllabi constitute suggestive ways of expanding the canon without abandoning survey courses in American literature and without abandoning aesthetic value as one criterion for works taught in those survey courses.[59] My affinity for what Lauter and his contributors are doing comes not only from an old concern with finding ways to bring neglected authors into survey courses; it also comes from the fact that what I have been up to for the last decade is simply another way of challenging the canon, asking not what we might teach *instead* of works like *The Red Badge of Courage* and *An American Dream* but what we teach when we *do* teach *The Red Badge of Courage* and *An American Dream*.

The second recent movement which I find encouraging is the return to the "historical method" now being promoted by Jerome J. McGann in a series of essays and in *A Critique of Modern Textual Criticism*. Although in practice, as I mentioned in Chapter 2 (n. 2), McGann has slighted the creative process, and although he has sometimes come perilously near the simplistic use of biographical evidence against which the original New Critics reacted so extremely, his approach by its nature

58. *Critical Inquiry* 10 (September 1983), the special issue on Canons edited by Robert von Hallberg. Smith's lead article, "Contingencies of Value," pp. 1-35, proceeds by ignoring most of the vagaries of recent critical theory.

59. Paul Lauter, ed., *Reconstructing American Literature: Courses, Syllabi, Issues* (Old Westbury, New York: The Feminist Press, 1983); the quotation is from the Introduction, p. xi.

should ultimately involve the study of the aesthetic implications of textual evidence, among other historical evidence.[60]

In detailing the waste of human effort in editing, criticism, and theory I have cited mainly writers of the 1950s, 1960s, and the early 1970s, but some younger academicians have been equally aloof from biographical, bibliographical, and textual scholarship, oblivious of it or contemptuous of it. The promising young post-Freudian structuralist Eric J. Sundquist relies placidly on unreliable biographical writing, as in his blithe repetition of a long-exploded legend ("the well-known fact that Melville, upon the birth of his second son, Stanwix, unwittingly entered his own mother's name in place of his wife's on the birth certificate").[61] Barbara Johnson, the translator of Derrida, gleefully pronounces that in *Billy Budd* "the very phrase 'the deadly space between' is, according to editors Hayford and Sealts, a quotation of unknown origin; the source of the expression used to designate what is not known is thus itself unknown"; but it was the benighted modern editors who did not know the phrase, not Melville, who, as the mere scholar Stanton Garner has shown, got it from Thomas Campbell.[62] Walter Benn Michaels writes on *Sister Carrie* and *The Financier*, oblivious to the possibility that their textual histories might

60. It is unfortunate that McGann, one of the foremost recent polemicists for a return to "extrinsic criticism," should fall into the sort of literal equating of the poem with real life which Wimsatt and Beardsley had so deplored in the biographical critics of the 1930s and early 1940s. Besides his *Critique* (Chicago: University of Chicago Press, 1983), see McGann's "The Text, the Poem, and the Problem of Historical Method," *New Literary History* 12 (1981): 282: "The hearse in the poem is on its way out Pleasant Street, past Emily Dickinson's house, to the cemetery located at the northern edge of the town, just beyond the Dickinson homestead."

61. Sundquist, *Home as Found: Authority and Genealogy in Nineteenth-Century American Literature* (Baltimore: Johns Hopkins University Press, 1979), 151.

62. *The Critical Difference*, pp. 93-94. Garner's discovery is in *English Language Notes* 14 (1979): 289-90. In his copy of *Paradise Lost*, Melville underlined "A dreadful interval" (Book VI, line 105) and noted at the bottom of the page "'The deadly space between'/Campbell." (This footnote to a footnote I include through the courtesy and kindness of Michael F. Robinson, who allowed me to examine Melville's two-volume set of *The Poetical Works of John Milton* at Phillips Galleries prior to their being auctioned on 27 March 1984.)

have some implications for interpretation.[63] The New Criticism may well be coming to a dead end not in the "newer criticisms" but in what Jay Martin identifies as the "new ignorance":[64]

> In order to write about the nineteenth-century American imagination of authority and genealogy, would it be necessary or even desirable to become acquainted with the major American intellectual historians of the period, or to know accurately the character and condition of family life, or law, or social relations on the East coast, or to become acquainted with the sociologists of American community and the anthropological investigations of American mores? . . . What must be called nothing less than the new ignorance is fully displayed in Eric J. Sundquist's *Home as Found*.

To the areas of "new ignorance" which Martin lists I would of course add literary history, biography, bibliography, and textual history.

All in all, we have paid a high price, and we have paid it over and over again, for the professional hubris which scorned "textual bibliography" and "textual criticism" while disproportionately rewarding critical essays then essays in literary theory. We have also paid a high price for the professional hubris which set editing apart as an inferior, barely ancillary service-industry (a make-work industry whose shoddy products critics and theorists grudgingly bought, sometimes, but never read the labels of, and tended not to use either in private or in public). A few of us have paid a high price, also, for the stranger hubris of the Newest Bibliography which at its worst barricaded editing within a mad-scientist laboratory more isolated from the author than any critic or theorist had yet been. Yet, as I have shown in earlier chapters, American literary scholarship has begun to flourish—even if it has done so, ironically, as a by-product of the great, flawed editorial enterprise of the 1960s, and even if it has often done so by documentation of particular

---

63. Walter Benn Michaels, "*Sister Carrie*'s Popular Economy," *Critical Inquiry* 7 (Winter 1980): 373-90; "Dreiser's *Financier*: The Man of Business as a Man of Letters," in *American Realism: New Essays*, pp. 278-95.

64. Review of Sundquist's *Home as Found* in *American Literature* 52 (January 1981): 654-55; the quotation is from p. 654.

biographical episodes or illumination of particular textual histories, without a sense of an author's life and writing as a whole and without a sense of the scholar's work in relation to that of other scholars, critics, and theorists—not to speak of the relationship of his or her work to that being pursued in other fields, such as clinical psychiatry and cognitive psychology.

My pleasure in promoting a new biographico-textico-aesthetico "movement" in the last decade would have been greater if I could have found a name for it. The search for a feminist aesthetic has so far been in vain, but at least there is a name for what the searchers want to find or produce. McGann's "the new historicism" has a cool, reassuring ring to it. Despairing of identifying myself by the term "textual critic" (J. Hillis Miller probably thinks *he's* a textual critic), I tried out "the New Scholarship," which was misleading because it left out the critical and aesthetic parts of the approach; worse, it conveyed all the bumptiousness of a new movement without the self-mockery it had been meant to carry. Textual bibliographers are not supposed to indulge in drollery. But after a decade and more of feeling very much an outsider—publicly condemned by Edmund Wilson, at odds with and even shut out by the editorial establishment, ignored (like all textualists) by critics and theorists—it is satisfying to finish this book after a little hunk of it has appeared in *Critical Inquiry*. Still more gratifying is the fact that in the last several years MLA programs in two Divisions, Nineteenth Century American Literature and Methods of Literary Research, have been devoted to The Aesthetic Implications of Textual Evidence, as have several sessions of the Bibliography and Textual Study Sections of regional MLA programs, particularly at the South Atlantic Modern Language Association (SAMLA) conventions. At the 1981 MLA, Steven Mailloux and I drew into one room an amazingly motley crowd where editors and textual bibliographers sat flank to flank, if not eye to eye, with literary theorists. At the 1983 MLA, J. A. Leo Lemay sponsored a splendid session in celebration of the Harvard Edition of Emerson's *Journals and Miscellaneous Notebooks* where the speakers repeatedly dwelt upon the aesthetic implications of the new textual evidence. The publication of Mailloux's *Interpretive Conventions* (1982) was another breakthrough, for he writes with equal familiarity of editorial

241

theory, speech act philosophy, and several varieties of literary theory. I take special pleasure now in the irony that the editor of this book, the director of Northwestern University Press, is best known as a literary theorist.

Having gained a hearing, I can admit to some earlier stridency of tone. In any case, G. R. Thompson has complained that I have been "railing against a lack of hardcore scholarship in Melville criticism for years, in *ALS* and elsewhere, calling for rejection of both narrow New Critical searches for textual 'unity' and fancy poststructuralist and deconstructionist wordgames."[65] But I have tried wooing rather than railing for some time (although perhaps still too roughly), as when I called on one critic to risk capture by a stoutly-linked row of scholars: "Red Rover, Red Rover, let WADLINGTON come over!"[66] Striving for a more overt erotics of textuality, I concluded a 1981 essay with what I thought was an irresistible appeal to deconstructionists and post-structuralist Freudians: "In this realm where biotextual evidence and creativity theory interplay with critical theory and aesthetic theory (a realm rife with suggestiveness) what you write has a chance of lasting a while."[67] There were no takers from that crowd, but I'm still hoping to lure some of the younger people into "doing" scholarship as well as "doing" theory. (Having renounced theory so early in their careers, Knapp and Michaels will *have* to take up something else.) Come over, come over. Even Robert Milder says that the "New

65. *American Literary Scholarship: An Annual, 1980* (Durham: Duke University Press, 1982), p. 41.

66. Once again I am singling out a fine critic to make a point about the pervasiveness of New Critical reflexes. See in *Studies in the Novel* 9 (Spring 1977): 102-05, my review of Warwick Wadlington, *The Confidence Game in American Literature* (Princeton: Princeton University Press, 1975). Wadlington uses the phrase "Scholarship has shown" (p. 202) in a situation where in fact scholarship had been erroneous. The discussion of *Innocents Abroad* cries out for textual corroboration at many points, as in the passage beginning on p. 190. Precisely how does the massive new research in Robert H. Hirst's 1975 Berkeley dissertation on "The Making of *The Innocents Abroad*: 1867-1872" complicate the possible analysis of Mark Twain's "opportunistic effects" (p. 192)? Wadlington's consideration of Hirst's evidence would be worth reading.

67. "The 'New Scholarship': Textual Evidence and Its Implications for Criticism, Literary Theory, and Aesthetics," *Studies in American Fiction* 9 (Autumn 1981): 181-97.

Scholarship" (or whatever we call it) may be "the most promising game in town."[68] There's nothing to lose but some misreadings, and a good deal to gain. You become an honest man or woman when you read *Pudd'nhead Wilson* in the light of its composition, acknowledging its virtues without exalting its formal perfection, and when you read the reconstructed *The Red Badge of Courage*, even though some of its crimson paint and gold leaf has been battered off irreparably, you hold what's left of an authentic textual icon.

68. *American Literary Scholarship: An Annual, 1981* (Durham: Duke University Press, 1983), p. 61.

Index

After a new project absorbed my attention (in a workaday analogue to the compulsive artistic behavior described by Albert Rothenberg), James Murphy took primary charge of the index, and Suzanne Hunger kindly helped him; Alma A. MacDougall saw it through its final stages.

244

245

James, Henry, 55, 58-59, 85-114, 210, 214, 228; *Ambassadors, The*, 90, 92, 93; 112; *American, The*, 88, 92, 94, 95, 96-97, 99, 100, 107-110, 109n, 111-12, 114; *American Scene, The*, 109; *Art of the Novel, The*, 108n; "Beast in the Jungle, The," 114; *Bostonians, The*, 97-98, 113; *Daisy Miller*, 40-41, 42n, 96; "Four Meetings," 97; *Notebooks*, 91, 103, 111, 225; "Pandora," 99, "Pension Beaurepas, The," 96; *Portrait of a Lady, The*, 89, 91, 96-97, 100, 100n, 107, 108, 113; *Princess Casamassima, The*, 93; *Roderick Hudson*, 92, 99, 108, 113; *Spoils of Poynton, The*, 90, 91, 113; *Turn of the Screw, The*, 97; *Watch and Ward*, 100; *What Maisie Knew*, 91; *Wings of the Dove, The*, 93, 101-4
James, William, 62; *Pragmatism*, 17n
Jasper (*Pudd'nhead Wilson*), 126, 127, 132
Jim (*Huckleberry Finn*), 4, 33
Johnson, Barbara, 232, 233, 233n, 239
Johnson, Lyndon B., 185, 185n
Jones, Howard Mumford, 163n
Juhl, P. D., Jr., 1-2

Kable, William S., 63
Kaplan, Sydney Janet, 236n
Katz, Joseph, 15, 147, 151, 156, 163, 174
Kelly, Barney Oswald (*An American Dream*), 183-84, 190, 195-96, 199, 204, 206-7
Kennedy, John F., 185-87, 191, 198
Kirkland, Caroline, 235
Kirkland, Joseph, 235
Knapp, Steven, 1-2, 86n, 213, 242
Knickerbocker, Conrad, 183n
Kolin, Philip C., 218n
Kolodny, Annette, 235-36, 236n, 238
Krause, Sydney J., 97, 98-99, 99-100, 101
Krieger, Murray, 3, 3n, 23-25, 26, 51, 82, 182
Krum (*The Sun Also Rises*), 44

LaFrance, Marston, 161, 168-69
Laurence, Dan H., 92
Lauter, Paul, 238
Leary, Lewis, 85
Leavis, F. R., 55, 92, 141
Lemay, J. A. Leo, 241
Levenson, J. C., 149, 152, 155, 172, 174
Lewis, Stuart A., 135n

Leznicki, Lt. (*An American Dream*), 198, 200-201, 203
Library of America, 68, 176
Linton, Marigold, 111n
Lipking, Lawrence I., x-xi, 86n, 213n
Lowes, John Livingston, 21
Lucid, Robert F., 182n, 208, 210
Luigi (*Pudd'nhead Wilson*), 5-6, 13, 115, 120-25, 127-32, 134-37, 139-40, 143
Luria, A. R., 113n

MacCallum, Buddy (*Flags in the Dust/ Sartoris*), 48
McGann, Jerome J., 18n, 221n, 238, 239n, 241
McKeithan, Daniel Morley, 117n, 120
McKerrow, Ronald B., 17-18, 19, 59, 61, 153
Mailer, Norman, xiv, 181-212; *Advertisements for Myself*, 183n; *American Dream, An*, 4, 10, 142, 181-212, 238; *Beyond the Law*, 202; *Deer Park, The*, 183
Mailloux, Steven, xii, 22n, 73n, 86n, 164, 165, 172, 220n, 241
Male, Roy R., 65
Mallet, Rowland (*Roderick Hudson*), 99
Malone, David H., 163, 163n
Mann, Charles W., 44-45
Mann, Karen, 142
Marcher, John ("The Beast in the Jungle"), 114
Marcus, Mordecai, 159,168
Mark Twain, 64, 114; *Huckleberry Finn*, 4, 33, 48, 49, 133, 144, 181, 218; *Innocents Abroad, The*, 242n; *Life on the Mississippi*, 144; *Mysterious Stranger, The*, 181; *Old Times on the Mississippi*, 144; *Pudd'nhead Wilson*, xiv, 4-5, 5-6, 5n, 8-9, 13-14, 28, 28n, 115-45, 166, 218-19, 225, 226n, 232, 243; *Those Extraordinary Twins*, 28, 115-45
Martin, Jay, 240
Martin, Shago (*An American Dream*), 191, 192, 194, 196, 197, 199, 200, 201, 204, 205, 206, 207
Maslin, Janet, xvi
Matthiessen, F. O., 11, 11n, 57-58, 94-95, 96, 97, 104, 136, 138
Mazzella, Anthony J., 100, 107
Melville, Gansevoort, 38

247

Melville, Herman, 33, 35-36, 49n, 64, 105, 209, 214n, 239, 242; "Benito Cereno," 37; *Billy Budd, Sailor*, 30-32, 30n, 58, 69-70, 71, 181, 233, 233n, 239; *Clarel*, 187; *Mardi*, 35, 36, 37; *Moby-Dick*, 20, 29, 36, 54, 56, 70-71, 82, 234; *Omoo*, 29, 37; *Piazza Tales, The*, 37; *Pierre*, 28-30, 29n, 173, 187, 190, 208, 225; *Redburn*, 29, 36, 37, 64n; *Typee*, 29, 37, 48, 49n; *White-Jacket*, 7-8, 29, 36, 37-39, 40, 57-58, 136
Melville, Stanwix, 239
Meriwether, James B., 43, 72, 151
Merle, Serena (*The Portrait of a Lady*), 100, 105
Michaels, Walter Benn, 1-2, 14n, 86n, 213, 239, 242
Milder, Robert, 216n, 242-43
Miller, Daisy (*Daisy Miller*), 40-41
Miller, J. Hillis, 233-34, 241
Millgate, Jane, xvi
Mitchell, Harry (*Sanctuary*), 47-48
Mitgang, Herbert, xvi, 176, 178, 209-10
Monroe, Marilyn, 186
Montoya (*The Sun Also Rises*), 46
Morewood, Sarah, 35n
Mumford, Lewis, 64n

National Endowment for the Humanities, 19, 19n, 151
Neisser, Ulric xiii, xiv
Nevius, Blake, 108, 147
New Criticism, x, xii, 2, 16, 16n, 20-21, 53, 54, 71-72, 73, 86, 87, 88-89, 91, 94-95, 100, 102, 103, 104, 105, 113, 114, 139, 140, 142n, 145, 155, 165, 166, 213-27, 229-33, 235, 236, 240
Newman, Christopher (*The American*), 96, 98, 100, 105, 109, 112
Nichol, John W. 11n, 58n
Nordloh, David J., 67-68, 156n, 164
North, Abe (*Tender is the Night*), 75

O'Brien (*An American Dream*), 200
O'Neill, Eugene, xiii, 189n
Old Coffee (*White-Jacket*), 37, 38
Osmond, Gilbert (*The Portrait of a Lady*), 100, 105

Parker, Hershel, 5n, 8n, 10n, 28n, 30n, 37n, 39n, 48n, 54, 67, 70, 73n, 76, 102, 148, 163, 172-75, 181n, 210, 216, 216n, 223n, 242n
Peinovich, Michael, 97-98
Perkins, D. N., 142n

Perkins, Maxwell, 26n, 46, 79
Perry, Bliss, 64n
Phelps, Peter, 156, 161, 167, 173
Pizer, Donald, 6n, 49, 156-57, 160, 161-63, 164, 165, 165n, 168, 169, 171-75, 172n, 179, 220-21n
Polk, Noel, 42n, 178
Popeye (*Sanctuary*), 42
Pound, Ezra, 43

Queequeg (*Moby-Dick*), 71

Rader, Ralph W., xiii, 144-45, 145n
Randel, William, 63
Rathbun, John W., 160
Raval, Suresh, 223-24
Ray, Gordon N., 92n, 148
Rechnitz, Robert M., 161
Reed, Elaine, 163
Register, Cheri, 236n, 237n
Reichert, John, 16n
Roberts, Detective (*An American Dream*), 10, 184, 190, 191, 192, 196, 197, 198, 199, 200-207
Rogers, Jimmie (*The Red Badge of Courage*), 160, 169, 170, 193n
Rojack, Deborah (*An American Dream*), 183-84, 185, 186, 186n, 190, 191, 193, 194, 195-96, 198, 199, 202, 203n, 206, 207
Rojack, Deirdre (*An American Dream*), 184, 186, 207
Rojack, Stephen Richards (*An American Dream*), 4, 10, 183-84, 185, 186, 186n, 187-207
Romeo (*An American Dream*), 10, 190, 191, 199, 204
Roper, Alan, 149
Rosenbaum, S. P., 88n, 90, 91, 101, 101n, 105
Ross, Michael L., 141
Rothenberg, Dr. Albert, xiii-xiv, 23, 24-25, 34n, 35, 51, 173, 173n, 182, 189n, 237
Rowlette, Robert, 141
Roxana (*Pudd'nhead Wilson*), 117, 119, 125, 126, 127, 128, 130, 131, 132, 135, 137, 138, 140, 141, 144
Roxon-Ropschitz, I., 189n
Ruta (*An American Dream*), 183, 190, 191, 198, 206
Ryle, Gilbert, 16n

"S" (mnemonist), 113
Sanderson, Kenneth, 116n

248